WITHDRAWN

Analyzing Workplace Arrogance and Organizational Effectiveness:

Emerging Research and Opportunities

Khaled Tamzini
University of Sousse, Tunisia

Tahar Lazhar Ayed
Umm Al-Qura University, Saudia Arabia

A volume in the Advances in
Human Resources Management
and Organizational Development
(AHRMOD) Book Series

Published in the United States of America by
    IGI Global
    Business Science Reference (an imprint of IGI Global)
    701 E. Chocolate Avenue
    Hershey PA, USA 17033
    Tel: 717-533-8845
    Fax: 717-533-8661
    E-mail: cust@igi-global.com
    Web site: http://www.igi-global.com

Library of Congress Cataloging-in-Publication Data

Names: Tamzini, Khaled, 1973- author. | Ayed, Tahar Lazhar, 1973- author.
Title: Analyzing workplace arrogance and organizational effectiveness :
  emerging research and opportunities / by Khaled Tamzini and Tahar Lazhar
  Ayed.
Description: Hershey : Business Science Reference, [2018]
Identifiers: LCCN 2017045868| ISBN 9781522555254 (hardcover) | ISBN
  9781522555261 (ebook)
Subjects: LCSH: Job satisfaction. | Organizational effectiveness.
Classification: LCC HF5549.5.J63 T33 2018 | DDC 658.3/1422--dc23 LC record available at
https://lccn.loc.gov/2017045868

This book is published in the IGI Global book series Advances in Human Resources Management and Organizational Development (AHRMOD) (ISSN: 2327-3372; eISSN: 2327-3380)

British Cataloguing in Publication Data
A Cataloguing in Publication record for this book is available from the British Library.

All work contributed to this book is new, previously-unpublished material.
The views expressed in this book are those of the authors, but not necessarily of the publisher.

For electronic access to this publication, please contact: eresources@igi-global.com.

Advances in Human Resources Management and Organizational Development (AHRMOD) Book Series

ISSN:2327-3372
EISSN:2327-3380

Editor-in-Chief: Patricia Ordóñez de Pablos, Universidad de Oviedo, Spain

MISSION

A solid foundation is essential to the development and success of any organization and can be accomplished through the effective and careful management of an organization's human capital. Research in human resources management and organizational development is necessary in providing business leaders with the tools and methodologies which will assist in the development and maintenance of their organizational structure.

The **Advances in Human Resources Management and Organizational Development (AHRMOD) Book Series** aims to publish the latest research on all aspects of human resources as well as the latest methodologies, tools, and theories regarding organizational development and sustainability. The **AHRMOD Book Series** intends to provide business professionals, managers, researchers, and students with the necessary resources to effectively develop and implement organizational strategies.

COVERAGE

- Human Relations Movement
- Skills Management
- Workplace Discrimination
- E-Human Resources Management
- Corporate governance
- Worker Behavior and Engagement
- Employee Benefits
- Disputes Resolution
- Outsourcing HR
- Organizational learning

IGI Global is currently accepting manuscripts for publication within this series. To submit a proposal for a volume in this series, please contact our Acquisition Editors at Acquisitions@igi-global.com or visit: http://www.igi-global.com/publish/.

Titles in this Series

For a list of additional titles in this series, please visit:
https://www.igi-global.com/book-series/advances-human-resources-management-organizational/73670

Creativity in Workforce Development and Innovation Emerging Research and Opportunities
Sally Blake (Flagler College, USA) and Candice M. Burkett (University of Illinois at Chicago, USA)
Business Science Reference • ©2018 • 152pp • H/C (ISBN: 9781522549529) • US $145.00

Evaluating Media Richness in Organizational Learning
Albert Gyamfi (Aalborg University Copenhagen, Denmark) and Idongesit Williams (Aalborg University Copenhagen, Denmark)
Business Science Reference • ©2018 • 328pp • H/C (ISBN: 9781522529569) • US $185.00

Teaching Human Resources and Organizational Behavior at the College Level
John Mendy (University of Lincoln, UK)
Business Science Reference • ©2018 • 305pp • H/C (ISBN: 9781522528203) • US $195.00

Handbook of Research on Organizational Culture and Diversity in the Modern Workforce
Bryan Christiansen (PryMarke LLC, USA) and Harish C. Chandan (Argosy University, USA)
Business Science Reference • ©2017 • 506pp • H/C (ISBN: 9781522522508) • US $255.00

Handbook of Research on Human Factors in Contemporary Workforce Development
Bryan Christiansen (PryMarke LLC, USA) and Harish C. Chandan (Argosy University, USA)
Business Science Reference • ©2017 • 563pp • H/C (ISBN: 9781522525684) • US $255.00

Driving Multinational Enterprises Through Effective Global Talent Management
Khaled Tamzini (University of Sousse, Tunisia) Tahar Lazhar Ayed (Umm Al-Qura University, Saudi Arabia) Aisha Wood Boulanouar (Sultan Qaboos University, Muscat, Oman) and Zakaria Boulanouar (Umm Al-Qura University, Saudi Arabia)
Business Science Reference • ©2017 • 191pp • H/C (ISBN: 9781522525578) • US $170.00

Exploring the Influence of Personal Values and Cultures in the Workplace
Zlatko Nedelko (University of Maribor, Slovenia) and Maciej Brzozowski (Poznan University of Economics and Business, Poland)
Business Science Reference • ©2017 • 458pp • H/C (ISBN: 9781522524809) • US $205.00

For an entire list of titles in this series, please visit:
https://www.igi-global.com/book-series/advances-human-resources-management-organizational/73670

701 East Chocolate Avenue, Hershey, PA 17033, USA
Tel: 717-533-8845 x100 • Fax: 717-533-8661
E-Mail: cust@igi-global.com • www.igi-global.com

Table of Contents

Preface

Arrogance is defined as that species of pride which consists in exorbitant claims of rank, dignity, estimation or power or which exalts the worth or importance of the person to an undue degree. Arrogance is engaging in behaviors intended to exaggerate a person's sense of superiority by disparaging others (Johnson et al., 2010).

Through actions associated with this inflated sense of entitlement and superiority, arrogant employees often impede effective organizational functioning (Johnson et al., 2010). Arrogant managers are therefore more likely to pursue failing courses of action that could otherwise have been prevented. Arrogant behavior can be an especially challenging problem to deal with due to the fact that arrogant individuals consider their own behavior acceptable and thus do not monitor their own actions when interacting with others.

A 2007 landmark study by the University of Akron investigated arrogance and its implications to an organization's morale and bottom line. According to the researchers, accounts of arrogant employees abound, but evidence is predominantly anecdotal and that there is little systematic research on arrogance within organizations, and sparse empirical data that verify the alleged negative relationship between arrogance and performance. The researchers developed the Workplace Arrogance Scale (WARS) to help obtain empirical data.

Among other things, Silverman et al. (2007) found empirical evidence to support the claim that the more arrogant a person is, the more self-centered and the less agreeable he is likely to be. Likewise, in another portion of the study which involved a 360-degree performance feedback survey, arrogance was shown to be negatively related to performance and cognitive ability. Competitive advantage might be gained by providing disincentives for arrogant behavior while providing for positive reinforcements for positive behaviors like humility.

While research in the area of worker arrogance is in its infancy, a negative relationship between performance and arrogance has been established.

Specifically, Leslie and Van Velsor (1996) note that arrogant behavior accelerates executive failure. They found that such behavior at the management level often causes belittlement of other employees leading to high employee turnover and overall organizational dysfunction.

Hence, despite the importance of understanding arrogant behavior at work and the exploration of the relationship between workplace arrogance and organizational performance, little systematic research has examined its occurrence and consequences in organizational settings. This is especially surprising given that personality is an important predictor of work outcomes (Day & Silverman, 1989).

The purpose of this book is to generate a collection of papers contributing to cope with the shortage of the academic research related to the concept of "workplace arrogance" in the field of strategic management. It focuses on the relationship between workplace arrogance and organizational effectiveness. Hence, some correspondences were developed between the former and some managerial concepts, namely: job performance, job satisfaction and organizational performance. This book bridges research in, and the practice, of workplace arrogance.

This book presents a collection of six chapters that address key themes, topics and approaches for managers, academics, and students: workplace arrogance, self-esteem, self-confidence, hubris, vanity, narcissism, job performance, job satisfaction, organizational performance, strategic scope, competence, among others.

Chapter 1, "Workplace Arrogance and Organizational Performance," aims to cope with the research scarcity on workplace arrogance and in order to explore and explain the relationship between workplace arrogance and organizational performance, the authors have made a focus on a various concepts: arrogance and its correlates, its relationship with firms' competitive advantage, strategic dynamism, strategic choices and company performance; arrogance selling, arrogance in advertising or brand arrogance and their implications on purchase intentions. Moreover, they have undertaken an empirical study to explore this relationship. The findings of this research were unexpected and first time discovered, such as the study of the dimensionality of the workplace arrogance.

Chapter 2, "Workplace Arrogance and Its Impact on the Organizational Performance in the Hospitality Industry," aims to test empirically the fundamental hypothesis highlighting the relationship between "workplace arrogance" and "organizational performance". The results of this study undertaken in the Tunisian hotel industry validate two hypotheses out of thirty and reach crucial findings: (1) workplace arrogance is a multidimensional variable (6 dimensions) and its dimensions are unidimensional; (2) workplace arrogance has a significant and negative impact on organizational performance measured by two dimensions: the customer satisfaction and the quality of service; and (3) workplace arrogance has a significant and positive impact on organizational performance measured by two dimensions: quality of service and financial performance. These findings could be considered as a theoretical contribution never been discovered before.

Chapter 3, "Workplace Arrogance and Job Satisfaction," aims to cope with the inadequacy of studies related to the job satisfaction and its relationship with workplace arrogance. This chapter consists of three main parts: the first deals with this notion of "job satisfaction". The second part focuses on the factors explaining job satisfaction with a focus on an empirical study entitled "Job satisfaction of operational employees in the tourism and hospitality sector in Tunisia". In fact, this study aims to enrich the literature by overcoming the deficit of international and Tunisian research on factors explaining the job satisfaction of the operational employees belonging to the tourism and hospitality industry. The results of this research provide the eight factors explaining the job satisfaction of employees belonging to this sector which are divided into factors of hygiene (pay and remuneration, social benefits, supervision, colleagues, equity) and motor factors (promotion, training, working environment). In addition, the results of this research demonstrate that (1) these factors explaining job satisfaction affect different groups of employees in different ways that the cluster analysis allowed them to extract. And that (2) these groups are distributed in a quasi-equal way in terms of demographic characteristics (age, gender, position held, etc.) contrary to the results of the majority of the research carried out in this field. Thus, these factors do not play an explanatory role for the differential of hotel staff satisfaction. Finally, the third part will focus on the relationship between job satisfaction and workplace arrogance based on the concept of self-esteem.

Chapter 4, "Workplace Arrogance and Job Performance," aims to cope with the scarcity of studies related to the job performance and its relationship with workplace arrogance. It consists of five main parts: the first deals with this notion of "job performance as a dynamic concept". The second part depicts the models of job performance by presenting the two main and the most known job performance models: (1) the Campbell et al.'s (1993) model and (2) the Borman and Motowidlo (1993) model. The third part deals with the predictors (antecedents or determinants) of job performance with a focus on an empirical study entitled "Job performance of nurses in hospitality sector in Qatar". In fact, this study aims to deepen our knowledge on the nurses` job performance in a particular environment: the gulf region and precisely in Aspetar, a multicultural hospital. It aims to explore the nursing job performance at Aspetar by studying its dimensionality by using the Schwirian Six Dimension Scale of Nursing Performance (Schwirian 1978). Finally, the fourth part will focus on the relationship between job performance and workplace arrogance.

Chapter 5, "How Do Competences Valorize Strategic Scope Dimensions?" deals with the concept of the competence as a main dimension of the organizational effectiveness and with its mysterious relation with the concept of the arrogance. In fact, competences are considered as a main driver of any company that drives it towards competitiveness but its definition remains very large to the extent that we mixed it with the concept of the arrogance. In order to explore the relationship between competence and arrogance, the authors attempted to answer the following question: how do competences valorize strategic scope dimensions? In fact, they tried to view empirically how the competences can impact the strategic scope dimensions of any business which are: Research and Development, Market and Resources.

Chapter 6, "Case Study: A Young Entrepreneur Agronomist Between Arrogance and Competence," is a pedagogical case addressed to students who would be entrepreneurs and studying in business administration and wishing to create their own projects It explores the relationship between competence and arrogance based on real facts that a young ergonomist entrepreneur was confronted with. In fact, the main question that the authors asked in this case: do we think that all these competences that entrepreneur should acquire cannot be done comparatively to his old age? In the reality, entrepreneur need only "over trust" and strong personality, an arrogance that permits to him to live more experience and then acquire expertise. This chapter is in the continuity of the previous. It offers to the reader a different perspective in order to investigate this ambiguous relationship between arrogance and competence in the field of entrepreneurship.

Khaled Tamzini
University of Sousse, Tunisia

Tahar Lazhar Ayed
Umm Al-Qura University, Saudi Arabia

REFERENCES

Borman, W. C., & Motowidlo, S. J. (1993). Expanding the Criterion Domain to Include Elements of Contextual Performance. In N. Schmitt & W. Borman (Eds.), *Personnel Selection in Organizations* (pp. 71–98). New York: Jossey-Bass.

Campbell, J. P., McCloy, R. A., Oppler, S. H., & Sager, C. E. (1993). A theory of performance. In C. W. Schmitt & W. C. A. Borman (Eds.), *Personnel Selection in Organizations* (pp. 35–70). San Francisco: Jossey Bass.

Day, D., & Silverman, S. (1989). Personality and job performance: Evidence of incremental validity. *Personnel Psychology*, *42*(1), 25–36. doi:10.1111/j.1744-6570.1989.tb01549.x

Johnson, R. E., Silverman, S. B., Shyamsunder, A., Yao. Swee, H., Rodopman, O. B., Cho, E., & Bauer, J. (2010). Acting Superior But Actually Inferior?: Correlates and Consequences of Workplace Arrogance. *Human Performance*, *23*(5), 403–427. doi:10.1080/08959285.2010.515279

Jones, J. (2016). *How Do Confidence and Arrogance Work in the Workplace? Organizational and Employee Development*. Society for Human Resource Management. Retrieved from https://www.shrm.org/resourcesandtools/hr-topics/organizational-and-employee-development/pages/how-do-confidence-and-arrogance-work-in-the-workplace.aspx

Leslie, J. B., & Van Velsor, E. (1996). *A look at derailment today: North America and Europe*. Greensboro, NC: Centre for Creative Leadership.

Meyer, G., Brünig, B., & Nyhuis, P. (2015). Employee competences in manufacturing companies – an expert survey. *Journal of Management Development*, *34*(8), 1004–1018. doi:10.1108/JMD-06-2014-0056

Padua, R. N., Lerin, M. M., Tumapon, T. T., & Pañares, Z. A. (2010). Patterns and Dynamics of an Arrogance-Competence Theory in Organizations. *Liceo Journal of Higher Education Research Cutting Edge Research*, *6*(2), 2094–1064.

Schwirian, P. (1978). Evaluating the performance of nurses: A multidimensional approach. *Nursing Research*, *27*(6), 347–351. doi:10.1097/00006199-197811000-00004 PMID:251246

Chapter 1
Workplace Arrogance and Organizational Performance

ABSTRACT

The aim of this chapter is to introduce the concept of "arrogance" in the psychological, sociological, and managerial field. The authors explore the origins and advance some definitions of arrogance. The relationship between this latter concept and its correlates (e.g., narcissism, hubris, self-confidence) are introduced and explained. The history of the organizational performance, its components, and the relationship between its three dimensions—culture, structure, and individuals and their behaviors—are empirically studied in the Tunisian agro-food industry. Moreover, this chapter is considered as a conceptual one necessary to the understanding of "workplace arrogance" and its implications on competitive advantage and organizational performance.

INTRODUCTION

The research on workplace arrogance are very scarce, especially the link between it and organizational performance. To cope with this research scarcity and in order to explore and explain the relationship between workplace arrogance and organizational performance, the authors have made a focus on a various concepts: arrogance and its correlates, its relationship with firms' competitive advantage, strategic dynamism, strategic choices and company performance; arrogance selling, arrogance in advertising or brand arrogance and their implications on purchase intentions.

DOI: 10.4018/978-1-5225-5525-4.ch001

This chapter is composed by three parts. The first part is an overview on one of the main concepts of this book: arrogance and its correlates and workplace arrogance. The second part describes the concept of organizational performance. The third part aims to investigate theoretically the relationship between these two concepts. This last part is considered as a base of an empirical study undertaken in the Tunisian hotel industry to test this relationship empirically.

ARROGANCE AND WORKPLACE ARROGANCE

Origins and Definitions of Arrogance

In order to define the notion of "arrogance", we will first focus on its etymological origins. For the Online Etymology Dictionary, "arrogance" finds its origins from the Middle English (13c) 'arrogant' which is rooted in the Old French 'arrogance' (12c.) and the Latin 'arrogantia' which means "presumption, pride, haughtiness".

For the Webster's Revised Unabridged Dictionary, "Arrogance" is a noun which means

The act or habit of arrogating, or making undue claims in an overbearing manner; that species of pride which consists in exorbitant claims of rank, dignity, estimation, or power, or which exalts the worth or importance of the person to an undue degree; proud contempt of others; lordliness; haughtiness; self-assumption; presumption.

The Century Dictionary defines "arrogance" as

The condition or quality of being arrogant; a manifest feeling of personal superiority in rank, power, dignity, or estimation; the exalting of one's own worth or importance to an undue degree; pride with contempt of others; presumption.

For the Webster's 21st Century Dictionary, arrogance means

Proud and insolent; disrespectful. Arrogance is a characteristic that people perceive in others rather than in themselves. An arrogant communication

2

indicates that the communicator is perceived to think that he/she is better than others. (Wosinska, Dabul, Whestone-Dion, & Cialdini, 1996; Wang et al. 2013: 919).

From these previous definitions, arrogance could be considered as a concept based on a personnel relationship area, behaviors, and pride. In fact, Brown (2012) argues that "arrogance has been defined as a chronic belief of superiority and exaggerated self-importance that is demonstrated through excessive and presumptuous claims (Hareli & Weiner, 2000; Kowalski, Walker, Wilkinson, Queen, & Sharpe, 2003; Leary, Bednarski, Hammon, & Duncan, 1997)" (p. 555). Hence, the personnel relationship between arrogant individual and its victims as argued by Kowalski et al. (2003 in Brown 2012). This personnel relationship finds its roots in the study undertaken by Tiberius and Walker (1998), who consider "arrogance as essentially an interpersonal matter". That is to say, that a dual behaviors perception exists between the two actors. These behaviors perceptions are considered by Tiberius and Walker (1998) as an arrogant person's interactions with others; these latter *"reveal the arrogant person's attitudes toward the relationships she stands in with those others"* (p. 381). Thus, for the first, it is a "chronic belief of superiority" (Brown 2012) exaggerated by a disrespectful behavior against others (Johnson et al. 2010 in Silverman et al. 2012). These notions of "superiority" and "disrespect" are often cited by authors who have studied "arrogance" in their different fields (sociology, psychology, education, management, etc). Johnson et al. (2010 in Silverman et al. 2012) argue that *"arrogance is engaging in behaviors intended to exaggerate a person's sense of superiority by disparaging others"* (p. 22). In addition, *"arrogance can be thought of as a cluster of behaviors that communicate one's superiority and importance relative to others (Johnson et al., 2010; Leary, Bednarski, Hammon, & Duncan, 1997)"* (Silverman et al. 2012: 23). For the second, they view arrogance as a negative behavior belonging to some marginal persons. Brown (2012) have advanced that *"victims of arrogance viewed the behavior more negatively than perpetrators of arrogance"* (p. 556). Moreover, Johnson et al. (2010) based on Ma and Karri (2005) stipulate that *"in its extreme form, arrogant behavior cultivates perceptions of the self as invincible and omnipotent"* (p. 405). These types of perceptions are based on the fact that arrogant people believe that they are smarter than others and they have exceptional skills and abilities such as high intelligence (Hareli & Weiner 2000 in Johnson et al. 2010). These perceptions highlight the nature of the relationship between competence and arrogance (the specific relationship between competence and workplace arrogance will be introduced later: see chapter 4). In fact, despite that these later are considered as opposite (good versus negative trait of a person), they are often related to each other as argued by Golson (2009 in Padua et al. 2010). One can say that there is a cause-effect relationship:

Being smart, bright and clever leads to competence in many areas related to success in one's career. But having these intellectual gifts also means that one gets used to being right, being perceived as a good problem-solver and being highly valued by others which, unfortunately, often lead to arrogance. (Golson, 2009; Padua et al. 2010: 83).

Finally, arrogance is defined by focusing on the concept of "pride". Padua et al. (2010) have defined arrogance *"as that species of pride which consists in exorbitant claims of rank, dignity, estimation or power or which exalts the worth or importance of the person to an undue degree"* (p. 77). They also consider "pride" as a positive aspect of arrogance, and "vanity" its negative aspect. In the same vein, *"Poggi and D'Errico (2011) classify arrogance as a type of pride and note that an arrogant person tends to believe that he or she has power over others"* (Wang et al. 2013: 919).

This section was devoted to introduce the concept of "arrogance" by focusing on its origins and some of its essential determinants. Therefore, this is not sufficient to define it. One shall enlarge the scope of reflection by emphasizing the link between "arrogance" and its correlates (Johnson et al. 2010) or its related constructs (Silverman et al. 2012; Tiberius & Walker 1998). This is the aim of the following section.

Arrogance and Its Correlates or Related Constructs

Almost all the literature which deals with the concept of arrogance has emphasized its relationship with some correlates or related constructs. For instance, Silverman et al. (2012) have cited some constructs related to arrogance: narcissism, hubris, and confidence. These later are considered by Silverman et al. (2012) as personality characteristics that are considered so close and so different from arrogance. For Johnson et al. (2010) *"taken together, arrogance differs from narcissism, hubris, and confidence in vital ways, and thus there may be value added by measuring arrogant behavior and identifying its correlates and consequences"* (p. 407). Before continuing, we should precise that it is important for the reader to stress that in this section we will present only the correlates and related constructs to arrogance and their similarities and differences (narcissism, hubris, confidence, humility). The impact or the consequences of arrogance on job performance and organizational performance will be discussed later (see chapter 3).

Arrogance vs. Narcissism

Before Freud's (1914) meta-psychological and clinical thinking considering narcissism as a focal construct, Ellis in 1898 introduced it (narcissism) in the psychological field. This latter *"used the term Narcissus-like to refer to "a tendency for the sexual emotions to be lost and almost entirely absorbed in self admiration" (Ellis, 1898)"* (Raskin & Terry 1988: 890). After Ellis (1898) Nacke in 1899 *"used the term Narcismus to refer to a sexual perversion whereby a person treats his or her own body as a sexual object"* (Raskin & Terry 1988: 890). This Nacke's vision of narcissism could be considered as the bases of Freud's (1914) meta-psychological and clinical thinking (Chatterjee and Hambrick 2007; Raskin & Terry 1988; O'Reilly et al. 2013).

As Raskin and Terry (1988) have argued, Freud has identified various uses for the term narcissism as either a meta-psychological construct or as a clinical construct. Firstly, as a meta-psychological construct, he

... used the term narcissism (a) to describe a stage of normal sexual development that occurred between the stages of autoeroticism and object love; (b) as the original source and energy for the development of the ego; (c) as a type of object (or interpersonal) choice in which the self plays a more important part in the object relationship than the real aspects of the object; (d) as a mode of relating to the environment that is characterized by a relative lack of object or interpersonal relations; (e) as a mechanism for the establishment of the ego's ideals; (f) as a primary ingredient in the development and maintenance of self-esteem; and (g) as a conditioning factor of repression (Freud, 1914/1957, 1923/1961; see also reviews on narcissism by Bing, McLaughlin, & Marburg, 1959; Duruz, 1981; Moore, 1975; Pulver, 1970; and Tiecholz, 1978). (Raskin & Terry 1988: 890).

Secondly, as a clinical construct Freud identified various manifestations of narcissism (considered as a behavioral phenomena), including:

(A) a set of attitudes a person has toward oneself, including self-love, self-admiration, and self-aggrandizement; (b) several kinds of fears or

vulnerabilities related to a person's self-esteem that include the fear of loss of love and the fear of failure; (c) a general defensive orientation that includes megalomania, idealization, denial, projection, and splitting; (d) motivation in terms of the need to be loved, as well as strivings for self-sufficiency and for perfection; and (e) a constellation of attitudes that may characterize a person's relationships with others. (Raskin & Terry 1988: 890).

Unlike this Freud's clinical vision of narcissism seen as a mental disorder (Chatterjee & Hambrick 2007), psychologists consider it as a personality dimension that one can measure it via Raskin and Hall's (1979) Narcissistic Personality Inventory (NPI)[1]. This latter is a psychometric scales for measuring narcissism and based on it *"individuals can be assigned scores along that dimension (Emmons, 1987; Raskin and Terry, 1988)"* (Chatterjee & Hambrick 2007: 353).

Based on this development, narcissism should be considered as different from arrogance in the way that narcissistic unlike arrogant person is focusing on its own person without disparaging others. As it was explained above, arrogance is based on a personnel relationship area (or interpersonal dynamics[2]). Unlike arrogant, narcissistic person doesn't need any interaction with others. Narcissism is a self-action as argued by Johnson et al. (2010)

… Narcissistic thoughts (e.g., fantasies of self-grandeur) and behaviors (e.g., excessive physical self-admiration) can occur in the absence of others. In fact, the term narcissism (meaning "self-love") is based on the Greek myth about Narcissus, who died alone while admiring his own reflection in a pool of water—a decidedly nonsocial event! (p. 406).

For Silverman et al. (2012),

Narcissism (or self-love) involves fantasies of self-grandeur and excessive self-admiration that can occur in the absence of others. Arrogance, on the other hand is manifested in interpersonal contexts by disparaging others. (p. 22).

This view that considers narcissism as a stable personality trait and occurs in absence of the others (Campbell et al. 2005 in O'Reilly et al. 2013), has been criticized by some authors. In fact, for Exline et al. (2004) and Vazire & Funder (2006) narcissists *"can be aggressive and hostile when confronted with criticism or negative feedback"* (O'Reilly et al. 2013: 2). Moreover, Brunell et al. (2008), Lubit (2002) and Rauthmann (2012) argued that *"narcissists lack true empathy and therefore can be exploitative, taking credit for others' accomplishments and shifting blame to others"* (O'Reilly et al. 2013: 2). In the same vein, Chatterjee and Hambrick (2007) have considered the *"... tendency to see others as an extension of one's self"* (p.353) as one of the various manifestations of narcissism.

This view is supported by focusing on the concept of "behavior" which is considered as a determinant of the arrogance (see paragraph I). In fact, Johnson et al. (2010) considered overt behaviors as essential to the manifestation of arrogance, while overt and covert behaviors are determinant for the manifestation of narcissism.

Arrogance vs. Hubris

Hubris term comes from the ancient Greeks (Owen 2016; Johnson 2010). For them the term hubris is linked to the act of the person who is based on an exaggerated pride and self-confidence with a behavior of insolence and contempt towards others. Thus, hubris (from ancient Greeks' vision) is based on a personnel relationship area or *"is manifested in interpersonal contexts by disparaging others"* (Silverman et al. 2012: 22). This behavior was severely punished and condemned as the following quotation from Owen (2016) illustrates:

Nemesis is the name of the goddess of retribution, and often in Greek drama the gods arrange nemesis because a hubristic act is seen as one in which the perpetrator tries to defy the reality ordained by them. The hero committing the hubristic act seeks to transgress the human condition, imagining himself to be superior and to have powers more like those of the gods. But the gods will have none of that, so it is they who destroy him. (p. 21).

This ancient Greeks' vision of hubris is not shared by the contemporary scholars. In fact, as narcissism and unlike arrogance, hubris is self-focused (Silverman et al. 2012) but doesn't need interactions with others and disparaging them. Hubris is based on the self-confidence and pride notions. In fact, hubris is considered by Hayward & Hambrick (1997 in Johnson et al. 2010) as *"an excessive proud of one's own successes, abilities, or attributes, despite any justification for such pride"* (p. 406). This excessive proud is considered by

Hayward (2007 in Johnson et al. 2010) as the result of decisions based on a false overconfidence unlike the authentic overconfidence that has no negative consequences.

Therefore, one can conclude that there is a high correlation between hubris, self-confidence (or overconfidence) and decision-making. In order to highlight and explore this correlation, the nature of the relationship between hubris and decision-making should be clarified. To do so, a focus on organizational context will be done.

For Li and Tang (2010) hubris can impact decisions (Kahneman et al. 1982 in Li & Tang 2010) in that way that they considered it as a "cognitive bias". This latter is the result of an individual's ability to made judgment which deviate from objective norms and rules (Hayward & Hambrick 1997; Hayward et al. 2006; Hiller & Hambrick 2005 in Li & Tang 2010). This "cognitive bias" is based on the individual's overconfidence that occurs when its *"certainty about his or her predictions exceeds the accuracy of those predictions"* (Li & Tang, 2010). Indeed, in the organizational context Malmendier and Tate (2003 in Pillal & Goldsmith 2006) *"found that overconfident CEOs overestimate their ability to generate returns"* and CEO's hubris pushes them to make decisions with unconsidered and unwarranted risks (Johnson et al. 2010). This view of hubris is the opposite of that of Pillal and Goldsmith (2006) who consider that hubris has a positive effect on beliefs and that making appropriate choices and decisions is necessarily based on overconfidence.

On the basis of the above, it could be argued that a more thorough investigation of this notion of "confidence" and its generics (sel-confidence, overconfidence...) is essential to understanding "arrogance."

Arrogance vs. Confidence

The distinction between arrogance and confidence rests on two fundamental elements. The first is based on how a person perceives himself without distorting reality. The second is related to the perception of one's position in relation to the others. In fact, the arrogant person is not only self-confident, but he cannot act without disparaging others. He acts in such a way as to make those around him feel inferior (Johnson et al. 2010). That is to say that self-confidence is a high estimation of talent and abilities of a person, whereas *"arrogance just consists in having too high an opinion of one's talents, skills, or accomplishments. It is characterized by false beliefs about one's skills and talents."* (Tiberius & Walker 1998)

Arrogance vs. Humility

Based on its etymological and lexical origins, humility could be understood as both negative and positive concept. Indeed, for the Latins and the Greeks, the term "humility" was treated differently. For the Latins, humility means literally *"humilis (i.e., lowly, humble, or literally "on the ground") and humus (i.e., earth)"* (Rowatt et al. 2006: 198). Thus, from a lexical point of view, humility is synonymous of lowliness, weakness and humiliation. This view has been adopted by some of the researchers belonging to pathological psychology thinking centered on the treatment of mental illness.

In contrast, the Greeks considered humility as a virtue (Morris et al. 2005). This understanding of humility has been shared by the proponents of the positive psychology. Indeed, Morris et al. (2005: 1330) states that *"Peterson and Seligman (2004) and others (Tangney, 2000, 2002), argued that humility was best understood as a positive human trait that is both stable and enduring"*.

Moreover, humility is considered and defined as psychological quality and a positive psychological construct. As a psychological quality, humility is *"characterized by being more humble, modest, down-to-earth, open-minded, and respectful of others (and less arrogant, immodest, conceited, closed-minded, or egotistical; cf. Exline et al., 2004; Exline & Geyer, 2004; Tangney, 2000, 2002)"* (Rowatt et al. 2006: 198). For Peterson & Seligman (2004 in Powers et al. 2007) humility is defined as "character strengths of temperance" (p. 77) and they also define temperance as "virtue of control over excess" (Powers et al. 2007: 77). This concept of virtue have been emphasized by Lee and Ashton (2004 in Peters et al. 2011) in order to define humility. For them, humility is considered as a *"personality dimension and conceptualized as a virtue or character strength (Exline et al., 2004; Tangney, 2002, 2009)"* (Peters et al. 2011: 155).

In contrast to humility, arrogance is considered as a negative psychological contrast (Powers et al. 2007) and it *"have been construed as sinful in many religious traditions, and could be conducive to hurting loved ones or even starting wars"* (Schimmel 1992 in Powers et al. 2007: 77). Peters et al. (2011) defined humility by contrasting it with arrogance. For them

Humility as a characteristic and enduring way of being more humble, modest, respectful, and open-minded than arrogant, self-centered, or conceited (...) That is, a humble person does not simply lack arrogance or self-focus, but

also possesses humble qualities like being modest or intellectually open (Roberts & Wood, 2003). (Peters et al. 2011: 155).

For other researchers, the difference between humility and arrogance resides in the fact that the former is high self-esteem and the latter is low self-esteem.

In fact, humility has much more in common with high self-esteem, while arrogance is more similar to low self-esteem (Ryan, 1983). Arrogance and low self-esteem lead one to evaluate life experiences in terms of their effect on self, while humility and high self-esteem have no urgency to deny praiseworthy achievements and no need to protect the self against criticism. (Elliott 2010: 7)

In the field of positive organizational psychology (Cameron et al., 2003) considered as the application of positive psychology in the organization (Morris et al. 2005), humility in contrast with arrogance *"prevents excessive self-focus, allowing leaders to develop perspective in relationships with employees."* (Silverman et al. 2012: 26). For Collins (2001 in Rowatt et al. 2006: 199) *"Chief Executive Officers who possessed a rare combination of extreme humility and strong professional will were catalysts for transforming a good company into a great one"*.

Throughout this section, the authors have introduced and explained the concept of arrogance by focusing on its origins. The authors emphasized the subtlety between arrogance and certain related concepts: narcissism, humility, self-confidence...

This subtlety is fundamental to understanding arrogance in the workplace and its relationship to organizational performance. In addition, this will increase certain research proposals in the field of management which are very limited until today.

Workplace Arrogance

Workplace arrogance is considered as the arrogant behavior in the organization. Studying this behavior is quite very important in order to understand and explain its implications on the organizations and specifically on their performance. As an emerging insight and based on the fact that it is rooted (as explained in section 1) on the psychology and sociology field, workplace arrogance was studied within Industrial Organizational Psychology (Swiden-Wick 2013). However, this field couldn't explain the relationship between workplace arrogance, competitive advantage, and organizational performance which should be treated within the strategic management field. Unfortunately, despite the critical implications of this negative human characteristic (see chapter 3), very little systematic and scientific research was conducted and examined its repercussions on work outcomes (Day & Silverman 1989 in Johnson et al. 2010) and organizational settings (Padua et al. 2010; Johnson et al. 2010). Moreover, Johnson et al. (2010) and Padua et al. (2010) argued simultaneously that

To date, existing evidence concerning arrogance is predominantly anecdotal"
and that "according to the researchers, accounts of arrogant employees
abound, but evidence is predominantly anecdotal and that there is little
systematic research on arrogance within organizations...

In addition, and in contrast with humility and narcissism, to date no studies have been undertaken in the strategic management field explaining the effect of workplace arrogance on job performance and on organizational performance as argued by Johnson et al. (2010):

Research conducted outside work contexts suggests that arrogance has
negative socio-emotional outcomes (e.g., decreased liking; Schlenker &
Leary, 1982), yet it is unclear whether these detrimental effects extend to job
performance. Although we suspect that arrogance may be negatively related
to job performance (e.g., because arrogance is associated with being closed
to other people's ideas and overreacting to criticism), this proposition has
not been empirically tested.

In the following, the authors will review some research relating humility and narcissism to competitive advantage and organizational performance in order to discuss the foundation of this supposed relationship between workplace arrogance and organizational performance.

Considering arrogance as a negative trait of personality and a negative psychological contrast (Powers et al. 2007), Padua et al. (2010) argued that *"competitive advantage might be gained by providing disincentives for arrogant behavior while providing for positive reinforcements for positive behaviors like humility"*. In the same vein, Vera and Rodriguez-Lopez (2004 in Johnson et al. 2011) considered humility as *"a source of competitive advantage linked to both personal and organizational performance"*. This statement is shared by Silverman et al. (2012) who have posited that *"curtailing arrogant behavior and instilling humility can provide organizations with a competitive advantage"*.

Following the above statements, it can be said that arrogance in the workplace does not allow the organization to have a competitive advantage and develop it. This conclusion is shared by Collins (2001 in Johnson et al. 2011) who *"found that companies with CEOs who possessed a combination of humility and strong professional will went from being "good" to "great" (with regard to stock performance)"*. More harmful than that, Ma and Karri (2005 in Johnson et al. 2010) consider arrogant behavior as "a leader-based trigger of destruction within organizations". For Levine (2005 in Johnson et al. 2010)

Arrogance is implicated as an attribute of corrupt organizations ... where "leaders of the greedy corporation substitute the goal of self-aggrandizement for the goals of honest dealing and doing the real work of developing and producing good products for their customers and making profit for their shareholders. (Levine, 2005, p. 726)

THE ORGANIZATIONAL PERFORMANCE

At the beginning of the 21st century, strategic management researchers brought new definitions to clarify existing nuances and ambiguities related to the concept of performance (Bowles & Coates 1993). Referring to the work of Sevcik (2003), the concept of performance goes through two types of attributes: the first refers to the management of assets which means the improvement of their efficiency. The second refers to the management of experience which means the valuation of expertise. On the other hand, some other authors such as Greene (2008), argued that it would be important to distinguish between performance and outcome. The author considered that the use of capital is made via performance solutions, and has a main objective which is value creation. Performance solutions are seen as inputs and can be human capital or any other type of capital that leads to a defined objective or outcome. Outcomes are considered to be generally economic and have value. The performance solutions are distinguished from the results produced. Indeed, the good use of time, knowledge, space, equipment, plans, supplies, and purchased services are seen as performance solutions that generate results (Almatrooshi et al. 2016). They are capital which is continually used to achieve a certain result. The result is a measurable output that must have a value and a lower cost than the performance solution (Greene 2008).

This section is composed by three parts. The first part is an overview on the history of the organizational performance development. The second part describes the elements that compose the organizational performance. The third part is an empirical study that aims to investigate the relationship between the three dimensions of the organizational performance: culture, structure and individuals and their behaviors. This study was undertaken is the Tunisian Agro-food industry.

Overview on the History of the Concept Development

In any organization, any manager is certainly called upon to combine resources strategically and effectively in order to achieve particular objectives (Lusthaus 2003). Experience has shown, however, that organizations have priorities in their objectives (Quinn & Rohrbaugh 1983). The design of organizational performance was based on the idea that organizations must have a good way of identifying rationally and assessing their performance.

Initially, researchers in the field of management developed a multitude of scientific methods in order to increase financial results. In addition, and to reinforce the achievement of this type of objectives, management researchers have identified ways to improve employee effectiveness. They put "optimal behaviors of people in specific organizational production systems" (Taylor 1947 quoted by Lusthaus et al. 2003).

From the 1940s, new conceptions of organizational performance emerged. Concepts such as employee efficiency, effectiveness and morale have emerged. Managers have realized that any company can only perform if it achieves its stated objectives (efficiency) and uses relatively few resources (efficiency). In this context, the objective that dominated most definitions of organizational performance is summed up in the development of the ability to survive (Lusthaus et al. 2003). The consideration of individuals as an organizational resource has highlighted the fact that human resources can have an impact on organizational performance. Some theories have been based on the idea that participatory management practices lead to better organizational performance.

In the fifties and sixties, research in the field of management began to analyze the organizational structures, work processes and behaviors of individuals. Later and especially in the seventies, new tests were carried out to study the factors of performance and to integrate as much as possible of organizational aspects. Specialists have begun to study the different human and interpersonal factors that can impact organizational performance, such as problem solving, teamwork, employee morale, communications, innovation and adaptation (Levinson 1972, quoted by Lusthaus et al. 2003; De Waal 2010).

Studies of organizational performance focused initially on the issue of financial performance. That means an organization is said to be performing if it made profits and it covered all expenses resulting from its activities. Gradually, other dimensions, more than financial, have been integrated. These are mainly social dimensions such as teamwork, morale, innovation, adaptation, openness to change, etc. (Lusthaus et al. 2003).

Elements of the Organizational Performance

Every organization must function in order to achieve the objectives set in advance. At this level, effectiveness and efficiency were at the same time the most commonly used concepts for organizational performance. Progressively, other variables associated with organizational performance have emerged, such as morale, values, adaptability and openness to change, all of which reflect culture. In some cases, performance refers to the extent to which an organization as a social system achieved its objectives. This means that the concept of organizational performance is based mainly on individuals. Moreover, the influence or the power of the management styles and the modes of division influence the organizational performance and reflect the setting up of a given structure. It implies, that organizational performance is always linked to three fundamental concepts namely culture, structure and individuals and their behaviors.

The Relationship Between Structure and Culture as a Dimension of Organizational Performance

According to Allaire and Firsiritou (1993: 387-396), the relationship between structure and culture should be in mutual support. The two dimensions are integrated and felt as a single and indivisible entity.

On the other hand, in some cases we can see a discrepancy between culture and structure. This is when structural changes do not go hand in hand with the values and expectations of the organization. Structural changes would thus be complex if its application requires the questioning and replacement of certain values and expectations of the organization. This situation will cause a great tension and a degradation of the performance of the organization. On the other side, structural change will be simple if it is legitimated within the framework of the organization's current values and beliefs. Thus, the relationship between culture and structure is as harmonious as the organizational performance is valued and reinforced (Beard 2016). Conversely, the more culture and structure are divergent, the more negatively the organizational performance is negatively affected.

Relations Between the Members of the Organization and the Cultural and Structural Dimensions

According to the research works of Allaire and Firsiritou (1993: 387-396), the members of an organization are sensitive to varying degrees, to the values and beliefs of the organization they learn, assimilate and generate. However, members of an organization do not generally distinguish between the cultural and the structural in an obvious way since they maintain a relationship with the whole organization. In the event of disagreements between cultural and structural aspects, the individual will tend towards reconciliation. In the event that the disharmony between the culture and the structure is strong and irremediable, the staff will then be in a state of very high stress and confusion which imperatively affects the organizational performance of the company. Thus, organizational performance is dependent on the individuals of a firm whose behavior implicitly depends on the harmony between cultural and structural aspects. On the other hand, if such a concordance exists, the individuals of the organization will automatically reestablish internal harmony by resorting to reinterpretations and selective perceptions. Moreover, for some members of the organization, culture and structure form a whole that only gradually changes under the internal and external pressures. Finally, individuals display several forms of integration into the organization. Their integration into the system of values and beliefs of the organization varies considerably in nature and intensity.

Flexibility

In the managerial literature, researchers dealing with organizational performance have begun to focus on an important dimension, which is flexibility in management (Boyle 2006). Indeed, to be flexible, it is essential to manage the individuals working in the organization while at the same time ensuring their diversity. In this perspective, it is a matter of grasping and recognizing the differences existing between the individuals of the organization and managing them for which they have a positive impact on the organization. Diversity should affect even the social and ethnic level of the members of a company since every organization is confronted with a very wide external environment. Every company recognizes today that cultural diversity is a necessary factor for competitiveness, especially in a multinational business environment (Chuang et al. 2004).

Likewise, all organizational processes should be flexible and primarily at the level of the learning process, which will allow new knowledge to be shared by the different members of the organization. In addition, the structures themselves must be flexible. Flexibility is important in the identification of strategies. This makes it possible to adapt the plans to the different environmental changes (Grewel & Tansuhaj 2001; Wojtczuk-Turek & Turek 2015).

The Absorption Behavior of Complexity

Any organization needs to practice different methods to absorb complexity, so it would be able to achieve its operating performance (Ashmos et al. 2000). It creates processes or structures that facilitate the exchange of information and allow for filtering, processing and better interpretations. These processes are characterized by a variety of information exchange mechanisms and the emergence of multiple interpretations. Complexity can affect objectives, strategy and interpersonal relationships among members of the organization (Parkinson et al. 2016).

The Organizational Commitment as a Responsible Behavior

Organizational commitment translates into ongoing commitment and identification to the organization (Continuance Commitment) (Allen & Meyer 1996). This commitment can be approved for the organization or for certain actions to be taken such as the implementation of new programs (Gupta et al. 1998). This commitment behavior leads the individual to adopt the values existing in the organization, to adhere to the group and to provide the good will to achieve the expected objectives. It must translate active research into new methods of implementation and continuous improvement of conditions (Zhou & George 2001).

Organizational Citizenship

Organizational commitment behavior sets the minimum required in the performance of tasks. Moreover, in some cases, any organization would need another type of behavior in order to achieve the good performance called Organizational Citizenship Behavior (Organ 1990; Robbins 2001; Appelbaum et al. 2004). This discretionary behavior was not part of the requirement informal employment, it promoted the effective functioning of the organization. Organ (1990) distinguishes a variety of behavioral categories of organizational citizenship. Thus, we find Conscientiousness which means that an employee must not only be aware of his responsibility but also of the proper execution of tasks. This execution must always be above the minimum level required. In addition, we find the altruism which means that every employee must be ready to give help to others who work with him in the same organization. Sportsmanship too, indicates that individuals should behave continuously with a positive attitude. Finally, courtesy, means that every employee treats others with respect. Trust contributes to the perception of fairness and impartiality of individuals and therefore to the valorization of this behavior (McAllister 1995; Erdem & Ozen 2003; Zayas-Ortiz et al. 2015).

Organizational Performance in Terms of Effectiveness, Efficiency, and Relevance

Organizational performance was analyzed in two different dimensions, namely the economic dimension and the organizational dimension called social (Allen & Helms 2002, Jashapara 2003). It should be noted that, from a traditional perspective, organizational performance has always been evaluated on the financial side, taking into account budgets, assets, operations, products and services, and markets. Over time it has taken another perspective by involving it with non-financial measures (Barker 1995; Yeo 2003). In the work of Lusthaus et al. (2003), we define organizational performance from the point of view of efficiency, efficiency and relevance.

Regarding the organizational effectiveness, this latter is defined as the extent to which an organization is able to achieve its goals (Lusthaus 2003).

17

These include issues related to the mission, the achievement of the charter's goals and measures, the use of quantitative and qualitative indicators, internal organizational monitoring, feedback, etc. (Handa 1996, Lusthaus et al. 1999).

Concerning the efficiency, any company is considered efficient if it uses few resources as possible to achieve its targets. In fact, it is a question of trying to relate the amount of resources used to the results achieved. In other words, how different working methods contribute to added value. The researchers Simons and Davila (1998) speak of an approach that allows the company to balance its policies, procedures and creative efforts by determining how roles and responsibilities help or hinder staff (Lusthaus et al. 2003).

Finally, relevance refers to the ability of the organization to ensure continuity of stakeholder satisfaction, innovation and adaptation to conditions. Several questions assessing the relevance of the organization can be asked and generally relate to its adaptation to changes over time, to the regular updating of programs in the light of context and capacity, to regular review of the context for ability to adapt strategy, encourage change and innovation, etc. (Lusthaus et al. 2003).

Do Organizations Work Well? The Case of Emerging Economy

We have shown that the organization consists of three main interrelated dimensions that are culture, structure and individuals and their behaviors. This organization can provide powerful solutions to achieve strategic objectives. According to researchers, defining the concept of performance requires leads to deal with how to manage assets, which concerns the improvement of efficiency and the management of experience, and its adaptation to practice. Performance can be considered as a mean of enhancing the company's ability to achieve specific objectives. In our case, we focused on the notion of the performance of the organization. The latter can be realized in several ways but essentially by dealing with the interrelation within the three main dimensions that are culture, structure and individuals with their behaviors. In this chapter, we started from the modeling of Allaire and Firsiritou (1993) which confirm that individuals inside their organization have to derive the legitimacy of their behavior from culture and structure. At the same time interrelation between culture and structure has to be of reinforcement, solid interaction and mutual support (see Figure 1 below).

Figure 1. The organization
Allaire and Firsiritou, 1993.

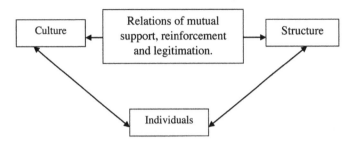

The Case of Tunisian Context

Some diagnoses and observations mission carried out with some Tunisian companies, have identified some salient features. Indeed, the number of hierarchical levels seems relatively high, despite that most of Tunisian companies are small and medium-sized enterprises (simple structure). At the same time, the management team is heterogeneous in terms of the nature of training (management, engineering), nature of experience, etc. Moreover, power is centralized and the style of leadership is rather authoritarian. Management is usually governed by informal principles (socio-emotional, family, friendship) rather than formal principles (rules, procedures, results, etc.) Moreover, according to the research work of Ben Turkia (1996: 72-73), entrepreneurs from the private sector are mainly concerned with the survival of their businesses. The style of management often depends on its environment, the culture of the country, traditions, social constraints, economic performance, banking system, social legislation and tax regulations. According to Ben Turkia (1996), it is recommended that Tunisian companies should involve psychologists and sociologists in their future projects and more particularly in the launching of new products, although at present they are dealing with the technical- Financial and neglect the cultural and innovation factors. The Tunisian management must go through the respect of all its variables (Ben Turkia 1996: 214-215).

EMPIRICAL STUDY

The Tunisian Agro-food companies have been chosen as our sample study to validate the model of organizational performance as their investments are very important in this sector. They usually try to review their functioning mode. Finally 66 companies have been questioned to see how their organizations are functioning. The method of collecting data which has been selected is the questionnaire. Culture items are mainly about change culture, interpretation of managerial choice, culture reinforcement of management system, etc. As for structure items, we put flexibility of management system, adaptation of the organization to the complexity of work, structure-environment relationship, monitoring system functioning, etc. Finally, for the items concerning the individuals, we focused especially on the working conditions, achievement of tasks, the sense of responsibility, the feeling of belonging to the organization, the collaborative working inside the organization, etc.

THE RESULTS

Analysis with SmartPLS software has been preceded firstly by verifying the validity and reliability conditions that it takes into consideration the limited number of respondents has shown the results below (see Table 1).

There are four criteria used in order to validate the validity and reliability of data collected. Cronbach's alpha and Composite reliability are used to evaluate reliability and should be between 0.7 and 0.9 (Hair et al. 2012). Results shown in the Table 1 are considered satisfactory. Regarding the convergent validity which ensures if the measures of the same construct are correlated (Carricano & Poujol 2008), should has Values of Average Variance Extracted (AVE) greater than 0.5 (Hair et al. 2012). Finally, to evaluate discriminant validity which indicates how much items of each construct represent only their construct, we used Fornell-Larcher analysis (Hair et al. 2012).

Table 1. Reliability and validity measurements

Variables	Reliability		Validity	
	Internal Consistency Reliability		**Convergent Validity**	**Discriminant Validity**
	Cronbach's Alpha	**Composite Reliability**	**Average Variance Extracted (AVE)**	**Fornell-Larcker Criterion**
Culture	0.682	0.820	0.611	0.782
Structure	0.731	0.825	0.543	0.737
Individuals	0.778	0.870	0.691	0.831

Once this completed, we pass to validate the structural model path coefficients. All the links are statistically significant (see Table 2) but it is more interesting to assess how strongly the exogenous variable explains endogenous variable. We have to take into consideration that a value of f square (f^2) between 0.02 and 0.15 indicates a weak effect whereas a value between 0.15 and 0.35 indicates a moderate effect while f square above 0.35 indicates a large effect (Cohen 1988).

According to these results, we noted the validation of the interrelations between the different components of the organization inside the Tunisian company but these interrelations are relative as the effect between culture and structure is moderate, between structure and individual is large and between culture and individual is moderate, close to weak.

Despite the fact that the validation of the links indicates a statistical significance of all structural links between the three dimensions of the organization, we cannot overlook some important remarks:

- The mutual support and reinforcement in the relation between culture and structure exist fairly. We observe the same effect but this effect is not yet large and this can involve that the organization in the Tunisian company is not considered yet solid. The Tunisian organization must get rid of the obsession of the authoritarian model, there must be more openness to other norms, traditions and culture of work that activate and impact positively the feasibility of any company.
- The effect of structure on individual is more important that the effect of the culture on the individual. This shows once again that the method of managing the system inside Tunisian companies has not yet been liberated yet from the centralization. Organization must be open to culture and new norms.

Table 2. Validation of structural links

Effects	Original Sample	T Statistics	p Values	f^2	Effect
Culture --> Individuals	0.343	3.654	0.000	0.173	Moderate effect close to weak
Structure--> Individuals	0.522	6.637	0.000	0.435	Large effect
Culture --> Structure	0.441	4.379	0.000	0.242	Moderate effect
Structure --> Culture	0.441	4.356	0.000	0.242	Moderate effect

Culture inside organization oriented to the adoption and introduction of innovations, develops and establishes values and attitudes that enable people to become involved in improvement processes and encourages individuals to develop the spirit of initiative which encourages them to embark on a competitive market. Flexible culture, can lead to the adoption of new methods of market development with a view to achieving a comparative advantage (Laforet 2016). On the other side, organizational structural often avoids inadequate support for strategic change and involvement in unrealistic expectations. Motivational behavior in the organization ensures goodwill, commitment and citizenship at all levels. Every organization must create a climate and a working environment of creativity both on the individual and collective level. Organizational performance at its cultural level establishes a process to maintain internal stability and control and achieve competitiveness in the market by favoring standards that allow new methods and conceptualizations of work. Organizational performance at its structural level can also control and monitor the execution of objectives, it serves to foster an adequate framework for listening to the expectations of clients and to organize tasks in order to deliver an efficient service (Marín-Idárraga & Cuartas 2016). Organizational performance at the level of motivational behaviors ensures goodwill, commitment and citizenship at all levels.

RELATIONSHIP BETWEEN WORKPLACE ARROGANCE AND ORGANIZATIONAL PERFORMANCE

In order to investigate the relationship between workplace arrogance and organizational performance, the authors will focus on the arrogance tendencies of a CEO and its repercussion on the dynamism of the company's strategy which is positively correlated to the organizational performance.

Due to the fact that no studies have been conducted to answer this issue, the authors have emphasized on the results of research studies that focalized on the relationship between narcissistic CEOs and firm performance.

Indeed, a study undertaken by Resick et al. (2009 cited by O'Reilly et al. 2013) showed two important results. The first, argue that more narcissistic CEOs of major league baseball organizations were less concerned with equitable rewards. The second is related to the fact that there is a significant and positive relationship between some of the CEOs' arrogance and firm performance, which was unexpected and surprising. Therefore, this is confirming the fact that *"there is sparse empirical data that verify the alleged negative relationship between arrogance and performance"* (Padua et al. 2010).

To go further in their analysis and to discover the nature of this relationship between workplace arrogance and organizational performance, the authors reviewed the results of a study conducted by Chatterjee and Hambrick (2007). Those latter have confirmed three basic hypotheses:

Hypothesis 1: The greater the narcissistic tendencies of a CEO, the greater the dynamism of the company's strategy.
Hypothesis 2: The greater the narcissistic tendencies of a CEO, the more extreme the company's performance.
Hypothesis 3: The greater the narcissistic tendencies of a CEO, the greater the fluctuation in the company's performance.

Knowing that narcissistic unlike arrogant person is focusing on its own person without disparaging others (see chapter 3) and knowing that the dynamism of the company's strategy (or strategic dynamism which means the degree of change in an organization's strategy and the degree to which an organization's strategy adapts to changing environments) is not only related to external factors[3] by also to internal factors such the volitional choices, experiences and preferences of executives, one can hypothesize that arrogant CEOs and arrogant top management team (TMT) will tend to lower firm's performance. In fact, successful response to change depends on strategic scope dimensions such as management strategy (see chapter 1) which is the responsibility of the CEOs and to TMT. Hence, strategic scope of a firm is function of the degree of arrogance of its CEOs and its TMT, which means that the greater the arrogance tendencies of a CEO and a TMT, the lower the dynamism of the company's strategy and consequently its organizational performance. In fact, developing a company's strategic scope required specific and high level competencies embedded in PDG and TMT. Those competencies are essential to build global company policy in collaboration with the stakeholders. This global company policy which summarizes the mission, the vision and the goals of the firm is considered as the backbone of its corporate strategy and business strategy. Those strategies are essential to achieve the strategic objectives and consequently the organizational performance. In addition and knowing that strategy is considered as a set of reflections, decisions, and actions undertaken by executives in order to enlarge the strategic scope of the firm and consequently its performance (Marchesnay, 2004). Based on the foregoing analyze and knowing *"that arrogant individuals tend to become less competent while humble individuals tend to be more competent*" as argued by Padua et al. (2010), one can conclude that workplace arrogance and particularly arrogant executives has a negative impact on organizational performance. This conclusion is supported by the findings of Leslie and Velsor (1996 cited in Brown 2012) who "*found that acting arrogant is one factor that precedes executive failure*", and those of Boyd (2001 cited in Brown 2010) and Ma and Karri (2005 cited in Brown 2010) who argued respectively that "*there is also some evidence that demonstrates that arrogance can result in organizational failure*" and "*can serve as a leader-based trigger of destruction within organizations*".

The same conclusion could be obtained by considering the relationship between workplace arrogance, job performance and organizational performance. In fact, knowing that arrogant behavior is negatively related to job performance (Silverman et al. 2012; Johnson et al. 2010) and that this latter is positively related to organizational performance (Padua et al. 2010), one can conclude that arrogant behavior is negatively related to organizational performance which is supported by the conclusion of Silverman et al. (2012) who argued the following:

Individuals who are arrogant at work make interpersonal interactions difficult, create an uncomfortable and potentially stressful work environment for others, and have poor performance ratings. This could ultimately influence feelings of customer satisfaction and loyalty, relationships among members of a work team or a leader and subordinate, and the organization's bottom line.

Another aspect of workplace arrogance concerns the employee's behavior towards the external environment, especially customers. In the following section, the authors focused on two types of arrogance: arrogance selling and arrogance in advertising and their implications on consumer's attitude and on purchase intentions and consequently on organizational performance.

Arrogance Selling and Arrogance in Advertising or Brand Arrogance

Arrogance selling is this arrogant behavior displayed by sellers and service employees towards customers. This arrogance is the result of the company's efforts to foster salespeople pride as a sales stimulator (Verbeke et al. 2004 cited in Wang et al. 2013). In fact, the marketers of MNCs operating in the luxury industry have observed and experienced that the higher the arrogance selling of their sellers, the greater the purchase intentions and the higher the sales growth. But this is only possible if the customer's self-esteem is low. In fact, researcher demonstrated that arrogance selling *"has direct negative impact on others' judgment of and attitudes toward the person showing it"* (Wang et al. 2013) especially customer with high self-esteem. Hence, arrogant selling should be related to the degree of customer self-esteem in order to maximize purchase intentions. Conversely,

… for people with high self-esteem, arrogance displayed by service employees makes a significantly negative difference on purchase intentions, thus likely stopping them from purchasing. They may instantly quit the buying process if treated badly (Wang et al. 2013).

The best way to achieve this adequacy is that

Marketers should continue to assess the self-esteem of their core customers through research before developing strategies. They might even provide training for their frontline staff on how to predict customers' self-esteem by the appearance, image, and/or body language. (Wang et al. 2013).

In the same vein, Brown (2012) has examined the effect of the use of arrogance in advertising on product and brand attitudes as well as purchase intentions. This arrogance is called "corporate or brand arrogance" and defined as *"behavior that communicates a company's or brand's exaggerated sense of superiority, which is often accomplished by disparaging others (Johnson, Silverman, Shyamsunder, Swee, Rodopman, Cho, & Bauer, 2010)"* (Brown 2012). The results of Brown's (2012) study have shown that the use of brand arrogance in advertising (*use of arrogance in commercials*) has an impact on the consumer's attitude which could be positive or negative depending on his previous experience with the brand or product. In fact,

Individuals who currently own target products react favorably to the use of arrogance in advertising by displaying higher attitudes toward the advertisement, brand, and product. Conversely, individuals who do not currently own target products react negatively to the use of arrogance in advertising by displaying lower attitudes toward the advertisement, brand, and product. (Brown 2012).

These opposite effects on consumers' attitudes are the same described and analyzed by Wang et al. (2013) who called it the 'dual attitudes'. *"This notion is in line with the dual attitudes literature that proposes the coexistence of both explicit negative attitudes and implicit positive attitudes (e.g., Chan & Sengupta, 2010)"* (Wang et al. 2013). In fact, the arrogant behavior of luxury brand employees affect negatively and explicitly the consumers' attitudes toward the brand. However, the past experience of these brand luxury consumers creates implicit attitudes toward these brands. Hence, this dual attitudes must be carefully managed by the marketers of firms operating in the luxury industry by taking into account the degree of consumer's self-esteem as mentioned above and by *"repeatedly associating luxury brands with desirable symbols and positive self-qualities"* in order to *"... reinforce the implicit positive attitudes (Fitzsimons, Chartrand, & Fitzsimons, 2008)"* (Wang et al. 2013).

Concerning the relationship between brand arrogance and the purchase intentions, scholars in this field argued that the use of arrogance in commercials or the exposure of an arrogant behavior by salespeople has a negative effect on the purchase intentions and by the consequence on the organizational performance (Wang et al. 2013; Brown 2012).

Following this analysis, the authors posit this main research hypothesis:

Workplace arrogance has a significant and negative impact on organizational performance.

This hypothesis will be verified empirically by the authors in the following chapter.

CONCLUSION

The fundamental objectives of this chapter was, first, to investigate theoretically the relationship between workplace arrogance on organizational performance and, second, to developed a conceptual model based on a review of the literature on this subject (workplace arrogance and organizational performance), that will be tested empirically (see Chapter 2).

Throughout this chapter, the authors introduced and explained the concept of arrogance by focusing on its origins. The authors emphasized the subtlety between arrogance and certain related concepts: narcissism, humility, self-confidence. This subtlety is fundamental to understanding arrogance in the workplace and its relationship to organizational performance. In addition, this will increase certain research proposals in the field of management which are very limited until today.

REFERENCES

Allaire, Y., & Firsiritou, M. E. (1993). *L'entreprise stratégique: penser la stratégie*. Édition Gaetan Morin.

Allen, R. S., & Helms, M. M. (2002). Employee perceptions of the relationship between strategy, rewards and organizational performance. *The Journal of Business Strategy, 19*, 115–139.

Almatrooshi, B., Singh, S. K., & Farouk, S. (2016). Determinants of organizational performance: A proposed framework. *International Journal of Productivity and Performance Management, 65*(6), 844–859. doi:10.1108/IJPPM-02-2016-0038

AppelBaum, S., Batolomucci, N., Beaumier, E., Boulanger, G., Corrigan, R., Doré, I., … Serroni, C. (2004). Organizational citizenship beahavior: a case study of culture, leadership and trust. *Management Decision, 42*(1), 13-40.

Ashmos, D. P., Duchon, D., & McDaniel, R. R. J. Jr. (2000). Organizational responses to complexity: The effect on organizational performance. *Journal of Organizational Change Management, 13*(6), 577–595. doi:10.1108/09534810010378597

Barker, R. C. (1995). Financial Performance Measurement: Not a Total Solution. *Management Decision, 33*(2), 31–39. doi:10.1108/00251749510081700

Beard, A. (2016). CEOs Shouldn't Try to Embody Their Firms' Culture. *Harvard Business Review*.

Ben Turkia, M. (1996). La culture du management tunisien. Centre d'études, de recherches et de publications.

Bowles, M. L., & Coates, G. (1993). Image and Substance: The Management of Performance as Rhetoric or Reality? *Personnel Review, 22*(2), 2, 3–21. doi:10.1108/00483489310028190

Brown, H. T. (2012). So What if I don't have an iPhone? The unintended consequences of using arrogance in advertising. *Journal of Applied Business Research, 28*(4), 555–562. doi:10.19030/jabr.v28i4.7040

Carricano, M., & Poujol, F. (2008). *Analyse de données avec SPSS* [Data analysis with SPSS]. Paris, France: Pearson Education.

Chatterjee, A., & Hambrick, D. C. (2007). It's All about Me: Narcissistic Chief Executive Officers and Their Effects on Company Strategy and Performance. *Administrative Science Quarterly, 52*(3), 351–386. doi:10.2189/asqu.52.3.351

Chuang, Y., Church, R., & Zikic, J. (2004). Organizational culture, group diversity and intra-group conflict. *Team Performance Management, 10*(1/2), 26–34. doi:10.1108/13527590410527568

Cohen, J. (1988). *Statistical power analysis for the behavioral sciences.* Mahwah, NJ: Lawrence Erlbaum.

De Waal, A. A. (2010). Performance-driven behavior as the key to improved organizational performance. *Measuring Business Excellence, 14*(1), 79–95. doi:10.1108/13683041011027472

Elliott, J. C. (2010). *Humility: Development and analysis of a scale* (PhD diss.). University of Tennessee. Retrieved from http://trace.tennessee.edu/utk_graddiss/795

Erdem, F., & Ozen, J. (2003). Cognitive and affective dimensions of trust in developing team performance. *Team Performance Management: An International Journal, 9*(5/6), 131-135.

Greene, H. (2008). Redefining BPM: Why Results and Performance Must Be Separated. *Business Performance Management Magazine, 6*(2), 4-12.

Grewel, R., & Tansuhaj, P. (2001). Building organisational capabilities for managing economic crisis: The role of market orientation and strategic felexibility. *Journal of Marketing, 65*(2), 67–80. doi:10.1509/jmkg.65.2.67.18259

Gupta, A., Prinzinger, J., & Masserschmidt, D. C. (1998). Role of organisational commitment in advanced manufacturing technology and performance relationship. *Integrated Manufacturing Systems, 9*(5), 272–278. doi:10.1108/09576069810230383

Hair, J. F., Jr., Ringle, C. M., & Sarstedt, M. (2012). Partial least squares: The better approach to structural equation modeling? *Long Range Planning, 45*(5/6), 312-319.

Hair, J. F., Sarstedt, M., Ringle, C. M., & Mena, J. M. (2012). An Assessment of the Use of Partial Least Squares Structural Equation Modeling in Marketing Research. *Journal of the Academy of Marketing Science, 40*(3), 414–433. doi:10.1007/s11747-011-0261-6

Handa, V., & Adas, A. (1996). Predicting the Level of Organizational Effectiveness: A Methodology for the Construction Firm. *Construction Management and Economics, 14*(4), 341–352. doi:10.1080/014461996373412

Jashapara, A. (2003). Cognition, culture and competition: An empirical test of the learning organisation. *The Learning Organization, 10*(1), 31–50. doi:10.1108/09696470310457487

Johnson, M. K., Rowatt, C. W., & Petrini, L. (2011). A new trait on the market: Honesty–Humility as a unique predictor of job performance ratings. *Personality and Individual Differences, 50*(6), 857–862. doi:10.1016/j.paid.2011.01.011

Johnson, R. E., Silverman, S. B., Shyamsunder, A., Yao. Swee, H., Rodopman, O. B., Cho, E., & Bauer, J. (2010). Acting Superior But Actually Inferior?: Correlates and Consequences of Workplace Arrogance. *Human Performance, 23*(5), 403–427. doi:10.1080/08959285.2010.515279

Laforet, S. (2016). Effects of organisational culture on organisational innovation performance in family firms. *Journal of Small Business and Enterprise Development, 23*(2), 379–407. doi:10.1108/JSBED-02-2015-0020

Li, J., & Tang, Y. (2010). CEO hubris and firm risk taking in China: The moderating role of managerial discretion. *Academy of Management Journal, 53*(1), 45–68. doi:10.5465/AMJ.2010.48036912

Lusthaus, C., Adrien, M. H., & Perstinger, M. (1999). *Capacity Building: Implications for Planning, Monitoring and Evaluation.* Montréal: Universalia.

Lusthaus, C., Adrien, M.H., Anderson, G., Carden, F., & Montalván, P. G. (2003). *Évaluation organisationnelle. Cadre pour l'amélioration de la performance.* Les Presses de l'Université Laval et le Centre de recherches pour le développement international.

Marín-Idárraga, D. A., & Cuartas, J. C. (2016). Organizational structure and innovation: Analysis from the strategic co-alignment. *Academia (Caracas)*, *29*(4), 388–406. doi:10.1108/ARLA-11-2015-0303

Mcallister, D. J. (1995). Affect and cognition based trust as foundations for interpersonal cooperation in organizations. *Academy of Management Journal*, *38*(1), 24–59. doi:10.2307/256727

Morris, J. A., Brotheridge, M. C., & Urbanski, J. C. (2005). Bringing humility to leadership: Antecedents and consequences of leader humility. *Human Relations*, *58*(10), 1323–1350. doi:10.1177/0018726705059929

O'Reilly, C. A., Doerr, B., Caldwell, D. F., & Chatman, J. A. (2013). Narcissistic CEOs and executive compensation. *The Leadership Quarterly*. doi:10.1016/j.leaqua.2013.08.002

Organ, D. W. (1990). The motivational basis of organizational citizenship behaviour. *Research in Organizational Behavior*, *12*, 43–72.

Owen, L. D. (2016). Hubris syndrome. *Entreprise Risk*, 20-24.

Padua, R. N., Lerin, M. M., Tumapon, T. T., & Pañares, Z. A. (2010). Patterns and Dynamics of an Arrogance-Competence. *Liceo Journal of Higher Education Research*, *6*(2), 76–97. doi:10.7828/ljher.v6i2.66

Parkinson, J., Schuster, L., & Russell-Bennett, R. (2016). Insights into the complexity of behaviours: The MOAB framework. *Journal of Social Marketing*, *6*(4), 412–427. doi:10.1108/JSOCM-10-2015-0071

Peters, A. S., Rowat, W. C., & Johnson, M. K. (2011). Associations between Dispositional Humility and Social Relationship Quality. *Psychology (Irvine, Calif.)*, *2*(3), 155–161. doi:10.4236/psych.2011.23025

Pillal, K. G., & Goldsmith, R. E. (2006). Calibrating managerial knowledge of customer feedback measures: A conceptual model. *Marketing Theory*, *6*(2), 223–243. doi:10.1177/1470593106063984

Powers, C., Nam, R. K., Rowatt, W. C., & Hill, P. C. (2007). Associations between humility, spiritual transcendence, and forgiveness. *Social Scientific Study of Religion*, *18*, 75–94.

Quinn, R.E., and J. Rohrbaugh, (1983). A Spatial Model of Effectiveness Criteria: Towards a Competing Values Approach to Organizational Analysis. *Management Science*, *29*, 363-377.

Raskin, R., & Terry, H. (1988). A Principal-Components Analysis of the Narcissistic Personality Inventory and Further Evidence of Its Construct Validity. *Journal of Personality and Social Psychology, 54*(5), 890–902. doi:10.1037/0022-3514.54.5.890 PMID:3379585

Robbins, S. P. (2001). *Organizational behaviour.* Prentice-Hall.

Rowatt, W. C., Powers, C., Targhetta, V., Comer, J., Kennedy, S., & Labouff, J. (2006). Development and initial validation of an implicit measure of humility relative to arrogance. *The Journal of Positive Psychology, 1*(4), 198–211. doi:10.1080/17439760600885671

Sevcik, P (2003). A framework for enterprise application performance. *Business Communications Review, 33*(11), 8.

Silverman, S. B., Johnson, R. E., McConnell, N., & Carr, A. (2012). Arrogance: A Formula for Leadership Failure. *The Industrial-Organizational Psychologist, 50*(1), 21–28.

Simons, R., & Dávila, A. (1998). *Harvard Business Review on Measuring Corporate Performance.* Cambridge, MA: Harvard Business School Press.

Swiden Wick, R. A. (2013). *Personality and interpersonal aspects of the work environment* (Honors thesis). University of Central Florida, Orlando, FL. Retrieved from http://stars.library.ucf.edu/honorstheses1990-2015/1469

Tiberius, V., & Walker, J. D. (1998). Arrogance. *American Philosophical Quarterly, 35*(4), 379–390.

Wang, X., Chow, C. W. C., & Leung Luk, C. (2013). Does Service Employee Arrogance Discourage Sales of Luxury Brands in Emerging Economies? *Psychology and Marketing, 30*(10), 918–933. doi:10.1002/mar.20655

Wojtczuk-Turek, A., & Turek, D. (2015). Innovative behaviour in the workplace: The role of HR flexibility, individual flexibility and psychological capital: the case of Poland. *European Journal of Innovation Management, 18*(3), 397–419. doi:10.1108/EJIM-03-2014-0027

Yeo, R. (2003). The tangibles and intangibles of organisational performance. *Team Performance Management: An International Journal, 9*(7-8), 199-204.

Zayas-Ortiz, M., Rosario, E., Marquez, E., & Gruñeiro, P. C. (2015). Relationship between organizational commitments and organizational citizenship behaviour in a sample of private banking employees. *The International Journal of Sociology and Social Policy*, *35*(1/2), 91–106. doi:10.1108/IJSSP-02-2014-0010

Zhou, J., & George, J M. (2001). When job dissatisfaction leads to creativity: encouraging the expression of voice. *Academy of Management Journal*, *44*(1), 31.

ENDNOTES

[1]   "Using the DSM-II (Diagnostic and Statistical Manual of Mental Disorders; American Psychiatric Association, 1968) behavioral criteria as a template, Raskin and Hall originally developed a 220-item instrument for measuring narcissism. Through a series of internal consistency tests, the instrument has been reduced to fewer items (reviewed in Raskin and Terry, 1988; Campbell, Goodie, and Foster, 2004), which have formed the basis for extensive subsequent tests and applications" (Chatterjee & Hambrick 2007: 356).

[2]   "Arrogance is more social in nature because it is manifested during interpersonal interactions—it encompasses actions and language that exaggerate one's own importance while also disparaging others (Leary et al., 1997; Schlenker & Leary, 1982)" (Johnson et al. 2010: 406).

[3]   "Researchers have found that industry conditions (Birkinshaw, Morrison, and Hulland, 1995), organizational size (Chen and Hambrick, 1995), slack (Singh, 1986), and other contextual factors affect the degree of dynamism observed in companies' strategies" (Chatterjee and Hambrick 2007).

Chapter 2

Workplace Arrogance and Its Impact on the Organizational Performance in the Hospitality Industry

ABSTRACT

The aim of this chapter is to test empirically the fundamental hypothesis highlighting the relationship between "workplace arrogance" and "organizational performance." The results of this study undertaken in the Tunisian hotel industry validate 2 hypotheses out of 30 and reach crucial findings: (1) workplace arrogance is a multidimensional variable (6 dimensions) and its dimensions are unidimensional; (2) workplace arrogance has a significant and negative impact on organizational performance measured by two dimensions: the customer satisfaction and the quality of service; and (3) workplace arrogance has a significant and positive impact on organizational performance measured by two dimensions: quality of service and financial performance. These findings could be considered as a theoretical contribution never been discovered before.

DOI: 10.4018/978-1-5225-5525-4.ch002

INTRODUCTION

As the authors have noted previously (see chapter 1), research on workplace arrogance are very scarce, especially the link between it and organizational performance. To cope with this research scarcity and in order to explore and explain the relationship between workplace arrogance and organizational performance, the authors have undertaken an empirical study to explore this relationship in the Tunisian hotel industry. The findings of this research were unexpected and first time discovered, such as the study of the dimensionality of the workplace arrogance.

This chapter is devoted to the presentation of the research methodology, its results, the discussion of the research methodology and the presentation of contributions, limitations and future research trajectories.

Research Model and Hypotheses

Knowing that the organizational performance is a multidimensional concept, the authors have chosen five dimensions to measure it: Customer satisfaction, Employee satisfaction, Financial Performance, Innovation, and Quality of service. Thus, the research model and the underlying hypotheses are the following (see Figure 1).

It can be deduced from the above conceptual model that workplace arrogance has a significant and negative impact on the dimensions of organizational performance. So:

H1: Workplace arrogance has a significant and negative impact on financial performance.

H2: Workplace arrogance has a significant and negative impact on customer satisfaction.

H3: Workplace arrogance has a significant and negative impact on employee satisfaction.

H4: Workplace arrogance has a significant and negative impact on quality of service.

H5: Workplace arrogance has a significant and negative impact on innovation.

To verify this set of hypotheses, the authors have followed the following method.

Figure 1. Initial conceptual model and hypotheses

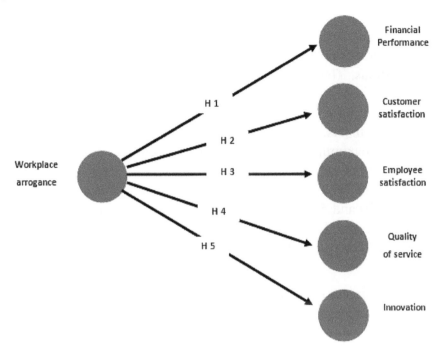

RESEARCH METHODOLOGY

Sampling and Data Collection

The choice of the hotel industry was motivated mainly by two reasons. First, few academic research has been carried out in Tunisia in this sector despite the recent crisis it has experienced in recent years (a drop of -9.2% in the hotel and catering sector). The latter was triggered by the 2011 revolution and aggravated by the wave of terrorist attacks between 2012 and 2015. Secondly, this industry is still of economic importance for Tunisia, contributing 7.5% of the product (GDP) and generates more than 400,000 direct jobs (ONEQ 2013).

This study was conducted in 2016 on a sample of hotel operators chosen by applying the non-probabilistic method by judgment which is a form of the non-probabilistic method by convenience (Malhorta 2012). These operatives belong to 5 stars hotels. Two of these hotels belong to internationally renowned chains and five belong to a local Tunisian group. These hotels are located in three locations (Gammarth, Carthage and Downtown) of Grand Tunis (the capital of Tunisia). This choice is supported by two main reasons: (1) they are known for their high quality of service; and (2) they are considered as business hotels.

The questionnaire was distributed directly to employees or via the human resources department of these hotels. Our sample is composed by 52 observations. The survey was conducted for 8 weeks (November and December).

The authors have chosen the traditional method of administering the questionnaire, that is, the face-to-face distribution of printed sheets in order to guarantee maximum answers and for a practical reason that they do not have the e-mail of all of respondents.

As shown in Table 1, the sample is predominantly male. Most of them are between 30 and 50 years old and have qualifications corresponding to License and Master. The majority has a salary between 1000 and 2000 dinars. As mentioned below (see Table 1), our sample is functional.

Table 1. Demographic characteristics

	Number	%
Gender		
Male	35	67
Female	17	33
Age		
Under 20 years	-	-
20-30 years	6	12
30-40 years	23	44
40-50 years	13	25
50-60 years	10	19
Above 60 years	-	-
Marital Status		
Single	13	25
Married	39	75
Seniority		
Under 1 year	3	6
1-5 years	16	31
5-10 years	20	38
10-15 years	8	15
Above 15 years	5	10

continued on following page

Table 1. Continued

	Number	%
Qualification		
BTS	9	17
BTP	4	8
BAC	4	8
License	16	32
Master	14	27
PhD	2	2
Other	3	6
Salary		
Under 500 DT	-	-
500 - 1000	6	11
1001 - 1500	13	25
1501 - 2000	18	35
Above 2000	15	29
Function		
Head bar	2	3.85
Head chef	2	3.85
Booking manager	2	3.85
Head of security	4	7.7
CFO	1	1.92
DGM	2	3.85
HRM	3	5.77
Development manager	1	1.92
Financial manager	3	5.77
Sales manager	3	5.77
Hosting manager	1	1.92
SPA Director	2	3.85
Catering manager	2	3.85
Technical manager	2	3.85
F&B	1	1.92
Executive Housekeeper	4	7.7
Health manager	1	1.92
Social media coordinator	1	1.92

RESEARCH VARIABLES MEASUREMENTS

Operationalization of Organizational Performance

The items related to each dimension of the organizational performance variable were identified from the review of the literature related to the study's subject (Bailey et al. 2000). The development of all these items followed three steps: (1) the creation of a set of items that reflected the distinctive characteristics of each dimension and were appropriate for use in a self-reported questionnaire; (2) the evaluation of the group of items by a group of university teachers; and (3) the evaluation of all these items by a sample of managers.

Table 2 summarizes the dimensions of the "organizational performance" variable studied and the number of items in each of them (20 items). For each dimension, respondents were asked to indicate their degree of agreement or disagreement with each proposal by choosing between 1 "very low" and 5 "very high". The question was: "Please indicate the "degree of development" of your hotel relative to the indicators mentioned below, for the past 3 years, in comparison with your two most important competitors".

Operationalization of Workplace Arrogance

Workplace arrogance as an independent variable was measured by using a specific scale developed by Johnson et al. (2010). This instrument is called Workplace Arrogance Scales (WARS), it is "a measure that has allowed for more efficient and reliable examination of arrogance in the workplace. Thanks in part to this measure, empirical evidence regarding the effects of workplace arrogance has begun to emerge" (Silverman et al. 2012). The WARS scale ($a = 0.93$) comprises 26 self-report items (see Table 3), scored on a five-point Likert scale.

RESULTS

Exploratory Factor Analysis (EFA)

In order to make our study more reasonable and well structured, the authors preceded firstly by the Exploratory Factor Analysis (EFA) in order view the dimensionality of the concept of Arrogance. We noted that the latent variable

Table 2. Dimensions of job satisfaction

Dimensions	Number of Items
Financial Performance	
1. Room occupancy rate 2. Market share gain 3. Average sales growth in the last five years 4. Income per room 5. Total gross profit 6. Gross profit per room 7. Wealth creation (accounting value of the firm with respect to its market value) 8. Capacity to generate profit in times of crisis	8
Customer Satisfaction Level	
9. Ability to adjust to guest needs and wants 10. Ability to meet customer requirements on time 11. Delivering guest products and services on time	3
Employee Satisfaction Level	
12. Number of employee training and development programs 13. Employee turnover surveys 14. Employee performance appraisal ratings	3
Quality of Service	
15. Maintaining hotel classification rating (e.g. five-star) 16. Guest evaluations of attitude, behavior, and expertise of employees 17. Guest evaluations of design facilities renovations and maintenance 18. Guest evaluations of benefits gained such as relaxation, exercise, and refreshment	4
Innovation	
19. Monitoring of performance of individual employee innovators 20. Number of product and services innovated per year	2

is represented by 26 items. The validity and reliability will be checked later using the SmartPLS software (Carricano and Poujol 2008; Akrout 2010). To perform this analysis, we began, firstly, by checking the adequacy of the data and their factorization. The index of Keyser Meyer Olkin (KMO) is about 0.809 and the Bartlett's test of sphericity equals to 0.000. This indicates factorable solutions. An orthogonal rotation (Varimax) helps simplify the interpretation of the factors (Hair et al. 2010). The results are shown in the Table 4.

The results obtained following the exploratory level indicate the adequacy of data. All items are selected with an acceptable variance (above the 50% threshold) and good performances qualities (above the 50% threshold). Only three items are removed which are Arrogance 18, 19 and 26. The adjustment provides six dimensions of Arrogance verified a good representation with high validity and reliability as will be show in the follow analysis.

Table 3. Workplace arrogance scale

Items	λ
1. Believes that s/he knows better than everyone else in any given situation	.78
2. Makes decisions that impact others without listening to their input	.78
3. Uses non-verbal behaviors like glaring or staring to make people uncomfortable	.76
4. Criticizes others	.75
5. Belittles his/her employees publicly	.75
6. Asserts authority in situations when s/he does not have the required information	.72
7. Discredits others' ideas during meetings and often makes those individuals look bad	.72
8. Shoots down other people's ideas in public	.71
9. Exhibits different behaviors with subordinates than with supervisors	.70
10. Makes unrealistic time demands on others	.70
11. Does not find it necessary to explain his/her decisions to others	.70
12. *Willing to listen to others' opinions, ideas, or perspectives	.69
13. *Welcomes constructive feedback	.69
14. *Takes responsibility for his/her own mistakes	.68
15. *Never criticizes other employees in a threatening manner	.67
16. *Realizes that it does not always have to be 'his/her way or the highway'	.67
17. *Avoids getting angry when his/her ideas are criticized	.66
18. Takes him/herself too seriously	.66
19. *Gives others credit for their ideas	.66
20. *Is considerate of others' workloads	.66
21. *Is willing to take credit for success as well as blame for failure	.66
22. *Does not mind doing menial tasks	.64
23. *Can get others to pay attention without getting emotionally 'heated up'	.64
24. *Promises to address subordinates' complaints with every intention of working to resolve them	.63
25. *Does not see him/herself as being too important for some tasks	.62
26. *Puts organizational objectives before his/her personal agenda .61	.61

Source: Johnson et al. (2010).

Note. a = .93.

* Reverse scored items.

In addition, each construct represents an acceptable internal reliability since as their alpha coefficients are all higher than the threshold of 0.7 (Anderson and Gerbing 1988; Hair et al. 2006).

Table 4. Results of exploratory analysis

Items	Loadings					
	D1	D2	D3	D4	D5	D6
Arrogance2	0.755					
Arrogance3	0.782					
Arrogance4	0.750					
Arrogance5	0.825					
Arrogance6	0.763					
Arrogance7	0.626					
Arrogance8	0.734					
Arrogance9	0.764					
Arrogance10	0.622					
Arrogance11	0.619					
Arrogance14		0.776				
Arrogance15		0.723				
Arrogance16		0.746				
Arrogance23		0.609				
Arrogance13			0.662			
Arrogance17			0.611			
Arrogance24			0.819			
Arrogance20				0.726		
Arrogance21				0.766		
Arrogance22					0.828	
Arrogance25					0.711	
Arrogance1						0.701
Arrogance12						0.607

KMO = 0.809 Bartlett's test of sphericity 0.000 communalities = verify the quality of representation DF = 253

Results of Measurement Model

As SmartPLS can function with small sample size and without distributional assumptions, the authors preceded in our study to perform the analysis taking into consideration the dimensionality results of the Arrogance variable generated by the SPSS.

The measurement model ensures the quality of the model and eliminates any unsuitable indicators related with its construct. All items of the research model contributing significantly to their assigned constructs (outer loadings values of items greater than 0.7 or even 0.8) will be kept (Henseler et al. 2009; Hair et al. 2012; Henseler et al. 2012). The detailed results are presented in the Table 5.

Table 5. Reliability and validity measurements

Variables	Dimension	Items Retained	Outer Loadings	Reliability	Validity	
				Internal Consistency Reliability	**Convergent Validity**	**Discriminant Validity**
				Composite Reliability	Average Variance Extracted (AVE)	Fornell-Larcker Criterion
Arrogance	Arrogance 1	Arrogance2	0.788	0.941	0.617	0.785
		Arrogance3	0.751			
		Arrogance4	0.818			
		Arrogance5	0.833			
		Arrogance6	0.793			
		Arrogance7	0.792			
		Arrogance8	0.856			
		Arrogance9	0.763			
		Arrogance10	0.720			
		Arrogance11	0.729			
	Arrogance 2	Arrogance14	0.836	0.883	0.655	0.809
		Arrogance15	0.860			
		Arrogance16	0.820			
		Arrogance23	0.712			
	Arrogance 3	Arrogance13	0.627	0.828	0.622	0.789
		Arrogance17	0.942			
		Arrogance24	0.765			
	Arrogance 4	Arrogance20	0.870	0.873	0.775	0.880
		Arrogance21	0.891			
	Arrogance 5	Arrogance22	0.912	0.893	0.807	0.898
		Arrogance25	0.884			
	Arrogance 6	Arrogance1	0.881	0.822	0.699	0.836
		Arrogance12	0.788			

continued on following page

Table 5. Continued

Variables	Dimension	Items Retained	Outer Loadings	Reliability	Validity	
				Internal Consistency Reliability	Convergent Validity	Discriminant Validity
				Composite Reliability	Average Variance Extracted (AVE)	Fornell-Larcker Criterion
Organizational performance	Customer satisfaction	Cust.Sat1	0.933	0.860	0.682	0.826
		Cust.Sat2	0.925			
		Cust.Sat3	0.566			
	Employee satisfaction	Empl.Sat1	0.807	0.890	0.804	0.897
		Empl.Sat3	0.978			
	Financial Performance	Finan.Perf1	0.711	0.922	0.598	0.774
		Finan.Perf2	0.783			
		Finan.Perf3	0.776			
		Finan.Perf4	0.814			
		Finan.Perf5	0.852			
		Finan.Perf6	0.866			
		Finan.Perf17	0.759			
		Finan.Perf8	0.596			
	Innovation	Innov1	0.847	0.872	0.773	0.879
		Innov2	0.910			
	Quality of service	Qual.Serv1	0.667	0.859	0.606	0.778
		Qual.Serv2	0.815			
		Qual.Serv3	0.824			
		Qual.Serv4	0.797			

In order to measure the validity and reliability of the variables, the authors used in this research work three measures. The Composite reliability in order to check internal consistency reliability, it should be greater than 0.7. The Average Variance Extracted (AVE) to check the convergent validity, it has to be greater than 0.5 to indicate a good measure and Fornell-Larcker Criterion to check the discriminant validity. This measure indicates how much items of each construct represents only their construct. The Fornell-Larcher analysis compares the square root of AVE with the latent variable correlations. This square root should be greater than the highest correlation of each construct. In this analysis it has been confirmed that all Fornell-Larcker values are greater than correlations (Hair et al. 2012). Since, all the measurement results are satisfactory; one can easily move to test the effect of all the dimensions of workplace arrogance on the dependent variables which are: the financial performance, the customer satisfaction, the employee satisfaction, the quality of service, and the innovation.

Before moving on to the results of the structural model, it should be noted that the initial conceptual model was modified (see Figure 2) following the results of the EFA studying the dimensionality of workplace arrogance. As a consequence, it should be noted that the number of the hypotheses has been changed (from 5 to 30).

It can be deduced from the above conceptual model the following set of hypotheses linking the 6 dimensions of workplace arrogance to the five dimensions of organizational performance.

Figure 2. Conceptual model after EFA

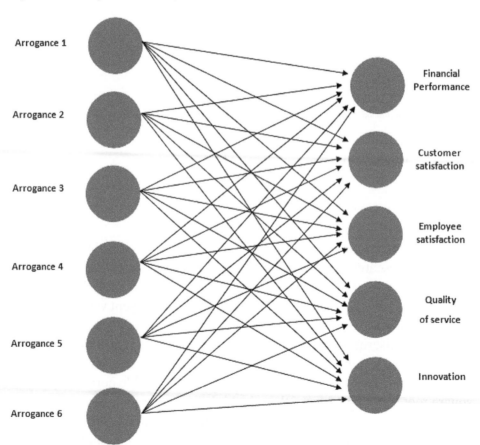

H1a: Workplace arrogance 1 has a significant and negative impact on financial performance.

H1b: Workplace arrogance 1 has a significant and negative impact on customer satisfaction.

H1c: Workplace arrogance 1 has a significant and negative impact on employee satisfaction.

H1d: Workplace arrogance 1 has a significant and negative impact on quality of service.

H1e: Workplace arrogance 1 has a significant and negative impact on innovation.

H2a: Workplace arrogance 2 has a significant and negative impact on financial performance.

H2b: Workplace arrogance 2 has a significant and negative impact on customer satisfaction.

H2c: Workplace arrogance 2 has a significant and negative impact on employee satisfaction.

H2d: Workplace arrogance 2 has a significant and negative impact on quality of service.

H2e: Workplace arrogance 2 has a significant and negative impact on innovation.

H3a: Workplace arrogance 3 has a significant and negative impact on financial performance.

H3b: Workplace arrogance 3 has a significant and negative impact on customer satisfaction.

H3c: Workplace arrogance 3 has a significant and negative impact on employee satisfaction.

H3d: Workplace arrogance 3 has a significant and negative impact on quality of service.

H3e: Workplace arrogance 3 has a significant and negative impact on innovation.

H4a: Workplace arrogance 4 has a significant and negative impact on financial performance.

H4b: Workplace arrogance 4 has a significant and negative impact on customer satisfaction.

H4c: Workplace arrogance 4 has a significant and negative impact on employee satisfaction.

H4d: Workplace arrogance 4 has a significant and negative impact on quality of service.

H4e: Workplace arrogance 4 has a significant and negative impact on innovation.

H5a: Workplace arrogance 5 has a significant and negative impact on financial performance.

H5b: Workplace arrogance 5 has a significant and negative impact on customer satisfaction.

H5c: Workplace arrogance 5 has a significant and negative impact on employee satisfaction.

H5d: Workplace arrogance 5 has a significant and negative impact on quality of service.

H5e: Workplace arrogance 5 has a significant and negative impact on innovation.

H6a: Workplace arrogance 6 has a significant and negative impact on financial performance.

H6b: Workplace arrogance 6 has a significant and negative impact on customer satisfaction.

H6c: Workplace arrogance 6 has a significant and negative impact on employee satisfaction.

H6d: Workplace arrogance 6 has a significant and negative impact on quality of service.

H6e: Workplace arrogance 6 has a significant and negative impact on innovation.

Results of PLS Structural Model

In this step, the authors evaluated the structural model path coefficients by running the bootstrapping (Hair et al. 2016). The *p values* reported the significant or not of the effects of all the dimensions on the dependent variables. The authors noted that the threshold of statistical significance which is the probability of the error permitted in this study is 0.10. Managerial research and more specifically regarding the data collected from companies can use a threshold of 10% and considers that all tests with values lower than 0.10 can be considered significant (Thietart et al. 2003).

According to this, with p values less than 0.1, one can confirm the existence of significant link (see Table 6 and Figure 3).

As shown on Table 7, only two hypotheses have been validated: H1b and H1d. That is, workplace arrogance 1 has a significant and negative impact on customer satisfaction and on the quality of service. That is, workplace

Table 6. Validation of structural links

Structural Links	Original Sample	T Statistics	*p* Values
Arrogance1 -> Cus.Sat	**-0.350**	**1.739**	**0.082**
Arrogance1 -> Empl.Sat	-0.152	0.641	0.521
Arrogance1 -> Fina.Perf	-0.025	0.095	0.925
Arrogance1 -> Innova	-0.277	1.125	0.261
Arrogance1 -> Qual.Serv	**-0.563**	**2.811**	**0.005**
Arrogance2 -> Cus.Sat	-0.328	1.140	0.254
Arrogance2 -> Empl.Sat	-0.160	0.559	0.576
Arrogance2 -> Fina.Perf	-0.234	1.009	0.313
Arrogance2 -> Innova	-0.149	0.586	0.558
Arrogance2 -> Qual.Serv	-0.235	1.182	0.237
Arrogance3 -> Cus.Sat	0.085	0.323	0.747
Arrogance3 -> Empl.Sat	0.089	0.492	0.622
Arrogance3 -> Fina.Perf	-0.013	0.064	0.949
Arrogance3 -> Innova	0.225	1.080	0.280
Arrogance3 -> Qual.Serv	**0.605**	**3.013**	**0.003**
Arrogance4 -> Cus.Sat	0.043	0.206	0.837
Arrogance4 -> Empl.Sat	0.228	1.179	0.238
Arrogance4 -> Fina.Perf	0.016	0.078	0.938
Arrogance4 -> Innova	0.069	0.371	0.711
Arrogance4 -> Qual.Serv	0.030	0.186	0.853
Arrogance5 -> Cus.Sat	-0.145	0.826	0.409
Arrogance5 -> Empl.Sat	-0.260	1.389	0.165
Arrogance5 -> Fina.Perf	0.055	0.324	0.746
Arrogance5 -> Innova	-0.285	1.392	0.164
Arrogance5 -> Qual.Serv	-0.039	0.274	0.784
Arrogance6 -> Cus.Sat	0.185	0.883	0.377
Arrogance6 -> Empl.Sat	-0.067	0.305	0.760
Arrogance6 -> Fina.Perf	**0.478**	**1.937**	**0.053**
Arrogance6 -> Innova	0.291	1.454	0.146
Arrogance6 -> Qual.Serv	-0.014	0.069	0.945

arrogance has a significant and negative impact on organizational performance measured by two dimensions: the customer satisfaction and the quality of service.

Figure 3. Final conceptual model

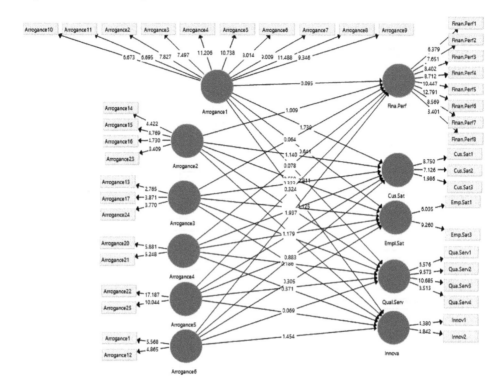

Another very interesting finding is that workplace arrogance 3 has a significant and positive impact on quality of service; and workplace arrogance 6 has a significant and positive impact on financial performance. In fact, whatever the nature of this workplace arrogance this result is crucial because it posits that workplace arrogance has a significant and positive impact on organizational performance (quality of service and financial performance) which is not common and shared by the previous findings in this field.

DISCUSSION

These unexpected results (in particular for the last two) should be discussed and explained by making the bridge with what the literature in this field has to tell us. However, to achieve this goal, it is essential to give meaning to the retained dimensions of workplace arrogance: workplace arrogance 1; workplace arrogance 3; and workplace arrogance 6.

Table 7. Validation of research hypotheses

Hypotheses	Validation
H1a: workplace arrogance 1 has a significant and negative impact on financial performance.	No
H1b: workplace arrogance 1 has a significant and negative impact on customer satisfaction.	Yes
H1c: workplace arrogance 1 has a significant and negative impact on employee satisfaction.	No
H1d: workplace arrogance 1 has a significant and negative impact on quality of service.	Yes
H1e: workplace arrogance 1 has a significant and negative impact on innovation.	No
H2a: workplace arrogance 2 has a significant and negative impact on financial performance.	No
H2b: workplace arrogance 2 has a significant and negative impact on customer satisfaction.	No
H2c: workplace arrogance 2 has a significant and negative impact on employee satisfaction.	No
H2d: workplace arrogance 2 has a significant and negative impact on quality of service.	No
H2e: workplace arrogance 2 has a significant and negative impact on innovation.	No
H3a: workplace arrogance 3 has a significant and negative impact on financial performance.	No
H3b: workplace arrogance 3 has a significant and negative impact on customer satisfaction.	No
H3c: workplace arrogance 3 has a significant and negative impact on employee satisfaction.	No
H3d: workplace arrogance 3 has a significant and negative impact on quality of service.	No
H3e: workplace arrogance 3 has a significant and negative impact on innovation.	No
H4a: workplace arrogance 4 has a significant and negative impact on financial performance.	No
H4b: workplace arrogance 4 has a significant and negative impact on customer satisfaction.	No
H4c: workplace arrogance 4 has a significant and negative impact on employee satisfaction.	No
H4d: workplace arrogance 4 has a significant and negative impact on quality of service.	No
H4e: workplace arrogance 4 has a significant and negative impact on innovation.	No
H5a: workplace arrogance 5 has a significant and negative impact on financial performance.	No
H5b: workplace arrogance 5 has a significant and negative impact on customer satisfaction.	No
H5c: workplace arrogance 5 has a significant and negative impact on employee satisfaction.	No
H5d: workplace arrogance 5 has a significant and negative impact on quality of service.	No
H5e: workplace arrogance 5 has a significant and negative impact on innovation.	No
H6a: workplace arrogance 6 has a significant and negative impact on financial performance.	No
H6b: workplace arrogance 6 has a significant and negative impact on customer satisfaction.	No
H6c: workplace arrogance 6 has a significant and negative impact on employee satisfaction.	No
H6d: workplace arrogance 6 has a significant and negative impact on quality of service.	No
H6e: workplace arrogance 6 has a significant and negative impact on innovation.	No

Workplace arrogance 1 is explained by 10 items (see Table 8).

What it can be concluded from these elements is a set of basic concepts of management, namely: decision, authority and communication. Obviously, the meanings of these concepts as presented by the ten items remind us of

Table 8.

Arrogance 2. Makes decisions that impact others without listening to their input
Arrogance 3. Uses non-verbal behaviors like glaring or staring to make people uncomfortable
Arrogance 4. Criticizes others
Arrogance 5. Belittles his/her employees publicly
Arrogance 6. Asserts authority in situations when s/he does not have the required information
Arrogance 7. Discredits others' ideas during meetings and often makes those individuals look bad
Arrogance 8. Shoots down other people's ideas in public
Arrogance 9. Exhibits different behaviors with subordinates than with supervisors
Arrogance 10. Makes unrealistic time demands on others
Arrogance 11. Does not find it necessary to explain his/her decisions to others

the classical school of management and its two principal precepts given by Taylor: the uniqueness of command principle and the authority principle. We are faced with authoritarian management characterized in this case by a "chronic belief of superiority" (Brown 2012) exaggerated by a disrespectful behavior against others (Johnson et al. 2010 in Silverman et al. 2012).

The authors called this kind of workplace arrogance: "Superiority/Disrespect based Workplace Arrogance".

Thereby, one could say that Superiority/Disrespect based Workplace Arrogance has a significant and negative impact on customer satisfaction and on the quality of service. The first finding supported and shared those of Silverman et al. (2012). For the second finding, there are no studies sharing it. It is the first time one concludes that workplace arrogance has a significant and negative impact on the quality of service.

Workplace arrogance 3 is explained by three items shown in Table 9.

The significant and positive impact of this workplace arrogance on quality of service has never been achieved before. However, this could be explained by focusing on the nature of the hotel industry which requires the application of a set of standards without criticizing them.

Table 9.

Arrogance 13. *Welcomes constructive feedback
Arrogance 17. *Avoids getting angry when his/her ideas are criticized
Arrogance 24. *Promises to address subordinates' complaints with every intention of working to resolve them

For the workplace arrogance 6 that is explained by two items (Table 10), one can conclude that it is based on the relationship between competence and arrogance. In fact, as it has been mentioned in chapter 3, "arrogant people believe that they are smarter than others and they have exceptional skills and abilities such as high intelligence (Hareli & Weiner 2000 in Johnson et al. 2010)".

The authors called this kind of workplace arrogance: "Competence based Workplace Arrogance".

Thereby, one could say that Competence based Workplace Arrogance has a significant and positive impact on financial performance. This discovery is unexpected and never realized before.

CONCLUSION

The fundamental objective of this research was to measure the impact of workplace arrogance on organizational performance of Tunisian hotels. In order to achieve this objective, the authors developed first a conceptual model based on a review of the literature on this subject (see chapter 1), which was translated into a set of research hypotheses showing the causal links between these two concepts. In a second phase, the authors carried out a survey of a sample of Tunisian hotels (5 stars) in order to verify their research hypotheses. The results of this study enabled them to validate two hypotheses out of thirty and reach crucial findings: (1) workplace arrogance is a multidimensional variable (6 dimensions) and its dimensions are unidimensional; (2) workplace arrogance has a significant and negative impact on organizational performance measured by two dimensions: the customer satisfaction and the quality of service; and (3) workplace arrogance has a significant and positive impact on organizational performance measured by two dimensions: quality of service and financial performance. These findings could be considered as a theoretical contribution never been discovered before (see discussion of results).

For the authors this research has an important contribution for the field of strategic management, as it increases the understanding of the workplace

Table 10.

Arrogance 1. Believes that s/he knows better than everyone else in any given situation
Arrogance 12. *Willing to listen to others' opinions, ideas, or perspectives

arrogance and its impact on the organizational performance of firms belonging to the service industry in general and the hospitality industry in particular.

From a managerial point of view, these results inform Tunisian hotel managers about the seriousness of workplace arrogance and how they would improve the performance of their establishment by avoiding this behavior or by managing it.

REFERENCES

Akrout, F. (2010). *Les méthodes des équations structurelles*. Sfax, Tunisie: Coopi.

Anderson, J. C., & Gerbing, D. W. (1988). Structural Equation Modeling in Practice: A Review and Recommended Two - Step Approach. *Psychological Bulletin, 103*(3), 411–423. doi:10.1037/0033-2909.103.3.411

Bailey, J. M., Dunne, M. P., & Martin, N. G. (2000). The distribution, correlates and determinants of sexual orientation in an Australian twin sample. *Journal of Personality and Social Psychology, 78*, 524–536. doi:10.1037/0022-3514.78.3.524 PMID:10743878

Brown, H. T. (2012). So What if I don't have an iPhone? The unintended consequences of using arrogance in advertising. *Journal of Applied Business Research, 28*(4), 555–562. doi:10.19030/jabr.v28i4.7040

Carricano, M., & Poujol, F. (2008). *Analyse de données avec SPSS*. Paris, France: Pearson Education.

Hair, Black, Babin, Anderson, & Ronald. (2006). *Multivariate data analysis* (Vol. 6). Upper Saddle River, NJ: Pearson Prentice Hall.

Hair, J., Black, W., Babin, B., & Anderson, R. (2010). *Multivariate data analysis* (7th ed.). Upper Saddle River, NJ: Pearson Prentice Hall.

Hair, J. F., Jr., Ringle, C. M., & Sarstedt, M. (2012). Partial least squares: The better approach to structural equation modeling? *Long Range Planning, 45*(5/6), 312-319.

Henseler, J., Fassott, G., Dijkstra, T. K., & Wilson, B. (2012). Analysing quadratic effects of formative constructs by means of variance-based structural equation modelling. *European Journal of Information Systems, 21*(1), 99–112. doi:10.1057/ejis.2011.36

Henseler, J., Ringle, C. M., & Sinkovics, R. R. (2009). The use of partial least squares path modeling in international marketing. *Advances in International Marketing*, *20*, 277–320.

Johnson, R. E., Silverman, S. B., Shyamsunder, A., Yao. Swee, H., Rodopman, O. B., Cho, E., & Bauer, J. (2010). Acting Superior But Actually Inferior?: Correlates and Consequences of Workplace Arrogance. *Human Performance*, *23*(5), 403–427. doi:10.1080/08959285.2010.515279

Li, J., & Tang, Y. (2010). CEO hubris and firm risk taking in China: The moderating role of managerial discretion. *Academy of Management Journal*, *53*(1), 45–68. doi:10.5465/AMJ.2010.48036912

Malhorta, N. K. (2012). *Basic Marketing Research* (4th ed.). Pearson Education.

ONEQ. (2013). *Rapport annuel sur le marché du travail en Tunisie*. Retrieved from http://www.emploi.gov.tn/uploads/tx_elypublication/Rapport_annuel_decembre_2013.pdf

Silverman, S. B., Johnson, R. E., McConnell, N., & Carr, A. (2012). Arrogance: A Formula for Leadership Failure. *The Industrial-Organizational Psychologist*, *50*(1), 21–28.

Chapter 3

Workplace Arrogance and Job Satisfaction

ABSTRACT

This chapter could be considered as an attempt to clarify the relationship between workplace arrogance and job satisfaction. Thus, the authors examine and study this relationship by focusing on the role of self-esteem between these two concepts. Hence, the main result of this theoretical study is that workplace arrogance is negatively related to job satisfaction. Although this finding could be considered as a theoretical contribution, more studies are requested to investigate the specific relationship between workplace arrogance, self-esteem, and job satisfaction with its two dimensions: extrinsic and intrinsic factors. Does self-esteem play a mediated or moderated role in this relationship?

INTRODUCTION

This chapter aims to cope with the inadequacy of studies related to the job satisfaction and its relationship with workplace arrogance. It consists of three main parts: the first deals with this notion of "job satisfaction". The second part focuses on the factors explaining job satisfaction with a focus on an empirical study entitled "Job satisfaction of operational employees in the tourism and hospitality sector in Tunisia". In fact, this study aims to enrich the literature by overcoming the deficit of international and Tunisian research on factors explaining the job satisfaction of the operational employees belonging to the tourism and hospitality industry. The results of this research provide

DOI: 10.4018/978-1-5225-5525-4.ch003

the eight factors explaining the job satisfaction of employees belonging to this sector which are divided into factors of hygiene (pay and remuneration, social benefits, supervision, colleagues, equity) and motor factors (promotion, training, working environment). In addition, the results of this research demonstrate that (1) these factors explaining job satisfaction affect different groups of employees in different ways that the cluster analysis allowed them to extract. And that (2) these groups are distributed in a quasi-equal way in terms of demographic characteristics (age, gender, position held, etc.) contrary to the results of the majority of the research carried out in this field. Thus, these factors do not play an explanatory role for the differential of hotel staff satisfaction. Finally, the third part will focus on the relationship between job satisfaction and workplace arrogance based on the concept of self-esteem.

JOB SATISFACTION

According to Sypniewska (2013), the concept of "satisfaction" originated in the work of Maslow and Herzberg, who are considered the founders of the Human Relations School. In fact, the economic crisis of 1929, with its social, economic and political realities, contributed to a strong rethinking of the postulates of total rationality that had prevailed up to that moment and gave birth to a new tendency of thought which has raised a set of useful questions to understand the functioning of organizations, such as the emergence of informal structures and their impact on formal structures, interpersonal power systems, the importance of statutes, …

The studies of these researchers tend to show that employee has complex motivations and not only reacts to the attraction of gain. Indeed, some intrinsic motivations for valuation can lead to qualitative and quantitative performances superior to those obtained by the principle of authority developed by Taylor.

Thus, in 1954, Maslow proposed the ranking of human needs in the form of a pyramid (the pyramid of Maslow) composed of five levels: physiological needs; safety needs; social needs; esteem needs and the self-actualization needs. In addition, Maslow (1954) proposed the idea that a need that is not satisfied would be a source of motivation until it is satisfied. Thus, the individual will seek to satisfy higher needs and so on.

Maslow described both the organization and functioning of motivations. So in the firm, why continue to offer safety when employees consider having it already by their professional status? It is preferable to try to develop rewards centered on belonging and social integration in the firm. Conversely, how can we expect motivated behavior by offering esteem or decoration to employees who consider that they are underpaid given their expense? Thus, it is necessary to begin by guaranteeing the basic needs and safety before being able to play on the grounds of the top of the pyramid.

In the 1960s, Herzberg, to complement Maslow's theory, sought to identify what are the sources of satisfaction and those which are sources of dissatisfaction. To do this, he conducts several studies in companies based on the "critical incidents" method. This method involves asking employees to remember the professional events in which they felt satisfied or dissatisfied, and then to describe the impact of this feeling of satisfaction or dissatisfaction on their efficiency, their relationships with others and with themselves. Following this study, Herzberg was able to distinguish two types of factors: the former are sources of satisfaction and the latter are sources of dissatisfaction.

In other words, this means that:

- Some factors only cause dissatisfaction when they are not taken into consideration. However, when taken into consideration, there is no satisfaction. These factors are called: factors of hygiene, because they are the basis of the "good health" of the human relations in the firm. These include: relationships with supervisors and co-workers or subordinates, benefits, pay and remuneration, working conditions, type of control exercised in the organization, etc.
- Some factors do not cause dissatisfaction when they are not considered. These are the driving forces, such as: promotion, training, responsibility, etc.

Overall, hygiene factors are related to the work environment and response to the needs of the lower Maslow pyramid (physiological and safety needs), while driving factors have similarities with higher levels of Pyramid (social needs; esteem needs and the self-actualization needs).

Despite its contributions, the Human Relations School has been partially criticized for various reasons: it has failed to balance or compensate for the excesses of the rational model. He is criticized for his "psychologism," which tends to reduce organizational problems to individual psychological problems. The unit of analysis is no longer the organization, but rather the members that compose it. The analysis of the motivations of the employees is mainly carried out in terms of psychological comparisons without mentioning the sociological and political components of the problems posed.

For Garcia-Bernal et al. (2005), satisfaction is expressed as the positive or negative attitude of the employee towards his or her job. Thus, job satisfaction is the perceived perception of the work of a person or organization in which he or she performs daily work (Qasim et al. 2012). Locke (1976 cited by Waqas et al. 2014) states that job satisfaction has a positive influence on the employee's job. As for Chaudhary and Banerjee (2004 cited by Qasim et al. 2012), they argue that in an organization, employee morale is a factor explaining the effectiveness of an organization. Schermerhorn (1993 cited by Parvin and Kabir 2011) defines job satisfaction as a moral or emotional response of the employee to different aspects of his job. For Mitchel and Hoppock (1987 cited by Waqas et al. 2014), job satisfaction is a feeling that defines an austerity or psychological, physiological or environmental disorder that allows an employee to define his or her state of satisfaction or dissatisfaction.

According to Mrzygłód (2004 cited by Sypniewska 2013), an employee's job satisfaction correspond to the quality of his work. In fact, if an employee feels satisfied with his work, this feeling will contributes to its performance. On the other hand, according to Hussaimi (2008 cited by Neog and Mukulesh 2014), satisfaction or dissatisfaction at work does not depend on the nature of the job, but on what the job offers to employees. It is not the nature of job that influences job satisfaction, but rather the aspects and economic and environmental factors and the conditions of this job that explain satisfaction and dissatisfaction.

Finally, several researchers have identified various elements and factors of job satisfaction. Thus, according to Isen (2005 cited by Sypniewska 2013), people generally participate in creating a positive environment and climate based on cooperation with others. Similarly, the effective work of a team creates positive communication and reduces the rate of conflict. In the same context, Argyle (2004 cited by Sypniewska 2013) states that a satisfied employee will present a high level of commitment to work and loyalty to his firm. Recent research, such as that undertaken by Biswas (2011), has shown that the more satisfied the employee is in his work, the greater the commitment to his firm. In addition, according to Denton (2000 cited by Ankit Laddha 2012 in Neog and Mukulesh 2014), satisfied and happy employees work tend to achieve quality job and take care of their clients. Finally, Maurer (2001 cited by Waqas et al. 2014) emphasized the link between business success and employee satisfaction at work.

Factors Explaining Job Satisfaction

Job satisfaction is considered as a multidimensional concept. Thus, according to Herzberg and Zalaweska (1965 and 2001 cited by Sypniewska 2013), job satisfaction consists of four factors: the economic aspect of work, interpersonal relationships, activities and tasks, and working conditions.

The economic aspect is all that is related to the remuneration, wages, benefits received by the employee in exchange for his effort or work done. Interpersonal relationships relate to the social climate within the firm (e.g. relationships between colleagues or between employees and managers). This aspect is a psychological factor in employee satisfaction at work, and it is a way to determine whether the work atmosphere is favorable or not. In terms of activities and tasks, they represent the type of work required, the type of tasks to be carried out and their relationship to job satisfaction; they favorably or adversely affect the employee's job satisfaction. Finally, the working conditions which guarantee comfort for employees as well as safety in the workplace. This aspect concerns generally work equipment, technology, transportation, etc.

Similarly, according to Armstrong (2005 cited by Sypniewska 2013), the basic factors that can guarantee job satisfaction are: high salary, promotion opportunities, relationship with supervisors or colleagues, working conditions and the nature of work.

In what follows, we present the thirteen individual factors that explain employee satisfaction in the work following a thorough review of the literature on this field that could be described as abundant.

Factors Explaining Job Satisfaction: Literature Review

Pay and Remuneration

The factor of remuneration and salary is undoubtedly one of the most cited factors in the literature and explaining the satisfaction of employees at work. For Parvin and Kabir (2011), remuneration is the amount of money paid to the employee in return for work done.

Researchers such as Kalleberg and Voydanoff (1977 and 1980 cited by Neog and Mukulesh 2014) confirm the importance of salary and remuneration factor to explain the degree of employee satisfaction. Arnold and Feldman (1996 cited by Qasim et al. 2012) argue that an employee is affected by this factor, because like every individual, he has infinite needs and tends to use pay to satisfy them.

According to Boggie (2005 cited by Qasim et al. 2012), "the lower the remuneration, the lower the job satisfaction." This is reflected empirically by a significant positive impact between remuneration and job satisfaction. On the other hand, some authors such as Bassett (1994 cited by Qasim et al. 2012) argue that there is no empirical study that explains that salary alone can influence job satisfaction.

Social Benefits

Extrinsic rewards (promotion, social benefits, job security, remuneration, better working conditions) are considered by many researchers (Speers 2004, Herzberg 1959, Porter & Steers 1973, Kalleberg 1977, Mottaz 1988, Mottaz 1985, Price & Muller 1986, Tausky 1984) as tangible rewards that companies try to provide to their employees to keep them motivated and satisfied.

Social benefits are optional, non-salary, paid to employees in addition to their salary or wages. These benefits may include group insurance (sickness, dental, life, etc.), disability insurance, a pension plan, child care, tuition reimbursement, funding for training, and flexible and unconventional working conditions (councilhc.ca).

Promotion

Several researchers have identified this causal relationship between the promotion offered by firms and their job satisfaction (Qasim et al. 2012, Pergamit & Veum 1999, Peterson et al. 2003, Sclafane 1999).

Promotion is a factor contributing to job satisfaction and is seen as a motivating factor, especially when the system is fair and equitable for all employees (Qasim et al. 2012). Otherwise, there is a risk of creating a sense of injustice and therefore dissatisfaction. Conversely, good management of the promotion policy will push employees to move forward and evolve in their careers.

Supervision

One factor influencing job satisfaction is the supervisory factor. Researchers such as Friedlander and Margulies (1969 cited by Neog and Mukulesh 2014) have shown that a relationship that is not too tense and more or less friendly between employees and their managers can create a pleasant atmosphere and favorable climate for developing job satisfaction. This justifies the need for executive support for employees.

Colleagues

This factor is seen in some cases as a more important factor than pay and remuneration. This was confirmed by the results of a survey[1] of more than 500 workers in Canada. In fact, at least 52% of respondents considered this factor "relationship with colleagues" to be the main factor explaining job satisfaction. In addition, the same survey showed that 43% of respondents would be close to not leaving their business just to maintain their relationships with colleagues.

Reward

The recognition and reward of employees within an organization are very important factors in ensuring employee satisfaction at work. It is about recognizing a personal effort provided by the employee through bonuses or financial or moral compensation such as encouragement or recognition of an employee's effort or success, which will be a source of motivation. This will push the employee to work more and exceed even the expectations of the company and this will improve self-esteem, which leads to the success of the whole team and the achievement of the firm objectives with better quality (Samra et al. 2012).

Jun et al. (2006) argues that reward and recognition are seen as explanatory factors for job satisfaction. For Piscaoe (2002 cited by Waqas et al. 2014), the lack of encouragement, recognition and reward is the result of a weak and very conventional organizational system that affects how supervisors promote their good work and improve their performance.

For Samra et al. (2012),

Employers' actions to emphasize and reward employees' work motivate them, create a desire for excellence, build self-esteem, encourage them to overcome expectations, and increase the success of the team. Employees develop additional energy and enthusiasm, as well as an increased sense of pride and investment in their work. Employees who are recognized at work are also more likely to treat colleagues and clients with courtesy, respect and understanding. (p.4).

To have a good return and a good result of work, the firm's managers must invest in the factor "reward" in order to increase the job satisfaction of their employees.

Working Conditions

For Brangier (2005), if one wants to understand the attitude or the behavior of an employee in one's firm, one must first study the impact of working conditions on the latter. These conditions include mainly work requirements, organizational rules and procedures, control and workload. In this context, good management of work requirements, in dimensions adapted to the capacities of the employees, can reduce the stresses of the employees and allow them to obtain a better performance.

Nature of Work

According to Arnold and Feldman (1996 cited by Speers 2004), employee satisfaction is explained by several factors: relationship with colleagues, working conditions, etc. However, he may be totally dissatisfied with the work itself, which is why the "nature of work" factor is considered as a very important mean to explain the degree of job satisfaction.

Thus, the enrichment of the tasks constitutes a factor of satisfaction. In fact, the more repetitive and limited the job, the more it reduces the employee's sense of pleasure. Nel et al. (2004 cited by Speers 2004) argue that an employee prefers a rich and interesting job where he can face challenges and develop his skills and self-esteem. Similarly, continuous employee monitoring can create dissatisfaction and reduce the ease of performing tasks (Knobloch 2013).

Communication

Organizational communication plays a major role in job satisfaction. This assertion is shared by several researchers. Thus, according to King et al. (1988) and Orpen (1977), there is a clear and positive relationship between communication and employee satisfaction at work.

The results of a survey conducted in the United States by Mercer Human Resources Consulting with 2,600 employees showed that "the communication factor is the most important factor in ensuring workers' commitment to their organizations. It is considered the first way to ensure employee loyalty". Similarly, most employees interviewed said that communication is more important than salary.

In the same context, Ilozor and Carr (2001) indicate that good, clear, coherent and direct communication could guarantee job satisfaction.

Working Environment

According to Robins (2001), the working environment plays an essential role in the working life of employees and can influence positively or negatively the activity of employees and their behavior (Qasim et al. 2012). On the other hand, researchers like George and Jones (1999 cited by Neog & Mukulesh 2014) have shown that an unfavorable working environment leads to employee dissatisfaction.

According to Waqas et al. (2014), the work environment can alter the mind and moral perception of employees. Baron and Greenberg (2003 cited by Qasim et al. 2012) argue that an unfavorable working environment tends to affect the physical and especially moral well-being of the employee. Similarly, Donald and Siu (2001 cited by Waqas et al. 2014) have established a link between the work environment and the physical and mental well-being of employee.

Equity

Equity is a critical factor influencing employee satisfaction at work. According to equity theory, receiving too much in terms of benefits, rewards or others, or receiving too little is classified as unfair (Qasim et al. 2012). Thus, fairness of treatment within a firm is an important factor in improving employee satisfaction at work.

Training and Skills Development

Staff training has traditionally been regarded as a fundamental practice of human resource management and as one of the factors explaining job satisfaction (Woodruffe 2000 cited by Parvin & Kabir 2011 and Legg 2011 cited by Satterfield 2015). The training allows the development of employees and the development of their skills in order to achieve the organizational objectives.

Balance Private/Professional life

Job satisfaction is indirectly related to the satisfaction of private life. This was confirmed by the Stepstone survey[2] conducted in 2012 (see Table 1), which indicates that working life has a negative impact on private life and that the impact of this latter on working life is rather positive.

According to Méda (2003), an employee has an interest in providing his or her efforts and spending energy for his/her family but also for his/her work in order to keep his/her position and develop his/her career. However, employers do not really contribute to highlighting this factor, which makes it difficult for the employee (male or female) to choose between his or her career or family.

Job Satisfaction of Operational Employees in the Tourism and Hospitality Sector in Tunisia

Understanding what explains job satisfaction is one of the important issues related to human resource management of organizations. Job satisfaction is determined not only by the objective situation of employees at work, but also by their subjective perception of their job (Mora & Ferrer-i-Carbonell 2009).

Table 1. Results of the Stepstone survey

Impact of Professional Life on Private Life	57,7%: Mainly negative impacts 27,1%: Mainly positive impacts 15,2%: No impact
Impact of Private Life on Professional Life	13,6%: Mainly negative impacts 38,1%: Mainly positive impacts 48,2%: No impact

Source: http://www.stepstone.fr/b2b/espace-recruteur/nos-conseils-recrutement/enquetes-internationales/upload/CR-enquete-bonheur-au-travail.pdf

In the tourism and hospitality industry, "employees are seen as important factors explaining service quality, customer satisfaction, loyalty and hotel performance" (Heskett et al. 1994). These authors state that in the service value chain, there are critical links between service quality and employee satisfaction/productivity. The value of services provides a customer satisfaction and an economic value to the company as a profit (Rosentbluth 1991; Zeithaml & Bitner 1996; Zeithaml et al. 2009).

Job satisfaction is an important indicator of how employees feel about their work and predicts workplace behavior such as absenteeism, turnover, etc. The study of job satisfaction allows the company to reduce the number of complaints, manage absenteeism, turnover and work stoppage and improve the punctuality and morale of its employees. Job satisfaction is also related to employees in good physical and moral health and has been considered as a good indicator of longevity.

Arasl and Baradarani (2014) demonstrated that there is a positive impact of employee satisfaction in hotels on their performance. The satisfaction of the hotel staff has a positive and significant impact on their job performance and on customer satisfaction (Ladkin 2002; Dunlap et al. 1988; Tansuhaj et al. 1988; Chowdhary 2003; Yang & Chen 2010).

A review of the literature on this topic revealed that although many international studies have investigated factors explaining job satisfaction (Garcia-Bernal et al. 2005; Sypniewska 2013; Qasim et al. 2012; Neog & Mukulesh 2014), very little research has been carried out in the tourism and hospitality sector, for example the work of Simons and Enz (1995), Siu et al. (1997) and Bettencourt and Brown (1997) on what motivates employees in the hotel industry in the United States, Canada and Hong Kong, respectively.

In Tunisia, there is practically no research on this issue and, in addition, in the tourism and hospitality sector despite its importance in the Tunisian economy[3], known since January 14, 2011 (date of the Jasmine revolution), "A constant decline in the socio-economic situation with double-digit declines: trade activity: -26.7%, Posts and telecommunications: -12.5%, Transport: -10.5% Hotel and restaurant sector: -9.2% "(Tamzini et al. 2016). Thus, from January 2011 to the end of August 2011, the number of tourists decreased by 39% compared to the previous year (Kalboussi 2011). Revenues decreased by 952.5 million dinars during the same period compared to 2010 (Gamha 2011). Average hotel occupancy was also down 46.3% from the previous year. Twenty-four hotels have ceased operations, contributing to the loss of more than 3,000 jobs (Kalboussi 2011). Since the Jasmine revolution, the entire sector has lost more than 22,000 jobs (Kalboussi 2011). In Djerba

Island, which is a major destination for European tourists, half of the hotels stopped operations a few days after January 14th (Watson 2011). The hotels of Hammamet have experienced the same situation. Shops that sell crafts and restaurants and bars are desperately empty (Alami 2011).

Table 2 explains the situation of this sector over the last three years (2014, 2015 and 2016).

Hence, the fundamental objective of this section is to overcome this lack of research in a hyper-turbulent environment by answering the following research question: what are the factors explaining the job satisfaction of employees belonging to the sector Tourism and hospitality in Tunisia?

In other words, it is a question of answering these two sub-questions:

1.   Do the individual factors that constitute the job satisfaction affect all employees in the tourism and hospitality industry in the same way?
2.   Do the demographic factors (age, gender, seniority, position, etc.) play an explanatory role in the differential of hotel staff satisfaction?

Thus, this study aims to deepen our knowledge on the job satisfaction of the hotel staff in this particular type of environment.

This section is devoted to the presentation of our research methodology, its results, the discussion of the research methodology and the presentation of contributions, limitations and future research trajectories.

Research Methodology

Sampling and Data Collection

This study was conducted in 2016 on a sample of hotel operators[4] chosen by applying the non-probabilistic method by judgment which is a form of the

Table 2. Achievements of the tourism sector in 2016 compared to 2015 and 2014

Settings	2014	2015	2016	Deviation in% 2016/2015	Deviation in% 2016/2014
Tourism receipts in MDT	3.136,2	2.153,2	2.000,8	-7,1	-36,2
Overnight stays	26.823.724	14.933.592	16.422.968	10	-38,8
Arrivals at the borders	6.341.554	4.653.127	4.810.760	3,4	-24,1

Source: Studies Direction, Tunisian Ministry of Tourism (www.tourisme.gov.tn).

non-probabilistic method by convenience (Malhorta 2012). The authors have chosen respondents who have the same working conditions with the same classification level for the hotel units in which they work.

Our questionnaire was distributed directly to employees or via the human resources department of these hotels. Our sample is composed by 222 observations.

We chose the traditional method of administering the questionnaire, that is, the face-to-face distribution of printed sheets in order to guarantee maximum answers and for a practical reason that we do not have the e-mail of all of our respondents.

As shown in Table 3, the sample is predominantly male. Most of them are between 20 and 40 years old and have qualifications corresponding to BTS and the license. On the other hand, a large majority does not have a diploma. The majority has a salary between 500 and 1000 dinars. As mentioned below (see Table 3), our sample is operational and the results show that most of them are heads of rank, clerks and receptionists.

Operationalization of Job Satisfaction Dimensions

The items related to each dimension of the job satisfaction variable were identified from the review of the literature related to the study's subject (Bailey et al. 2000). The development of all these items followed three steps: (1) the creation of a set of items that reflected the distinctive characteristics of each dimension and were appropriate for use in a self-reported questionnaire; (2) the evaluation of the group of items by a group of university teachers; and (3) the evaluation of all these items by a sample of managers.

Table 4 summarizes the dimensions of the "job satisfaction" variable studied and the number of items in each of them (78 items). For each dimension, respondents were asked to indicate their degree of agreement or disagreement with each proposal by choosing between 1 "strongly disagree" and 5 "strongly agree".

Data Analysis

All statistical analyzes were performed using the SPSS software using factor analysis, cluster analysis, and variance analysis with the post-Hocs averaging tests. Indeed, a first step was to retain the dimensions and items that satisfied the conditions of reliability and validity (Hair et al. 2010). Then,

Table 3. Demographic characteristics

	Number	%
Gender		
Male	159	71.6
Female	63	28.4
Age		
Under 20 years	94	42.3
20-30 years	90	40.5
30-40 years	27	12.2
40-50 years	10	4.5
Marital Status		
Single	101	45.5
Married	119	53.6
Qualification		
BTS	60	27.0
BTP	15	6.8
BAC	6	2.7
License	51	23.0
Master	2	0.9
Other	88	39.6
Salary		
<500 DT	30	13.5
500 - 1000	164	37.9
1001 - 1500	27	12.2
1501 - 2000	1	0.5
Function		
Baggiest	13	5.8
Barman	11	4.9
Head of rank	59	26.6
Head of Reception	10	4.5
Clerk	50	22.5
Hostess	8	3.6
Maitre d'hotel	12	5.4
Receptionist	42	18.9
Waiter	17	7.6

Table 4. Dimensions of job satisfaction

Dimensions	Number of Items
Pay & Remuneration	11
Social benefits	4
Promotion	6
Supervision	10
Colleagues	8
Reward	4
Working conditions	4
Nature of work	4
Communication	4
Working environment	11
Equity	4
Training and skills development	5
Balance Private/Professional life	3

the classification was aimed at extracting the characteristics of the selected groups according to their satisfaction with their tasks.

RESULTS

According to Table 5, eight of the thirteen dimensions were selected. The "Social benefits", "Supervision", "Equity" and "Training" constructs are the most unidimensional since they represent the highest total extracted variances (Kim et al. 2016). All constructs retained verify their reliability conditions with Cronbach's Alpha indicators above the allowable limit and therefore ensure the internal consistency of each dimension or concept used in the analysis. Validity, which refers to the ability of the concepts to apprehend the phenomenon, has also been approved by the *Average Variance Extracted* (AVE) indicators since the values are all above the allowed limit of 0.5. More precisely, an AVE greater than the threshold indicated confirms the convergent validity which determines to what extent the measurements of the same concept (or construct) by two different methods converges. As for the discriminant validity which demonstrates the non-correlation of the construct with others of the same analysis, is approved when we applied the method of Fornell and Larker (1981) and found that the correlations between the constructs are no more than the value of the Cronbach coefficient of each construct (Akrout 2010).

Since the hierarchical classification method is cumbersome to manipulate beyond the threshold of 100 observations, we have focused on the application of the K-Means classification method with the ultimate objective of extracting a number of homogeneous groups of respondents in their vision (Saunders 1994). The specificity of this method is that it gives us the possibility of fixing the number of groups at the beginning of the process. We are called to make several attempts until the best solution is identified (Carricano & Poujol 2008).

Finally, the results of the cluster analysis allowed us to extract three groups as shown in Table 6.

The three groups selected after the cluster analysis were distributed in a quasi-equal manner in terms of demographic characteristics, as shown in Table 3.

Table 5. Indicators related to reliability and validity

Dimensions	Selected Items	Total Variance Extracted	Cronbach's Alpha	Average Variance Extracted (AVE)
Pay & Remuneration	6 Items	0.545	0.830	0.541
Social benefits	2 items	0.728	0.674	0.530
Promotion	5 items	0.550	0.794	0.545
Supervision	7 items	0.611	0.893	0.603
Colleagues	4 items	0.546	0.716	0.543
Working environment	5 items	0.532	0.779	0.529
Equity	3 items	0.652	0.732	0.651
Training and skills development	4 items	0.618	0.792	0.613

Table 6. Distribution of groups selected according to the method "K-Means cluster"

Groups	Frequency	Percentage
1	82	37%
2	76	34%
3	64	29%
Total	222	100

After choosing the appropriate solution for the number of groups following the cluster analysis "K-Means", it was necessary to carry out the analysis of the variances (ANOVA) followed by the Post-Hoc tests as the number of groups is greater than three. The results of the analysis revealed that the three groups had significant differences in the analysis dimensions used (Sig values below the allowed threshold 0.05). Thus, Table 7 presents the details of these characteristics after analyzing the details of the differences between the three groups.

Group 1: The first group is generally considered satisfied except for the following factors: Supervision, Colleagues and Working Environment, where it is moderately satisfied.

Group 2: This group is not satisfied above all for the factors: " Social benefits ", " Supervision " and " Colleagues ". For the rest it did not reach a level of high satisfaction.

Group 3: This third group is very close to the second group in its characteristics. It is not very satisfied with the various factors. However, he is dissatisfied, especially at the level of "Pay and Remuneration", "Social benefits", "Promotion" and "Working Environment".

To conclude, the strong satisfaction is only found in the first group whereas the non satisfaction is specific to groups 2 and 3.

The dimensions that have different assessments are "Pay and Remuneration" and "promotion" because at the first factor, the first group is satisfied, the second is moderately satisfied and the third is not satisfied. As for the second

Table 7. Characteristics of groups using the ANOVA method with Post-Hocs

Dimensions	Group 1	Group 2	Group 3	Sig.
Pay & Remuneration	S	M-S	NS	0.000
Social benefits	S	NS	NS	0.000
Promotion	S	M-S	NS	0.000
Supervision	M-S	NS	M-S	0.000
Colleagues	M-S	NS	M-S	0.000
Working environment	M-S	M-S	NS	0.000
Equity	S	M-S	M-S	0.000
Training and skills development	S	M-S	M-S	0.000

(Categorization according to Scheffe's test).
S = Satisfied * M-S = Moderately Satisfied * NS = Not satisfied

dimension, the first group is satisfied, the second is moderately satisfied, and the third is not satisfied.

In order to better evaluate the distances of the differences between the three groups, we performed a discriminant analysis to determine the dimension that discriminates most between the three groups (Hair et al. 2010). Thus, we obtained the results shown in Table 8.

Indeed, the discriminant analysis confirms that the most discriminating dimension between the three groups is that of "Pay and remuneration" since it has the lowest Wilks lambda value. The Wilks lambda value is interpreted inversely. A value that tends to 0 indicates a strong effect and vice versa (Hair et al. 2010). The highest F value also indicates the most discriminating dimension. The second dimension discriminating between the three groups is "social benefits".

Discussion

Discussion of the results of this research will focus on two aspects. First, the nature of the factors explaining the job satisfaction of the employees belonging to the tourism and hospitality sector in Tunisia based on the work of Herzberg (1959). Second, the link between these results and those related to the research carried out in the particular context of the "crisis".

Concerning the first aspect, the results of our research indicate that the eight factors (of the original thirteen) explaining the job satisfaction of the selected hotel staff are mainly "hygiene" (or extrinsic) factors according to the terminology of Herzberg (1959). Extrinsic satisfaction is satisfaction arising from extrinsic circumstances such as: remuneration and compensation,

Table 8. Discriminant analysis

Dimensions	Lambda of Wilks	F	Sig.
Pay & Remuneration	0.575	81.091	0.000
Social benefits	0.582	78.540	0.000
Promotion	0.620	67.131	0.000
Supervision	0.845	20.061	0.000
Colleagues	0.837	21.258	0.000
Working environment	0.593	75.039	0.000
Equity	0.724	41.649	0.000
Training and skills development	0.849	19.497	0.000

social benefits, relationship with superiors (or supervision), relationship with colleagues and equity. In contrast, promotion, training and working environment (intrinsic factors, motor factors, or motivators) are less represented by our research. Intrinsic satisfaction is the individual satisfaction expressed by the possibilities of success, creativity, personal advancement, etc. This approach to job satisfaction reflects cognitive assessments of job satisfaction and internal cost-benefit analyzes conducted by the employee (Brief 1998 cited by Markovits et al. 2013).

One can conclude that the employees of the tourism and hospitality sector in Tunisia are rather attracted by extrinsic satisfaction than by intrinsic satisfaction. This result is in line with those related to a research conducted in the context of a crisis and dealing with factors explaining job satisfaction. In order to discuss this second aspect, we take the example of a research carried out by Markovits et al. (2013), which examined the impact of the recent economic crisis in Greece on job satisfaction, commitment and self-regulation. The results of this research - although the nature of the crisis in Tunisia and Greece is not the same - demonstrate certain similarities. Indeed, Markovits et al. (2013) demonstrated that the extrinsic satisfaction of Greek employees is very strongly affected (negatively) by the crisis, whereas their intrinsic satisfaction is not. In fact, in period of crisis, employees are prepared to accept precarious employment conditions in order to preserve their positions. These results are partially confirmed by this study, since extrinsic satisfaction as well as the intrinsic satisfaction of Tunisian employees are affected by the seriousness of this rather alarming period that has been going through the tourism sector in Tunisia since 2010 (see the characteristics of Group 2 and 3 in Table 6). Similarly, Markovits et al. (2013) demonstrated that employees faced with an economic crisis are very unhappy with hygiene factors such as pay and job security. This is the case for employees in groups 2 and 3 of this study who are not only not satisfied with all five factors of hygiene (pay and remuneration, social benefits, supervision, colleagues and equity), but also for all motivating or motivating factors (promotion, training, working environment). Employees belonging to the first group seem to escape these conclusions, since they are highly satisfied with all the hygiene and motor factors.

Moreover, according to the results of the discriminant analysis carried out in order to better evaluate the distances of the differences between the three groups, the most discriminating dimensions between the three groups are: Pay and remuneration, social benefits (in fact this dimension is related to pay) and working environment. Thus, one can deduce that the appreciation of salary by operational employees varies. This could be explained by the sensitivity of the current period in which this sector is moving. In fact, respondents assess remuneration in relation to the context and, among other things, their personal circumstances. The third most discriminating dimension is "Working environment". The question that arises here: do the working conditions differ or the respondents' appreciation?

CONTRIBUTIONS, LIMITATIONS, AND FUTURE RESEARCH TRAJECTORIES

The results of this research conducted in the tourism and hospitality sector in Tunisia, based on the adaptation and validation of measurement scales, and statistical analyzes carried out using the SPSS software in applying factorial analysis, variance analysis methods with post-Hoc comparison tests of averages, allowed the authors to answer their fundamental research question by demonstrating that the factors explaining the job satisfaction of employees belonging to this sector are eight divided into factors of hygiene (pay and remuneration, social benefits, supervision, colleagues, equity) and motor factors (promotion, training, working environment).

In addition, the results of this research allowed the authors to respond to their two sub-questions (announced at the introduction of this section) by demonstrating that (1) these factors explaining job satisfaction affect different groups of employees in different ways that the cluster analysis allowed them to extract. And that (2) these groups are distributed in a quasi-equal way in terms of demographic characteristics (age, gender, position held, etc.) contrary to the results of the majority of the research carried out in this field. Thus, these factors do not play an explanatory role for the differential of hotel staff satisfaction.

The main contribution of this research work is the enrichment of the literature by overcoming the deficit of international and Tunisian research on factors explaining the job satisfaction of the operational employees belonging to the tourism and hospitality industry. Similarly, it is important to note that despite the fact that two groups of operational employees are not satisfied, there is a third group composed of almost all satisfied operational staff. This contradicts and relativizes the results of almost all research that has demonstrated the overall negative impact that a crisis could have on the degree of employee satisfaction.

These results have an important managerial contribution as they enable the various managers of the hotel industry to have a first reading of the factors that explain the satisfaction of their human resources. This will allow them to predict their behavior at work (absenteeism, turnover, etc.), reduce the number of complaints, effectively manage absenteeism, turnover and work stoppage, and improve employee punctuality and morale; and to have a positive and significant impact on employee performance at work, customer satisfaction and operational performance of the hotel.

The limitations of this research correspond mainly to the restrictive choice of the characteristics of the study sample. It might be wiser to extend our study sample to all socio-professional categories of hotel employees and to all types of hotels (not 4 and 5 star hotels only) for greater representativeness and generalization of findings and recommendations.

Despite these limitations, at least three major research opportunities can be identified. The first is to determine and measure the impact of the crisis in the tourism and hospitality sector in Tunisia, on job satisfaction of employees and hence on quality of service, customer satisfaction, loyalty and hotels' performance. The second is to address the link between employee job satisfaction and human resource strategies to ensure alignment with corporate strategy. Finally, the third opportunity consists of a comparative study carried out in the countries where the tourism and hospitality industry has experienced the same behavior.

WORKPLACE ARROGANCE AND JOB SATISFACTION

In order to analyze the relationship between workplace arrogance and job satisfaction, the authors focused on the notion of self-esteem.

The results of a meta-analysis undertaken by Judge and Bono (2001) have shown that the 4 traits — self-esteem, generalized self-efficacy, locus of control, and emotional stability (low neuroticism) — are among the best dispositional predictors of job satisfaction and job performance. These results confirm that self-esteem is positively related to job satisfaction.

Inkson (1978) has assessed the role of self-esteem as a moderator of the relationship between job performance and job satisfaction based on a sample of 93 meat-processing workers and he has demonstrated (based on the Korman's self consistency theory) that self-esteem exercised a significant moderating effect on correlations between performance and intrinsic satisfaction, but not on correlations between performance and extrinsic satisfaction.

These results were confirmed by those of a research conducted by Adler (1980) who, following balance theory[5], argued that business students high in self-esteem were significantly more internal in their attributions for satisfaction than those low in their attributions for dissatisfaction.

In contrast to the previous researches, Alavi and Askaripur (2003) have demonstrated in examining the relationship between self-esteem and job satisfaction in government organizations, that there is a significant relationship between self-esteem and extrinsic factors (nature of work; supervision; co-workers or colleagues; promotion; salary and wages)

Faragher et al. (2005) have concluded, on the basis of a systematic review and meta-analysis of 485 studies with a combined sample size of 267 995 individuals, that there is a significant relationship between job satisfaction and mental/psychological problems such as burnout, self-esteem, depression, and anxiety. The correlation with subjective physical illness was more modest.

In the same vein, Kikangras and Kinnunen (2003) have investigated the roles of self-esteem and optimism in the relationship between psychosocial work stressors and well-being for a sample of Finnish employees (n=457). They have concluded based on the results of the moderated hierarchical regression analyses that low levels of self-esteem and optimism had a direct negative effect on emotional exhaustion and mental distress among men employees. Furthermore, self-esteem moderated the relationships between poor organizational climate and emotional exhaustion and mental distress among male employees. Among female employees, optimism moderated the relationships between time pressures at work, job insecurity and poor organizational climate on mental distress.

Altogether, this study suggested that self-esteem and optimism are important resources which both have main effects as well as moderator effects on well-being, although these effects are gender specific.

Knowing that arrogant person is low self-esteem (see chapter 1), one can conclude that workplace arrogance is negatively related to job satisfaction. In fact, Locke et al. (1996 cited in Judge and Bono 2001) have noted that

A person with a high self-esteem will view a challenging job as a deserved opportunity which he can master and benefit from, whereas a person with low self-esteem is more likely to view it as an undeserved opportunity or a chance to fail. (p. 21)

Moreover, the Korman's (1970) self consistency theory suggests "*that individuals with high self-esteem choose occupations consistent with their interests, which would lead to greater levels of job satisfaction*" (Judge & Bono 2001). In addition, Dodgson and Wood (1998 in Judge and Bono (2001) have noted that "*individuals with high self-esteem maintain optimism in the face of failure, which makes future success (and thus future satisfaction) more likely*".

CONCLUSION

This chapter is considered as an attempt to clarify the relationship between workplace arrogance and job satisfaction. Thus, the authors examined and studied this relationship by focusing on the role of self-esteem between these two concepts. Hence, the main result of this theoretical study is that workplace arrogance is negatively related to job satisfaction. However, more studies are requested to investigate the specific relationship between workplace arrogance, self-esteem and job satisfaction with its two dimensions: extrinsic and intrinsic factors. Does self-esteem play a mediated or moderated role in this relationship?

REFERENCES

Adler, S. (1980). Self-esteem and causal attributions for job satisfaction and dissatisfaction. *The Journal of Applied Psychology*, *65*(3), 327–332. doi:10.1037/0021-9010.65.3.327

Akrout, F. (2010). *Les méthodes des équations structurelles*. Sfax, Tunisie: Coopi.

Alami, A. (2011). Tunisia's tourism hit by unrest. *Global Post*. Retrieved from http://www.globalpost.com/dispatch/news/regions/africa/110325/tunisia-tourism-%20%20economy

Alavi & Askaripur. (2003). The Relationship between Self-Esteem and Job Satisfaction of Personnel in Government Organizations. *Public Personnel Management*, *32*, 4.

Arasl, H., & Baradarani, S. (2014). European Tourist Perspective on Destination Satisfaction in Jordan's industries. *Procedia: Social and Behavioral Sciences*, *109*, 1416–1425. doi:10.1016/j.sbspro.2013.12.645

Bettencourt, L. A., & Brown, S. W. (1997). Contact employees: Relationships among workplace fairness, job satisfaction and pro-social behavior. *Journal of Retailing, 73*(1), 39–61. doi:10.1016/S0022-4359(97)90014-2

Biswas, S. (2011). Psychological Climate and Affective Commitment as Antecedents of Salespersons Job Involvement. *Management Insight, 7,* 2.

Brangier, E. (2005). Comment améliorer la performance de l'opérateur par des dispositifs d'aide au travail? In Management des organisations (pp. 429-450). Paris: Éditions d'organisation.

Carricano, M., & Poujol, F. (2008). *Analyse de données avec SPSS*. Paris, France: Pearson Education.

Chowdhary, N. (2003). Learning to Service. *CUTSA Transportes. Manage. Case Stud. J., 3*(1), 20–33.

Dunlap, B. J., Doston, M., & Chambers, T. M. (1988). Perceptions of real estate brokers and buyers: A sales orientation, customer orientation approach. *Journal of Business Research, 17*(2), 175–187. doi:10.1016/0148-2963(88)90050-1

Faragher, E. B., Cass, M., & Cooper, C. L. (2005). The relationship between job satisfaction and health: A meta-analysis. *Occupational and Environmental Medicine, 62*(2), 105–112. doi:10.1136/oem.2002.006734 PMID:15657192

Fornell, C., & Larcker, D. F. (1981). Evaluating structural equation models with unobservable variables and measurement error. *JMR, Journal of Marketing Research, 18*(1), 39–50. doi:10.2307/3151312

Gamha, E. (2011). Tourism income decreases 39%. *Tunisia Live.* Retrieved from http://www.tunisia-live.net/2011/08/07/tourism-income-dicreasing-by-39

Garcia-Bernal, J., Gargallo-Castel, A., Marzo-Navarro, M., & Rivera-Torres, P. (2005). Job satisfaction: Empirical evidence of gender differences. *Women in Management Review, 20*(4), 279–288. doi:10.1108/09649420510599098

Hair, J., Black, W., Babin, B., & Anderson, R. (2010). *Multivariate data analysis* (7th ed.). Upper Saddle River, NJ: Pearson Prentice Hall.

Heskett, J. L., Jones, T. O., Loveman, G. W., Sasser, W. E. Jr, & Schlesinger, J. A. (1994). Putting the service-pro"t chain to work. *Harvard Business Review, 72,* 164–174.

Inkson, J. K. (1978). Self-esteem as a moderator of the relationship between job performance and job satisfaction. *The Journal of Applied Psychology, 63*(2), 243–247. doi:10.1037/0021-9010.63.2.243 PMID:659355

Judge, T. A., & Bono, J. E. (2001). Relationship of Core Self-Evaluations Traits—Self-Esteem, Generalized Self-Efficacy, Locus of Control, and Emotional Stability—With Job Satisfaction and Job Performance: A Meta-Analysis. *The Journal of Applied Psychology, 86*(1), 80–92. doi:10.1037/0021-9010.86.1.80 PMID:11302235

Jun, M., Cai, S., & Shin, H. (2006). TQM practice in maquiladora: Antecedents of employee satisfaction and loyalty. *Journal of Operations Management, 24*(6), 791–812. doi:10.1016/j.jom.2005.09.006

Kalboussi, R. (2011), Tourism sector shows large losses. *Tunisia Live.* Retrieved from http://www.tunisia-live.net/2011/08/29/tourism-sector-shows-large-losses

Kalleberg, A. L. (1977). Work values and job rewards: A theory of job satisfaction. *American Sociological Review, 42*(1), 124–143. doi:10.2307/2117735

Kim, Y. H., Duncan, J. L., & Jai, T. C. (2016). Segmenting the collegiate football game spectator: A cluster analysis approach, *Sport, Business and Management International Journal (Toronto, Ont.), 6*(1), 76–96.

King, W. Jr, Lahiff, J., & Hatfield, J. (1988). A discrepancy theory of the relationship between communication and job satisfaction. *Communication Research Reports, 5*(1), 36–43. doi:10.1080/08824098809359798

Ladkin, A. (2002). Career analysis: A case study of hotel general managers in Australia. *Tourism Management, 23*(4), 379–388. doi:10.1016/S0261-5177(01)00092-9

Maˇkikangas, A., & Kinnunen, U. (2003). Psychosocial work stressors and well-being: Self-esteem and optimism as moderators in a one-year longitudinal sample. *Personality and Individual Differences, 35*(3), 537–557. doi:10.1016/S0191-8869(02)00217-9

Malhorta, N. K. (2012). *Basic Marketing Research* (4th ed.). Pearson Education.

Markovits, Y. D. B., & Dick, R. V. (2013). Economic crisis and the employee: The effects of economic crisis on employee job satisfaction, commitment, and self-regulation. *European Management Journal.* doi:10.1016/j.emj.2013.09.005

Maslow, A. (1954). *Motivation and personality.* New York: Harper.

Méda, D. (2003). *Propos statistique, sociologique et philosophique, in L'égalité entre femmes et hommes et la vie professionnelle.* Paris: Dalloz, Coll. Thèmes et commentaires.

Mora, T., & Ferrer-i-Carbonell, A. (2009). The job satisfaction gender gap among young recent university graduates: Evidence from Catalonia. *Journal of Socio-Economics, 38*(4), 581–590. doi:10.1016/j.socec.2009.02.003

Mottaz, C. J. (1985). The Relative Importance of Intrinsic and Extrinsic Rewards as Determinants of Work Satisfaction. *The Sociological Quarterly, 26*(3), 365–385. doi:10.1111/j.1533-8525.1985.tb00233.x

Mottaz, C. J. (1988). Determinants of Organizational Commitment. *Human Relations, 41*(6), 467–482. doi:10.1177/001872678804100604

Neog, B. B., & Mukulesh, B. (2014). Factors Influencing Employee's Job Satisfaction: An Empirical Study among Employees of Automobile Service Workshops in Assam. *The SIJ Transactions on Industrial Financial & Business Management, 2*, 7.

Parvin, M. M., & Kabir, M. M. N. (2011). Factors affecting employee job satisfaction of the pharmaceutical sector. *Australian Journal of Business and Management Research, 1*(9), 113–123.

Pergamit, M. R., & Veum, J. R. (1999). What is a promotion? *Industrial & Labor Relations Review, 52*(4), 581–601. doi:10.1177/001979399905200405

Peterson, D. K., Puia, G. M., & Suess, F. R. (2003). Yo Tengo La Camiseta (I Have the Shirt On): An Exploration Of Job Satisfaction and Commitment Among Workers In Mexico. *Journal of Leadership & Organizational Studies, 10*(2), 73–88. doi:10.1177/107179190301000208

Porter, L. W., & Steers, R. M. (1973). Organizational Work and Personal Factors in Employee Turnover and Absenteeism. *Psychological Bulletin, 80*(2), 151–176. doi:10.1037/h0034829

Price & Mueller. (1986). *Absenteeism and Turnover in Hospital Employment.* JAI Press.

Qasim, S., Cheema, F. E. A., & Syed, N. A. (2012). Exploring Factors Affecting Employees Job Satisfaction at Work. *Journal of Management and Social Sciences*, *8*(1), 31–39.

Robins, S. P. (2001). *Organizational behavior.* New Delhi: Prentice – Hall.

Rosentbluth, H. (1991). Tales from a nonconformist company. *Harvard Business Review*, *69*, 26–36. PMID:10114928

Samra, J., Gilbert, M., Shain, M., & Bilsker, D. (2012). Guarding Minds @ Work: Psychosocial factors. Vancouver, Canada: Centre for Applied Research in Mental Health and Addictions (CARMA).

Satterfield, J. M. (2015). Cognitive Behavioral Therapy: Techniques for Retraining Your Brian. *The Great Courses.* Retrieved from http://www. thegreatcourses.com/courses/cognitive-behavioral-therapy-techniques-for-retraining-your-brain.html

Saunders, J. (1994). Cluster analysis. *Journal of Marketing Management*, *10*(3), 13–28. doi:10.1080/0267257X.1994.9964257

Sclafane, S. (1999). MGA Managers in Sync with Employees on Job Satisfaction Issues, Survey Finds. *National Underwriter.*, *103*(22), 4–24.

Simons, T., & Enz, C. A. (1995). Motivating Hotel Employees. *The Cornell Hotel and Restaurant Administration Quarterly*, *36*(1), 20–27.

Siu, V., Tsang, N., & Wong, S. (1997). What Motivates Hong Kong's Hotel Employees? *The Cornell Hotel and Restaurant Administration Quarterly*, *38*(5), 44–49. doi:10.1177/001088049703800534

Spears, L. C. (2004). Practicing servant-leadership. *Leader to Leader*, *204*(34), 7–11. doi:10.1002/ltl.94

Sypniewska, B. (2013). Evaluation of factors influencing job satisfaction. *Contemporary Economics*, *8*(1), 57–118. doi:10.5709/ce.1897-9254.131

Tamzini, K., Mehrez, K., & Ayed, T. L. (2016). Le profil du dirigeant dans un environnement hyper-turbulent (EHT): le cas du dirigeant tunisien dans un environnement post-révolution. Article publié dans les actes de la XXVème conférence internationale de l'AIMS (31 Mai, 1er et 2 juin, Hammamet, Tunisie).

Tansuhaj, P., Randall, D., & McCullough, J. (1988). A Service Marketing Management Model: Integrating Internal and External marketing Functions. *Journal of Services Marketing*, 2(1), 31–38. doi:10.1108/eb024714

Tausky, C. (1984). *Work and society: an introduction to industrial sociology*. Itasca, IL: F. E. Peacock.

Waqas, A., Bashir, U., Sattar, M. F., Abdullah, H. M., Hussain, I., Anjum, W., & Arshad, R. et al. (2014). Factors Influencing Job Satisfaction and Its Impact on Job Loyalty. *International Journal of Learning and Development*, 4(2), 2. doi:10.5296/ijld.v4i2.6095

Watson, K. (2011). Bare beaches. *BBC News*. Retrieved from http://breakingnews24hrs.net/world-news/bare-beaches/

Yang, K. J., & Chen, S. H. (2010). The comparison and analysis of employee satisfaction improvement in the hot spring and financial industries. *African Journal of Business Management*, 4(8), 1619–1628.

Zeithaml & Bitner. (1996). Services marketing. New York: McGraw-Hill.

Zeithaml, V., Bitner, M. J., & Gremler, D. (2009). *Services Marketing*. New York: McGraw-Hill.

ENDNOTES

[1] This survey was conducted by the Canadian Job Site Canadian Jobboom. com.

[2] Survey of Personal and Professional Happiness in 2012.

[3] This strategic sector contributes up to 7.5% of the national Gross Domestic Product (GDP) and generates more than 400,000 direct jobs.

[4] These operatives belong to 4 and 5 stars hotels. Three of these hotels belong to internationally renowned chains and three belong to a local Tunisian group. These hotels are located in two regions: Tunis and Sousse. This choice is supported by two main reasons: 1. Their ability to stay open throughout the year and even during crises and low season; 2. These hotels have gastronomic restaurants or lounge restaurants that are renowned in these areas and are open to guests even those who come from outside the hotel. Unlike other hotels, they were not forced to close during the off-season, or because of cyclical and security problems such as terrorism, etc.

5   This theory hypothesizes that self-esteem would interact with whether an incident was one of satisfaction or dissatisfaction in determining the extent to which causality of the incident was attributed to the self or to external agents.

Chapter 4

Workplace Arrogance and Job Performance

ABSTRACT

This chapter is an attempt to clarify the relationship between workplace arrogance and job performance. Thus, the authors focus and define a set of four fundamental concepts—task performance, contextual performance, social support, and self-efficacy—in order to examine and explore this relationship. Hence, the main result of this theoretical study is that workplace arrogance is negatively related to job performance. Although this finding could be considered as a theoretical contribution, more studies are requested to investigate the specific relationship between workplace arrogance and job satisfaction with its two dimensions: task and contextual factors.

INTRODUCTION

This chapter aims to cope with the scarcity of studies related to the job performance and its relationship with workplace arrogance. It consists of four main parts: the first deals with this notion of "job performance as a dynamic concept". The second part depicts the models of job performance by presenting the two main and the most known job performance models: (1) the Campbell et al.'s (1993) model and (2) the Borman and Motowidlo (1993) model. The third part deals with the predictors (antecedents or determinants) of job performance with a focus on an empirical study entitled "Job performance of nurses in hospitality sector in Qatar". In fact, this study aims to deepen our

DOI: 10.4018/978-1-5225-5525-4.ch004

knowledge on the nurses` job performance in a particular environment: the gulf region and precisely in Aspetar, a multicultural hospital. It aims to explore the nursing job performance at Aspetar by studying its dimensionality by using the Schwirian Six Dimension Scale of Nursing Performance (Schwirian 1978). Finally, the fourth part will focus on the relationship between job performance and workplace arrogance.

Job Performance as Dynamic Concept

In order to investigate the concept of "job performance", one should begin by studying two fundamental aspects or issues: (1) the difference between performance and effectiveness such as Campbell et al. (1970) showed; and (2) does job performance has a behavioral aspect or outcome aspect?

Before going on the exploration of these two main issues, the authors will introduce the epistemological ground of this concept known as "job performance". In fact, this central concept of our study finds its origins in the Industrial / Organizational psychology. For many researchers as Austin and Villanova (1992); Campbell (1990); Murphy and Cleveland (1995); Schmidt and Hunter (1992)… *"job performance is a central construct in industrial/ organizational psychology"* (Viswesvaran and Ones 2000).

The difference between "performance" and "effectiveness" is based on the notion of "action". For Campbell (2012), *"performance is the action, not the thinking that preceded the action"*. Moreover, Campbell (1990); Campbell et al. (1993); Kanfer (1990); and Roe (1999) argue that action is considered as the "behavioral" aspect of performance unlike its outcome aspect (Sonnentag and Frese 2002).

In fact, all what an individual does in the work setting is referred to the behavioral aspect. That is to say all technical tasks which a person should execute when he was hired by a firm. *"Performance is what the organization hires one to do, and do well"* (Campbell et al. 1993: 40 cited by Sonnentag and Frese 2002). For Wetzels et al. (2000) *"job performance as the degree to which employees execute tasks, responsibilities, and assignments"* (Knight et al. 2007). However, Sonnentag and Frese (2002) argue that not all behaviors could be considered as related to the performance concept. Only those that are considered as relevant for the achievement of the firm goals. Moreover, for Campbell et al. (1993) if an action could not be measured, it will not be considered to constitute a performance. That is why the effectiveness indicators (e.g. sales volume) are very important to judge the individual performance, but only if they are related to the goals of the firm. Otherwise,

The specifications for individual performance are wrong and need changing, or conversely the organization is pursuing the wrong goals (...) If the variability in an effectiveness indicator is totally under the control of the individual then it is a measure of performance. (Campbell 2012).

Hence, it is essential to determine which actions constitute performance. What means, among all these actions which are relevant for organizational goals. To answer to this question, Sonnentag and Frese (2002), argue that the role of outcome aspect of performance is crucial in this quest. In fact, "The outcome aspect refers to the consequence or result of the individual's behavior (...) such as numbers of engines assembled, pupils' reading proficiency, sales figures, or number of successful heart operations. (Sonnentag and Frese 2002). For instance, and as Bush et al. (1990) argued, "retail salespeople's job performance evaluations should be multidimensional and include both outcome (e.g. sales) and behavior (e.g. customer orientation) components." (Knight et al. 2007).

According to the above development, one can conclude that job performance is a dynamic concept since "action" was considered as its core aspect. However, this dynamic aspect of job performance could be explained by focusing at least on two concepts: knowledge and learning.

The Campbell's (1990) model distinguished three determinants of job performance: (1) declarative knowledge (DK), (2) procedural knowledge and skills (PKS), and (3) motivation (M). Thus, one can note that knowledge and skills are the main two factors explaining job performance. And knowing that *"knowledge is essentially related to human action"* (Nonaka and Takeuchi 1995 in Tsoukas & Vladimirou 2001) and knowing that "action" is essential to define "knowledge" and emphasize its dynamic character as argued by Davenport and Prusak (1998 in Tsoukas and Vladimirou 2001: 974):

Knowledge is a flux mix of framed experiences, values, contextual information, and expert insight that provides a framework for evaluating and incorporating new experiences and information. It originates and is applied in the minds of individuals. In organizations it becomes embedded not only in documents or repositories but also in organizational routines, processes, practices, and norms.

one can emphasize the dynamic character of "job performance".

For Sonnentag and Frese (2002), the more an individual learns, the more his/her job performance increases. In fact, *"studies showed that performance initially increases with increasing time spent in a specific job and later reaches a plateau (Avolio, Waldman, & McDaniel, 1990; McDaniel, Schmidt, & Hunter, 1988; Quinones, Ford, & Teachout, 1995)"* (Sonnentag and Frese 2002). Moreover, there is a dynamic relationship between phases of the learning process and job performance. In fact,

During early phases of skill acquisition, performance relies largely on 'controlled processing', the availability of declarative knowledge and the optimal allocation of limited intentional resources, whereas later in the skill acquisition process, performance largely relies on automatic processing, procedural knowledge, and psychomotor abilities (Ackerman, 1988; Kanfer & Ackerman, 1989). (Sonnentag and Frese 2002).

Models of Job Performance

Modeling job performance has been and remains one of the most recent issues at least from the perspective of organizational behavior research, although it has been studied for decades. In fact, since mid-1980's several researchers (see Borman & Brush 1993; Borman & Motowidlo 1993; Campbell, McCloy, Oppler, & Sager 1993; Griffen et al. 2007; Murphy 1989; Organ 1988; Yukl, Gordon, & Taber 2002 Cited by Poropat 2002) have undertaken studies in order to determine the dimensionality of performance in general and job performance in particular. These studies have led to what is called "job performance models". These latter offer differing specificities of the nature of these construct.

In the following, the authors will present the two main and the most known job performance models: (1) the Campbell et al.'s (1993) model and (2) the Borman and Motowidlo (1993) model.

Campbell et al.'s (1993) model is considered as one of these famous models dealing with the complexity of job performance. This model is composed by three determinants and eight factors explaining job performance. These three determinants were introduced above: (1) declarative knowledge (DK), (2) procedural knowledge and skills (PKS), and (3) motivation (M).

Unlike the cognitive sciences, which provide a range of knowledge, management retains only two types of knowledge, namely: (1) "declarative knowledge" which consists on a set of technical, scientific and administrative knowledge. It is a relatively formal and explicit knowledge (Spender 1996; Nonaka 1994); and (2) "procedural knowledge" that encompasses both know-how and procedures. For *Sonnentag and Frese (2002), « procedural knowledge and skills include cognitive and psychomotor skills, physical skill, self-management skill, and interpersonal skill"*. However, Girod (1995) has added a third type of knowledge called "knowledge of judgment" that enables the organization to behave well at the right time and effectively (see Table 1). Concerning motivation, Campbell et al. (1993) argue that it *"comprises choice to perform, level of effort, and persistence of effort" (Sonnentag and Frese 2002)*.

Campbell et al.'s (1993) model consists of eight factors explaining job performance (see Table 2).

All these factors are not relevant to all kinds of jobs. Only three are considered as that: job-specific technical task proficiency; demonstrating effort; and maintaining personal discipline.

The second popular job performance model was developed in 1993 by Borman and Motowidlo. This same model is known as Task and Citizenship Performance model or Technical Core and Contextual Performance model. In fact, Borman and Motowidlo (1993) developed a model of job performance which includes two types of behaviors or activities, namely: task and contextual performance.

Task performance is also known as In-role performance. This latter is defined as *"those officially required outcomes and behaviors that directly*

Table 1. The subsystems of the organizational memory

Levels of Processing	Components		
	Declarative (Knowledge)	**Procedural (Know "How to")**	**Of Judgment (Know "What to Do")**
Individual	Knowledge held by each individual (brain and documents) and placed at the service of the organization	Know-how of each individual (essentially in his brain) and placed at the service of the organization	Prospective memory of the individual and know how to interpret based on his experience and placed at the service of the organization
Collective non-centralized	Acquisition of knowledge from another individual or creation of new knowledge through interaction	Creation of a common know-how by a common work	Creation of a common interpretation
Collective centralized	Knowledge held in the centralized databases	Procedures set out in the manuals	Legitimized culture, formalized as documents

Source: Girod (1995).

Table 2. A taxonomy of higher-order performance components

---

1. Job-specific technical task proficiency

The first factor reflects the degree to which the individual performs the core substantive or technical tasks that are central to his or her job. They are the job-specific performance behaviors that distinguish the substantive content of one job from another. Constructing custom kitchens, doing word processing, designing computer architecture, driving a bus through Chicago traffic, and directing air traffic are examples.

2. Non-job-specific technical task proficiency

This factor reflects the situation that in virtually every organization, but perhaps not all, individuals are required to perform tasks that are not specific to their particular job. For example, in research universities the faculty must teach classes, advise students, make admission decisions, and serve on committees. All faculties must do these things, in addition to practicing chemistry, psychology, economics, or electrical engineering.

3. Written and oral communication task proficiency

Many jobs in the work force require the individual to make formal oral or written presentations to audiences that may vary from one to tens of thousands. For those jobs, the proficiency with which one can write or speak, independent of the correctness of the subject matter, is a critical component of performance.

4. Demonstrating effort

The fourth factor refers to the consistency of an individual's effort day by day, the frequency with which people will expend extra time when required, and the willingness to keep working under adverse conditions. It is a reflection of the degree to which individuals commit themselves to all job tasks, work at a high level of intensity, and keep working when it is cold, wet, or late.

5. Maintaining personal discipline (Counterproductive Work Behavior)

The fifth component is characterized by the degree to which negative behavior, such as alcohol and substance abuse at work, law or rules infractions, and excessive absenteeism, is avoided.

6. Facilitating peer and team performance

Factor 6 is defined as the degree to which the individual supports his or her peers, helps them with job problems, and acts as a de facto trainer. It also encompasses how well an individual facilitates group functioning by being a good model, keeping the group goal directed, and reinforcing participation by the other group members. Obviously, if the individual works alone, this component will have little importance.

7. Supervision/leadership

Proficiency in the supervisory component includes all the behaviors directed at influencing the performance of subordinates through fact-to-face interpersonal interaction and influence. Supervisors set goals for subordinates, they teach them more effective methods, they model the appropriate behaviors, and they reward, punish, or are supportive in appropriate ways. The distinction between this factor and the preceding one is a distinction between peer leadership and supervisory leadership.

8. Management/administration

This factor is intended to include the major elements in management that are distinct from direct supervision. It includes the performance behaviors directed at articulating goals for the unit or enterprise, organizing people and resources to work on them, monitoring progress, helping to solve problems or overcome crisis that stand in the way of goal accomplishment, controlling expenditures, obtaining additional resources, and representing the unit in dealings with other units, with other organizations, or with the public.

Source: Campbell (2012).

serve the goals of the organization (Motowidlo & Van Scotter, 1994)" (Bakker et al. 2004). For Behrman and Perreault (1984 cited by Bakker et al. 2004), "*among other things, in-role performance includes meeting organizational objectives and effective functioning*". For Coleman & Borman (2000 cited by Greenslade and Jimmieson 2007), task performance is defined as "*behaviours that contribute directly to the organization's technical core and includes those activities that are typically recognized as part of a workers job*". Whence, the term "Technical Core and Contextual Performance model" to designate the job performance model. For Borman and Motowidlo (1997), core technical task performance is defined as,

... Activities that contribute to the organization's technical core either directly by implementing a part of its technological process, or indirectly by providing it with needed materials or services. Examples of task performance dimensions for a sales job might include, Product Knowledge, Closing the Sale, and Organization and Time Management. For a firefighter job, Performing Rescue Operations, Conducting Salvage Operations, and Applying Ventilation Procedures are good examples of task dimensions.

For Sonnentag et al. (2010), there is a tight correspondence between the eight factors of Campbell et al.'s (1993) job performance model and task performance. In fact,

Among these eight factors, five refer to task performance: (1) job-specific task proficiency; (2) non-job-specific task proficiency; (3) written and oral communication proficiency; (4) supervision, in case of leadership position; and partly (5) management/administration. Each of these five factors itself consists of subfactors which are differently important for various jobs. For example, the supervision factor includes (1) guiding, directing, and motivating subordinates and providing feedback, (2) maintaining good working relationships, and (3) coordinating subordinates and others resources to get the job done (Borman and Brush, 1993). (Sonnentag et al. 2010).

Another correspondence between the two models has been emphasized by some authors (Cai & Lin 2006; Griffin, Neal & Neale 2000 cite by Rosman et al. 2014) who argued that "*the core activities include procedural and declarative knowledge, ability, experience and technical tasks involved in the job*" (Rosman et al. 2014).

Cai and Lin (2006 cited by Rosman et al. 2014) argued that beside behaviors that are related to technical core activities and are source of job performance, other behaviors that are not related to technical core activities but they are so much crucial to enhance job performance. That is why researchers as Motowidlo (2003) argued that "*the job performance should not only measure the core activities (task performance) but also other activities (contextual performance)*" (Rosman et al. 2014).

For Borman and Motowidlo (1997), contextual performance consists of activities that

Contribute to organizational effectiveness in ways that shape the organizational, social, and psychological context that serves as a catalyst for task activities

and processes. Contextual activities include volunteering to carryout task activities that are not formally part of the job and helping and cooperating with others in the organization to get tasks accomplished.

For Podsakoff and MacKenzie (1994 cited by Bakker et al. 2004), Extra-role performance (a.k.a. contextual performance) *"is defined as discretionary behaviors on the part of an employee that are believed to directly promote the effective functioning of an organization, without necessarily directly influencing a person's target productivity"*.

For some researchers (Makin et al. 1996; Goodman & Svyantek 1999 cited in Bakker et al. 2004) contextual performance is related to the psychological contract between employees and organization. In fact, if this latter reward its employees for their efforts above their core activities, they will be willing to give more and more. Thus, for Coleman and Borman (2000 cited by Greenslade and Jimmieson 2007)

The behaviours that represent contextual performance are more stable across roles and include organizational support, job-task support and interpersonal support (...). Organizational support refers to behaviours that assist the organization through compliance with organizational rules as well as loyalty and allegiance. Job-task support refers to behaviours that go beyond job requirements, demonstrate dedication and persistence and maximize performance. Interpersonal support refers to behaviours that support the organization through interpersonal interfaces such as helping co-workers.

However, there are some required individual behaviors corresponding to the contextual performance that are not formally rewarded, but they could be otherwise by the organization. These behaviors are called "Organizational Citizenship Behavior" (OCB). These latter (OCB) has been defined by Organ (1988) as *"individual behavior that is discretionary, not directly or explicitly recognized by the formal reward system, and that in the aggregate promotes the effective functioning of the organization"*. Organ (1988) has identified some dimensions of the OCB, namely: altruism, courtesy, cheerleading, sportsmanship, civic virtue, and conscientiousness.

For some researchers as Moorman & Blakely (1995) and Williams & Wong (1999), the antecedents of OCB comprise employee attitudes, role perceptions, demographics, stress, job satisfaction, interpersonal trust, organizational commitment and employee mood (Basu et al. 2017). As consequences of the

OCB on individuals and organizations, Whiting et al. (2008) reported that OCB had a significant effect on performance evaluation decisions (Basu et al. 2017). MacKenzie et al. (1991 cited by Choi and Moon 2017) have studied the positive contribution of OCB on the sales and Walz and Niehoff (2000 cited by Choi and Moon 2017) have concluded that OCB have a positive impact on customer satisfaction.

Predictors (Antecedents or Determinants) of Job Performance

The psychology literature review provides us with a large set of job performance's predictors. The most popular or known are: the "Big Five" personality factors (Tett et al. 1991); the psychological well-being and job satisfaction (Wright and Cropanzano 2000); conscientiousness (Mount and Barrick 1995); self-esteem, locus of control, neuroticism, and generalized self-efficacy (Judge and Bono 2001); locus of control, job enrichment, demographic and situational variables (Miller 1984). However, there are others that are not widely known or used, namely: social support and self efficacy (Baumgärtner et al. 2014; AbuAlRub 2014).

The authors will focus on these predictors in order to explore, later, their relationship with workplace arrogance.

Social Support and Job Performance

Social support is defined by Shumaker and Brownell (1984 cited by Zimet et al. 1988) as "*an exchange of resources between at least two individuals perceived by the provider or the recipient to be intended to enhance the well-being of the recipient*". For Lin (1986 cited by Zimet et al. 1988) social support is a "perceived or actual instrumental and/or expressive provisions supplied by the community, social networks, and confiding partners". More lately, some researchers as Bakker et al. (2004) have defined social support as a high job resource that could reduce job demands. In fact, job resources are "...*those physical, psychological, social, or organizational aspects of the job that are (1) functional in achieving work goals; (2) reduce job demands and the associated physiological and psychological costs; or (3) stimulate personal growth and development*" (Bakker et al. 2014). Examples are salary, career opportunities, job security, supervisor and coworker support, team climate, role clarity, participation in decision making, performance feedback, skill variety, task significance, task identity, and autonomy. Whilst job demands are considered as

Those physical, psychological, social, or organizational aspects of the job that require sustained physical and/or psychological (cognitive and emotional) effort and are therefore associated with certain physiological and/ or psychological costs. Examples are a high work pressure, role overload, emotional demands, and poor environmental conditions. (Bakker et al. 2014).

Moreover, the findings of their study are crucial in specifying the relationship between social support and job performance. In fact, Bakker et al. (2014) have concluded that: (1) Job resources ... are the most important predictors of extra-role performance, through their influence on disengagement; and (2) job demands are the most important antecedents of in-role performance, primarily through the experience of exhaustion. Hence, one could conclude that social support as a job resource is a predictor of job performance, especially contextual or extra-role performance. This latter finding is supported by the results of a study undertaken by Baumgärtner et al. (2014) who have posit that there are three reasons behind the fact that social support has a significant impact on job performance: (1) it facilitates coping with work-related problems (Burns et al. 2007); (2) it is important for organizational socialization (Fisher 1985; Major et al. 1995; Colella 1994); and (3) has a positive influence on employees' health (Karpur and Bruye`re 2012; Allen et al. 2005; Frese 1999).

Self-Efficacy and Job Performance

Sonnentag and Frese (2002) defined self-efficacy as the belief that one can execute an action well. In fact, *"the concept of self-efficacy explains that individual's perception about their ability to achieve certain task motivates them to achieve their objectives at work place and in personal life"* (Bhatti et al. 2013).

Several researchers considered it as a relevant concept for performance (Bandura 1997; Stajkovic & Luthans 1998 cited by Sonnentag and Frese 2002) and widely used to explain employee performance (Bhatti et al. 2013). Thus, Stajkovic and Luthans (1998 cited by Bhatti et al. 2013) found that *"self-efficacy enhances job performance up to 28 per cent"*. As to Claus et al. (2011 cited by Bhatti et al. 2013), they argued that *"low self-efficacy leads to poor performance, absenteeism and high intention to search for a job whereas high*

self-efficacy leads to better performance and high organizational commitment".
Moreover, Baum et al. (2001 cited by Sonnentag & Frese 2002) posit that
self-efficacy is related to task performance. In fact, Bandura (1997 cited by
Bhatti et al. 2013) explains "*those individuals high on self-efficacy tend to
be more for initiating tasks, consistent efforts to achieve tasks and persistent
with problems even in the face of failure*". In the same vein, Baumgärtner et
al. (2014) argued that

*High self-efficacious individuals believe in their abilities and are motivated
to utilize them to achieve positive results. They tend to be persistent in
achieving their work-related goals, which has been demonstrated to positively
relate to their job performance. Low self-efficacious individuals, in contrast,
lack confidence in their abilities, which leads to mechanisms that are
counterproductive for good job performance.*

As to Speier and Frese (1997 cited by Sonnentag & Frese 2002) and
Frese et aL. (1999 cited by Sonnentag & Frese 2002), they have argued
that self-efficacy - respectively as personal initiative and developing ideas
and suggestions within an organizational suggestion system - is related to
contextual performance.

Job Performance of Nurses in Hospitality Sector in Qatar

As mentioned previously, employees are the most important resources of
each organization especially in more humanity jobs such as nursing. How
they feel about the work and the results from it, have a direct impact on
the organization's performance and ultimately its stability. In fact, Patient
satisfaction and the measurement of the quality of care are the most used
clinical indicators to determine the nurse's performance and satisfaction. For
example, if nurses are happy and satisfied with their work, they will be highly
motivated to perform the best of their ability to achieve their own goals and
the goals of the organization that they belong to, the first line to see that will
be patient satisfaction which leads to good reputation of the organization
and quality of care.

Nurses spend more time with patients than do any other health care providers
and patient outcomes are affected by nursing care quality. Thus, improvements
in patient safety can be achieved by improving nurse performance.

However, nursing performance includes cognitive, physical, and
organizational factors and the nurse's work system often does not accommodate

human limits and capabilities and that nurses work under cognitive, perceptual, and physical overloads. Specifically, nurses engage in multiple tasks under cognitive load and frequent interruptions, and they encounter insufficient lighting, illegible handwriting, and poorly designed labels. They spend a substantial amount of their time walking, work long shifts, and experience a high rate of musculoskeletal disorders. In order to improve nurses performance and patient safety, research in the areas of cognitive processes in nursing, effects of interruptions on nursing performance, communications during patient handoffs, and situation awareness in nursing has to improve and be more beneficial for patients and nurses.

Moreover, a number of studies have noted that nurses engage in both task and contextual performance behaviors.

For example, Kidder (2002) examined citizenship behaviors across professions and found that nurses performed a large number of altruistic citizenship behaviors (interpersonal support) as part of their job. Further, Bakker et al. (2005) noted that nurses engaged in both in-role (task) and extra-role (contextual) behaviors and that the performance of these was influenced by the nurses' level of burnout. Further, the Borman et al. model is in line with research from the patient satisfaction literature, which suggests that patient satisfaction is determined by both technical care and contextual factors. (Greenslade and Jimmieson 2007).

Numerous other studies examining continuity of care find that: "in wards where nurses work together to provide continuous care, patient satisfaction is higher than where traditional care is provided" (Waldenstro et al. 2000).

Accordingly, we can conclude that where nurses engage in contextual performance behaviors, such as assisting each other, patient satisfaction is improved. Therefore, making a distinction between task and contextual performance provides a sound theoretical base for the measurement of nursing performance.

In order to create a culture of continuous improvement requires knowing exactly what the organization is striving for and due to the importance of quality of care in any nursing department, this means the entire organization should understand the concept of excellence and continually look for ways to do things better and more efficiently, resulting in higher levels of effectiveness. To achieve excellence, nurses need to have a systematic approach to improvement initiatives that result in positive change for the organization.

Thus, this study aims to deepen our knowledge on the nurses` job performance in a particular environment: the gulf region and precisely in Aspetar, a multicultural hospital. It aims to explore the nursing job performance at Aspetar by studying its dimensionality by using the Schwirian Six Dimension Scale of Nursing Performance (Schwirian 1978).

Aspetar is a modern 25 plus bed facility therefore it is the only orthopedic and sports Medicine hospital in the Gulf Region. It provides the highest possible medical treatment for sports – related injuries non-sports related injuries and it is stuffed by some of the world`s leading sports medicine practitioners and researchers.

It is located in Doha the capital of Qatar and is a part of the Aspire Zone Foundation (AZF) known also as Doha sports City which is a 250-hectar sporting complex located in AlWaab (a district of Doha). It was established in order to be an international sports destination in 2003 and in 2004 an educational Centre for the development of sporting champions (aspire academy) started. Aspire Zone is an important feature in 2022 FIFA World Cup Bid submitted by the Qatar Football Association and the complex was central to the Doha Bid for the Summer Olympics in 2016 by Qatar Olympic Committee. Aspire Zone is also home to Doha`s tallest structure: The aspire Tower and it is adjacent to Villaggio Mall, the most popular mall in Qatar.

In addition, Aspetar has employees from more than 50 countries which make it unique and special with huge differences between countries, cultures, religions, languages.

Aspetar was chosen due to the diversity of its employees. They originate from a wide variety of countries which makes it a unique, special and interesting population to research. The mission and vision of Aspetar revolves around excellence. This latter cannot be achieved without proper job performance, and as nursing is one of the main pillars of medicine, the authors begun by exploring the nursing specificities in Aspetar.

The Nursing department at Aspetar is a very important department that reports directly to the General Director. Nursing department started since the first opening of Aspetar, there were not more than 10 nurses in 2006, today they are 85 nurses and the number will be higher in the coming years due to the increase of number of patients seen daily and the strategy that Aspetar is adopting.

Nursing department has a subcommittee in quality, infection control, risk management, education and patient safety. To achieve excellence, Aspetar develops and implements a patient safety plan supported by all departments mainly the nursing department by:

1. Collating/trending of incident reporting data/infection control data,
2. Performance improvement project workgroups,
3. Hospital Clinical and Non-clinical Committee review,
4. External safety consultant review,
5. Emergency drill review,
6. Table top exercises (Middle Eastern Respiratory Virus MERS to occur in August),
7. Department safety huddles,
8. Failure Modes Effects Analysis,
9. Risk assessment (likelihood and severity index),
10. Department risk registers,
11. Risk Management department reviews,
12. Environmental Rounds Assessment.

This section is devoted to the presentation of our research methodology, its results, the discussion of the research methodology and the presentation of contributions, limitations and future research trajectories.

Research Methodology

Sampling and Data Collection

This study was conducted over a three-month period between February and May 2017 at Aspetar Hospital.

Nurses not practicing under the umbrella of the nursing department were excluded due to their sub-specialization in their particular field. These included:

*   Radiology nurses
*   Dentistry nurses
*   Laboratory nurses
*   Materials officer nurses
*   National Sports Medicine Program nurses

These nurses, specialized in their relevant area, have a different scope of practice and have not practiced general nursing for more than 5 years. Thus, they may not be able to answer to the proposed questionnaire properly.

There were 80 licensed nurses working in the Nursing Department under the general nursing scope of practice. These included anesthesia and recovery nurses, Recovery nurses, Scrub nurses, Ward nurses, Outpatient department nurses, Pre-admission clinic nurses, Athlete screening nurses, Nurse Educators, Infection control nurses and Nursing supervisors. These were the target sample for the study.

Approvals were obtained from the relevant departments of Aspetar Hospital: Director of Nursing department, Director of Education department, Ethics Committee, Risk management and the Director General.

Nurses were assured that all data collected was confidential and that no individual data would be identifiable and provided to the hospital or used in any publications.

The questionnaire was sent to these 80 nurses at Aspetar via the intranet of the hospital. After two weeks, there were 40 completed responses that had been returned. To encourage more response, face to face interviews were undertaken. Two weeks later, the final response total was 57, which corresponds to a response rate of 71.25%.

As shown in Table 1, the sample is predominantly female. Most of them are between 30 and 50 year old and have qualifications corresponding to License. The qualifications of the participants were varied – according to country of origin, adopted education and professional level. Whether a diploma, a degree, a masters or some other type of qualification (in which circumstance Human Resources at Aspetar uses the UK and USA education equivalent). They are from more than 20 different nationalities - which make this survey particularly interesting due to the different cultural aspects of its participants. As mentioned below (see Table 3), the most of participants to the study are Senior registered Nurse.

Operationalization of Nursing Job Performance

Nursing Job performance - defined as the effectiveness of the nurse in carrying out his or her roles and responsibilities related to direct patient care - was measured with the Schwirian Six Dimension Scale of Nursing Performance (Schwirian 1978 cited by AbuAlRub 2004).

Table 4 summarizes the dimensions of the "Nursing job performance" variable studied and the number of items in each of them (78 items). For each dimension, respondents were asked to indicate "How well does this nurse perform these activities in his/her current job?" by choosing between 1 "not very well", 2=satisfactory, 3=well, and 4 "very well".

Table 3. Demographic characteristics

	Number	%
Gender		
Male	15	26
Female	42	74
Age		
20-30 years	1	2
30-40 years	37	65
40-50 years	13	23
50-60 years	6	10
More than 60 years old	-	-
Qualification		
Diploma	17	30
License	30	53
Master	10	17
Other	-	-
Experience		
Less than 1 year	3	5
1-5 years	19	33
5-10 years	27	48
More than 10 years	8	14
Positions		
Head Nurse	6	10
Registered Nurse	6	10
Team Leader	1	2
Senior registered Nurse	44	67
Nursing Supervisor	4	7
Assistant Director Of Nursing	1	2
Director Of Nursing	1	2

Data Analysis

All statistical analyzes were performed using the SPSS software using Exploratory Factor Analysis (EFA). Indeed, this analysis has as objective to retain the dimensions and items that satisfied the conditions of reliability and validity (Hair et al. 2010). That is to say, that is the best analysis to study the dimensionality of any variable.

Table 4. Dimensions of nursing job performance

Dimensions	Number of Items
Leadership	5
Critical Care	7
Teaching and collaboration	11
Planning and evaluation	7
Interpersonal relations and communications	12
Professional development	10

RESULTS

Sample with less than 100 of respondent is not considered as satisfactory to do such research (Wiktorowicz 2017), but this study remains a preliminary essay to exploit the dimensions of the job performance in context so interesting such as a hospital in the Middle East. The Exploratory Factor Analysis is a strong method that verifies the validity of a construct with its dimensions assumed to be measured (Carricano & Poujol 2008; Akrout 2010). Exploratory factor analysis leads to understand the dimensionality (represented by some items retained during the analysis) of a variable (Dobni 2008). It was to say that doing Exploratory Factor Analysis with putting all the items of the dimensions at the same time is more rigorous but as it said, this study is a first essay with a limited number of respondents. Maybe this is among the recommendations that we have to take into consideration in the future in order to improve the quality of the results.

In order to carry out this analysis, we tried firstly to ensure that the data were adequate and factorizable. Acceptable Values of Keyser Meyer Olkin Index (KMO) and Bartlett sphericity test indicate if we have factorizable solutions or not. An orthogonal rotation (Varimax) helps to simplify the interpretation of the factors (Hair et al. 2006). The tables below demonstrate the details of the results.

Dimension "Leadership"

The test identified that a total of four items retained explain the dimension "Leadership" (see Table 5). Value of Keyser Meyer Olkin Index (KMO) in the 0.80s is meritorious (Kaiser, 1974). The Bartlett's test of sphericity should be significant (p<0.05) to verify that data are factorizable and to show that

Table 5. Exploratory Factor Analysis (EFA) results dimension "leadership"

Dimension	Items	Items Retained	Communalities	Loadings	KMO	Variance	α
Leadership (L)	5	L1	0.766	0.875	0.767	74.57%	0.881
		L2	0.694	0.833			
		L4	0.853	0.924			
		L5	0.670	0.819			

"final factor solution indicate that the correlation matrices are representative identity matrices suitable for multivariate analysis" (Wiktorowicz 2017). An orthogonal rotation (Varimax) helps to simplify the interpretation of the factors (Hair et al. 2006).

Results obtained at the exploratory level indicate the adequacy of the data. All items are selected with an acceptable variance (above the 50% threshold) and good representation (Values of communalities) of all the items selected (above the 50% threshold). Moreover, each construct represents acceptable internal coherence reliability since Alpha coefficient is above the threshold of 0.7 (Anderson & Gerbing 1988; Hair et al. 2006).

Within this dimension, from 5 items only one dropped and the other 4 were retained, the "leadership" of Aspetar nurses is well correlated to teaching patient's family members about the patient's needs, coordinating the plan of nursing care with the medical plan of care, teaching preventive health measure to patients and their families and identifying and using community resources in developing a plan of care for a patient and his/her family. However, giving praise and recognition for achievement to those under his/her direction is an item that dropped explaining the non-correlation with other components.

Dimension "Critical Care"

Concerning the second dimension which is "Critical Care", results showed that six items are retained among seven put in the analysis (see Table 6). As we can see all values and indices respect the norms of good quality of results. Value of Keyser Meyer Olkin Index (KMO) which is in the 0.90s confirms that adequacy is marvelous. The Bartlett's test of sphericity is under the value of 0.05. This indicates that the correlation matrices are representative (Wiktorowicz 2017).

The Variance is above the threshold requested which is 50%. The values of communalities too are above 50% which show a good quality of representation

Table 6. Exploratory Factor Analysis (EFA) results dimension "critical care"

Dimension	Items	Items Retained	Communalities	Loadings	KMO	Variance	α
Critical Care (CC)	7	CC1	0.850	0.922	0.871	78.91%	0.946
		CC2	0.808	0.899			
		CC3	0.691	0.831			
		CC4	0.851	0.922			
		CC5	0.862	0.929			
		CC7	0.672	0.820			

of the items retained. Finally, the coefficient of reliability shows an acceptable internal coherence as Alpha coefficient is above 0.7 (Anderson & Gerbing 1988; Hair et al. 2006).

Critical care dimension includes 7 items, out of them one eliminated and 6 items retained. The critical care made at Aspetar by nursing staff is considered as highly performed with a good cohesion between care plans anticipated changes in patient's conditions, evaluating results of nursing care, promoting the inclusion of patient's decision and desires concerning nurses' care, develop a plan of nursing care for a patient and adapt teaching methods and materials to the understanding of the particular audience: e.g., age of patient, educational background and sensory deprivation.

Dimension "Teaching/Collaboration"

Regarding the dimension "Teaching/Collaboration", results are not good as on 11 items only 4 are retained (see Table 7). But the latter retained in the analysis respected all the norms requested concerning communalities,

Table 7. Exploratory Factor Analysis (EFA) results dimension "teaching/collaboration"

Dimension	Items	Items Retained	Communalities	Loadings	KMO	Variance	α
Teaching/Collaboration (TC)	11	TC8	0.738	0.859	0.838	75.58%	0.891
		TC9	0.687	0.829			
		TC10	0.793	0.891			
		TC11	0.806	0.898			

KMO, variance, value of Alpha and loading (see the table results Teaching/Collaboration).

Teaching and collaboration of nurses at Aspetar is well performed considering the cohesion and the correlation in communicating verbally facts, ideas, and feelings to other health care team members, promoting the patients' rights to privacy, contributing to an atmosphere of mutual trust, acceptance, and respect among other health team members and in delegating responsibility for care based on assessment of priorities of nursing care needs and the abilities and limitations of available health care personnel.

Dimension: "Planning/Evaluation"

Concerning "Planning/Evaluation", it is the only dimension that all their items put in the analysis are retained (see Table 8). Value of Keyser Meyer Olkin Index (KMO) is the 0.90s which indicates that it is marvelous (Kaiser 1974). The Bartlett's test of sphericity is significant (p= 0.000<0.05) that shows that "final factor solution indicate that the correlation matrices are representative identity matrices suitable for multivariate analysis" (Wiktorowicz 2017). Variance is acceptable (above the 50% threshold) and items have good representation (Values of communalities are above the 50% threshold). The whole construct represents acceptable internal coherence reliability as its Alpha coefficient is above the minimum requested 0.7 especially in the exploratory analysis (Dobni 2008).

Aspetar nurses are performing very well in planning and evaluation dimension of the Schwirian Six Dimension Scale of Nursing Performance. In fact, planning and evaluation of Aspetar nurses is demonstrated in nursing

Table 8. Exploratory Factor Analysis (EFA) results dimension "planning/evaluation"

Dimension	Items	Items Retained	Communalities	Loadings	KMO	Variance	α
Planning/Evaluation (PE)	7	PE1	0.564	0.751	0.859	66.58%	0.915
		PE2	0.724	0.851			
		PE3	0.705	0.840			
		PE4	0.725	0.851			
		PE5	0.677	0.823			
		PE6	0.688	0.830			
		PE7	0.577	0.759			

explaining procedures to patients prior to performing any nursing activity, guidance of other health team members in planning for nursing care, acceptance of responsibility for the level of care under his/her direction, performing appropriate measures in emergency situations, promote the use of interdisciplinary resource persons, the use of teaching aids and resource materials in teaching patients and their families and in performing nursing care required by critically ill patients.

Dimensions "Interpersonal Relations/ Communication" and "Professional Development"

Finally for the two last dimensions, a considered number of items have been removed compared to the total items in the analysis to reach the norms requested. "Interpersonal Relations/Communication" only 6 items retained compared to 12 extracted in the analysis. For "Professional Development" only 5 items retained on 10 put in the analysis. (see table 9 of dimensions Interpersonal Relations/Communication and Table 10 of Professional Development)

Interpersonal Relations and Communication of Aspetar nurses is explained by these 6 retained items translated in identifying and using resources within the appropriate policies and procedures in developing a plan of care for patient and his/her family, using nursing procedures as opportunities for interaction with patients, recognizing and meeting the emotional needs of a dying patient, communicating facts, ideas, and professional opinions in writing to patients and their families, in planning for the integration of patient needs with family needs and functioning calmly and competently in emergency situations.

Table 9. Exploratory Factor Analysis (EFA) results dimension: Interpersonal relations/communication

Dimension	Items	Items Retained	Communalities	Loadings	KMO	Variance	α
Interpersonal Relations/ Communication (IRC)	12	IRC2	0.600	0.775	0.877	69.37%	0.908
		IRC3	0.711	0.843			
		IRC7	0.719	0.848			
		IRC8	0.638	0.799			
		IRC9	0.780	0.883			
		IRC10	0.713	0.845			

Table 10. Exploratory Factor Analysis (EFA) results dimension: Professional development

Dimension	Items	Items Retained	Communalities	Loadings	KMO	Variance	α
Professional Development (PD)	10	PD1	0.799	0.894	0.859	71.07%	0.897
		PD2	0.690	0.831			
		PD3	0.788	0.888			
		PD4	0.662	0.814			
		PD7	0.615	0.784			

Finally for the two last dimensions, a considered number of items have been removed compared to the total items in the analysis to reach the norms requested. "Interpersonnel Relations/Communication" only 6 items retained compared to 12 extracted in the analysis. For "Professional Development" only 5 items retained on 10 put in the analysis. (See table of dimensions Interpersonnel Relations/Communication and Professional Development).

Professional Development of Aspetar nurses are explained by the use of learning opportunities for ongoing personal and professional growth, by displaying self-direction, accepting responsibility for own actions and assuming new responsibilities within the limits of capabilities.

DISCUSSION

Discussion of the results of this research will focus on two aspects. First, the nature of the dimensions explaining nurses' job performance in Aspetar (Qatar). That is to say, which of them are considered as task performance and which of them are considered as contextual performance? Second, the evaluation of the adjustment between these dimensions, the vision, the mission and the strategic objectives of Aspetar.

Concerning the first aspect and based on the prior research in this field, it is argued that leadership, critical care, teaching and collaboration, planning and evaluation, and professional development are considered as task performance (Motowidlo and Van Scotter 1994; Conway 1996). As argued by Greenslade and Jimmieson (2007)

Past measures of nursing performance, including the Slater Nursing Competencies Rating scale (Wandelt & Phaneuf 1974) and the Schwirian six-D scale (Schwirian 1978), have focused on task performance and incorporated components such as planning and evaluation of care, critical care, communication and professional development.

In contrast, the dimension "interpersonal relations and communications" is considered as a contextual performance. In fact, Greenslade and Jimmieson (2007) posit that

Contextual performance refers to those behaviours that maintain the broader social environment in which the technical core must function. It includes more discretionary behaviours that assist the hospital to function (Borman & Motowidlo 1993).

Concerning the evaluation of the adjustment between these dimensions, the vision, the mission and the strategic objectives of Aspetar, the authors will focus on some official documents and reports provided by the hospital.

Aspetar nursing leadership is considered as an important dimension of job performance, as meritorious, and it is one of the most important criteria in the recruitment of nurses. In addition, the leadership is considered as one of the Aspetar strategic objectives (see Table 11) and as a Key Aspetar Strategies supported by the nursing unit (see Table 12). Moreover, the Aspetar

Table 11. AZF and Aspetar mission and vision

AZF Mission: We enhance sports performance **AZF Vision:** By2020, we will be the reference in sports excellence word wide
Aspetar Mission: We assist athletes to achieve their maximum performance and full potential **Aspetar Vision:** To be a global leader in sports medicine and exercise science by 2020
Aspetar Strategic Objectives: 1. Establish world best clinical outcomes 2. Enhance Athletic performance 3. Provide world best integrated medical education and training 4. Contribute to successful international competitions / world cups 5. Retain and grow customer base 6. Maximize revenue to promote sustainability 7. Capitalize on research & innovation 8. Optimize internal operations and processes and maximize use of IT 9. Improve market perception and reach of Aspetar 10. Enhance leadership and governance at all levels 11. Attract, develop and retain talent

Table 12. Operational Plan 2017

Nursing Director Office 2017
Unit Objective: Establish world best Nursing outcomes for sports medicine and exercise science Establish efficient and effective patient flow strategy, entry to discharge and referral
Key Aspetar Strategies supported by the Unit: Establish world best clinical outcomes Optimize internal operations and processes and maximize use of IT Enhance leadership and governance at all levels Enhance Athletic performance Improve market perception and reach of Aspetar Capitalize on research and innovation.

Strategic Planning Process is guided by the higher authority of Qatar and led by the Executive Management Committee of the hospital. The process is supported by Corporate Planning and also by the Aspire Zone Foundation (AZF) Strategy Advisor and his team of experts. The Aspetar four Strategy Teams are composed of leaders and members of staff from all departments all important statements are developed with guidance and support of: The Higher Authority, the Aspetar Scientific Advisory Board, the Executive Management Committee of Aspetar, and the Chief Medical Office.

Although the critical care is considered as out of the scope of practice of Aspetar unless emergency or unpredicted situations, the results of this study have showen that it is one of the dimensions of nurses' job performance.

Aspetar nurses reported satisfied skills in teaching and collaboration. In Aspetar, education, teaching and collaboration are very important and effective component. In fact, nursing department is actively participating in the education process of Aspetar:

- A monthly journal club with evidence based practice researches study
- Each nurse has to be involved in a minimum of one presentation or talk on the assigned topic
- Each nurse is responsible for license renewal and CPD points
- First symposium in the region

In fact, nurses at Aspetar are working all over the hospital, nursing supervisor and ward nurses cover 24 hours and 7 days. Operating theater nurses work 8 hours a day and are on call for the rest of hours and the weekend. Nurses learn from events that occur by:

- Improving systems and processes by using FOCUS PDSA (the performance improvement methodology).
- Preventing recurrence through sharing and improving what we do based on best practice
- Working and communicating in multidisciplinary care teams
- Sharing our experiences at the Quarterly Safety Forum (Auditorium)
- Discussing safety issues and concerns at Department Safety Huddles
- Being open during Department Meetings about safety concerns
- Addressing issues at Aspetar Committees
- Participating in Leadership Rounds when executive management visits and enquires about safety

The ability to effectively communicate with other people in Aspetar is a very critical point because of the different languages spoken by nurses and their belonging to different cultures. Interpersonal relationship and communication skills are vital to effective job performance. The employment of new medical technology and instruments requires continuous educational training for nurses to maintain and improve their level of job performance (Ma and Jiang 2007). Professional development is one of the six dimensions explaining the nurses' job performance, however at Aspetar there is a lack of investment in professional development in nursing.

Nurses differed in the planning/evaluation aspect of job performance, just as they differed in initiating planning and evaluation of nursing care with others. Knowledgeable and autonomous nurses may be predicted to perform well in their job (Wade 1999). Nurses also differed in terms of their interpersonal relations and communication, particularly with regard to their patients and their patients' families. Family/community involvement was significantly correlated with nurses' job performance (Schwirian 1978): the greater the nurse's involvement in family and community, the higher the nurse's predicted job performance.

CONTRIBUTIONS, LIMITATIONS, AND FUTURE RESEARCH TRAJECTORIES

Although most scholars and managers would agree that employee performance is of utmost importance for organizations' effectiveness, thus far, research on nurse' job performance in multicultural hospital has been scarce and produced mixed findings. We argued that the main reason for these mixed findings is a lack of a sound theoretical basis.

This study therefore sought to measure nurses` job performance. Hence, the fundamental objective of this research is to explore the dimensionality of the nurses` job performance in the gulf region and precisely in Aspetar, a multicultural hospital.

The main contribution of this research work is the enrichment of the literature by confirming that nurse's job performance is multidimensional and explained by six dimensions (leadership, critical care, teaching and collaboration, planning and evaluation, Interpersonal relations and communications, and professional development) as argued by Schwirian (1978).

These results have an important managerial contribution as they enable the various managers of nursing department to have a first reading of the factors that explain the job performance of their nurses. This will allow them to predict their behavior at work (absenteeism, turnover, etc.), reduce the number of complaints, effectively manage absenteeism, turnover and work stoppage, and improve employee punctuality and morale; and to have a positive and significant impact on nurses' performance at work, patients satisfaction and operational performance of the hospital.

The limitations of this research correspond mainly to the use of the *Schwirian six-D scale* to measure the nurses' job performance. In fact, "Despite the importance of effective performance in nursing, few scales have been developed to measure how well nurses perform their job tasks. Further, those scales that have been developed have limitations, which may act to reduce their utility. Specifically, the majority of scales, such as the Schwirian six-D scale (Schwirian 1978) and the Slater Nursing Competencies Rating scale (Wandelt and Phaneuf 1974) were developed in the 1960s and 1970s (Redfern and Norman 1990). However, a more fundamental limitation of these scales is that they focus on a limited domain of task-specific behaviors that nurses perform within their roles, such as the provision of care and interpersonal support for patients. However, research from the job performance literature has noted that such task-specific behaviors are not the sole predictor of positive outcomes for clients (Bell and Menguc 2002).

Nowadays nurses are committed into a wider range of behaviors that are more discretionary in nature but important in the promotion of quality care overall. Such as, behaviors that assist other nurses and the hospital to function effectively have largely been ignored from past nursing performance scales, but have been demonstrated to have an impact on client outcomes (Bell and Menguc 2002).

Workplace Arrogance and Job Performance

In order to analyze the relationship between workplace arrogance and job performance, the authors focused on four concepts: (1) the two types of job performance, namely: task and contextual performance; and (2) the two main predictors of job performance, namely: social support and self efficacy.

Several researchers have argued that arrogance has a negative impact on the two types of job performance. Johnson et al. (2010) were the first researchers who have assessed the consequences of workplace arrogance on job performance and they found that arrogance was negatively related to self-reported OCB. These authors posit that

... Arrogant individuals would engage in less frequent acts of OCB because they likely see themselves as too important to "waste" their time helping colleagues and listening to others' problems. Arrogant individuals also place their own welfare and agenda ahead of the organization and its members, which serves to decrease their performance of OCB. (Johnson et al. 2010).

Moreover, they have undertaken a 360-degree evaluation of employees regardless of who (self, supervisor, peer, or direct report) rated their arrogance and performance. The results of this survey showed that arrogance was negatively related to task performance. Hence, as consequences of Johnson et al. (2010) study, one can conclude that workplace arrogance is associated with poor task performance and low organizational citizenship behaviors.

The findings of the exploratory study of Johnson et al. (2010) were confirmed by Silverman et al. (2012). In fact, Silverman et al. (2012) concluded that *"high levels of arrogance are associated with low self-esteem, low general intelligence, poor job performance, and low organizational citizenship behaviors"*. Moreover, they attempt to explain this paradox (Employees who act superior in actuality have inferior performance. What might account for this effect?) by focusing on the findings of two main research undertaken by Bauer et al. (2008) and Johnson et al. (2010). In fact, the latter through their empirical research found that: (1) arrogance is negatively related to cognitive ability and self-esteem (see chapter 1); and (2) arrogance is negatively associated with having a learning orientation. In fact, arrogant employees focus on how they show others that they are more proficient by wasting time in comparison and lowering them rather than spending time to improve their skills and abilities.

… Arrogant employees pay little attention to diagnostic information in their environment. Instead, arrogant individuals adopt a performance orientation, as they are more interested in how their skills and performance levels stack up against others rather than on improving their skills. (Silverman et al. 2012).

Based on these findings, one could underline the relationship between social support, self-efficacy and workplace arrogance. Indeed, arrogant individuals have negative behaviors that "*cultivate poisonous climates*" and "*they also do not engage in citizenship behaviors that cultivate positive social climates at work*" (Silverman et al. 2012). Thus, a negative relationship exists between workplace arrogance and social support considered as job resources. Moreover, knowing that this latter is negatively related to job demands (e.g. high work pressure, role overload, emotional demands, and poor environmental conditions cited by Bakker et al. 2004), one could conclude that the more workplace arrogance increase the more job demands increase yet.

Considering arrogant employees as persons who have strong individual identities (Bauer et al. 2008 cited by Silverman et al. 2012), one could conclude that their self-efficacy is very high as well as their confidence. And knowing that high self-efficacious person has a high job performance, one could conclude that arrogant individuals are high self-efficacious. However, these latter unlike arrogant persons act to achieve their occupational goals without disparaging others. Johnson and Saboe (2011 cited by Silverman et al. 2012) posit that "*when employees have a strong individual identity, it is much easier to act in a harmful and hostile manner towards others because actors are less sensitive to the well-being of other people*", while Osman-Gani and RockstuhI (2008 cited by Bhatti 2013) who undertaken a study on expatriates adjustment and job performance,

Argue that self-efficacy influences job performance through social networks. Expatriates high on self-efficacy may interact with people more positively which helps them to extend their social network.

Moreover, Johnson et al. (2010) argued that arrogant persons are not self-confident by analyzing the impact of their behavior on their job performance. They have concluded that arrogance is related to low job performance. In addition, as argued by Bauer et al. (2008 in Silverman et al. 2012) low job performance of arrogant person is related to a low level of its competences.

... Confident individuals are expressing genuine beliefs, whereas arrogant individuals may be attempting to hide insecurity and poor performance by exaggerating their own competence and importance.

Consistent with this development based on the self-efficacy and confidence concept, the authors posit that workplace arrogance is negatively related to job performance.

CONCLUSION

This chapter is considered as an attempt to clarify the relationship between workplace arrogance and job performance. Thus, the authors examined and studied this relationship by focusing on four concepts: task performance; contextual performance; social support and self-efficacy. Hence, the main result of this theoretical study is that workplace arrogance is negatively related to job performance as it argued by Silverman et al. (2012)

Workplace arrogance can be a serious problem. Arrogant employees are poor performers who negatively impact social exchange in the workplace. They make little effort to engage in citizenship behaviors and discount feedback that would otherwise help improve their performance.

However, more studies are requested to investigate the specific relationship between workplace arrogance and job satisfaction with its two dimensions: task and contextual factors.

REFERENCES

AbuAlRub, R. F. (2004). Job Stress, Job Performance, and Social Support Among Hospital Nurses. *Journal of Nursing Scholarship, 36*(1), 73–78. doi:10.1111/j.1547-5069.2004.04016.x PMID:15098422

Akrout, F. (2010). *Les méthodes des Equations Structurelles, 1 ère édition.* URM.

Anderson, J.C and Gerbing D.W (1988). Structural Equation Modeling in Practice: A Review and Recommended Two-Step Approach. *Psychological Bulletin, 103*(3), 411-423.

Austin, J. T., & Villanova, P. (1992). The criterion problem: 1917-1992. *The Journal of Applied Psychology*, *77*(6), 836–874. doi:10.1037/0021-9010.77.6.836

Bakker, A. B., Demerouti, E., & Verbeke, W. (2004). Using the job demands-resources model to predict burnout and performance. *Human Resource Management*, *43*(1), 83–104. doi:10.1002/hrm.20004

Basu, E., Pradhan, R. K., & Tewari, H. R. (2017). Impact of organizational citizenship behavior on job performance in Indian healthcare industries: The mediating role of social capital. *International Journal of Productivity and Performance Management*, *66*(6), 780–796. doi:10.1108/IJPPM-02-2016-0048

Baumgärtner, M. K., Böhm, S. A., & Dwertmann, D. J. G. (2014). Job performance of employees with disabilities: Interpersonal and intrapersonal resources matter, *Equality, Diversity and Inclusion. International Journal (Toronto, Ont.)*, *33*(4), 347–360. doi:10.1108/EDI-05-2013-0032

Bell, S. J., & Menguc, B. (2002). The employee–organization relationship, organizational citizenship behaviors, and superior service quality. *Journal of Retailing*, *78*(2), 131–146. doi:10.1016/S0022-4359(02)00069-6

Bhatti, M. A., Battour, M. M., & Ismail, A. R. (2013). Expatriates adjustment and job performance: An examination of individual and organizational factors. *International Journal of Productivity and Performance Management*, *62*(7), 694–717. doi:10.1108/IJPPM-12-2012-0132

Borman, W. C., & Motowidlo, S. J. (1993). Expanding the Criterion Domain to Include Elements of Contextual Performance. In N. Schmitt & W. Borman (Eds.), *Personnel Selection in Organizations* (pp. 71–98). New York: Jossey-Bass.

Borman, W. C., & Motowidlo, S. J. (1997). Task performance and contextual performance. The meaning for personnel selection research. *Human Performance*, *10*(2), 99–109. doi:10.1207/s15327043hup1002_3

Campbell, J. P. (1990). Modeling the Performance Prediction Problem in Industrial and Organizational Psychology. In M. D. Dunnette & L. M. Hough (Eds.), Handbook of Industrial and Organizational Psychology. Palo Alto, CA: Consulting Psychologists Press.

Campbell, J. P. (2012). Behavior, performance, and effectiveness in the 21st century. In S. W. J. Kozlowski (Ed.), The Oxford handbook of organizational psychology (pp. 159–194). New York: Oxford Press.

Campbell, J. P., Dunnette, M. D., Lawler, E. E., & Weick, K. E. (1970). *Managerial behavior, performance, and effectiveness.* New York: McGraw-Hill Book Company.

Campbell, J. P., McCloy, R. A., Oppler, S. H., & Sager, C. E. (1993). A theory of performance. In C. W. Schmitt & W. C. A. Borman (Eds.), *Personnel Selection in Organizations* (pp. 35–70). San Francisco: Jossey Bass.

Carricano, M., & Poujol, F. (2008). *Analyse de données avec SPSS* [Data analysis with SPSS]. Paris, France: Pearson Education.

Choi, B. K., & Moon, H. K. (2017). Subordinates' helping, voice, and supervisors' evaluation of job performance: The moderating effects of supervisor-attributed motives. *Career Development International, 22*(3), 222–240. doi:10.1108/CDI-04-2016-0058

Conway, J. M. (1996). Additional construct validity evidence for the task-contextual performance distinction. *Human Performance, 9*(4), 309–329. doi:10.1207/s15327043hup0904_1

Dobni, C. B. (2008). Measuring innovation culture in organizations: The development of a generalized innovation culture construct using exploratory factor analysis. *European Journal of Innovation Management, 11*(4), 539–559. doi:10.1108/14601060810911156

Girod, M. (1995). La mémoire organisationnelle. *la Revue Française de Gestion*, 30-42.

Greenslade, J. H., & Jimmieson, N. L. (2007). Distinguishing between task and contextual performance for nurses: Development of a job performance scale. *Journal of Advanced Nursing, 58*(6), 602–611. doi:10.1111/j.1365-2648.2007.04256.x PMID:17442026

Hair, Black, Babin, Anderson, & Ronald. (2006). *Multivariate data analysis* (Vol. 6). Upper Saddle River, NJ: Pearson Prentice Hall.

Johnson, R. E., Silverman, S. B., Shyamsunder, A., Yao. Swee, H., Rodopman, O. B., Cho, E., & Bauer, J. (2010). Acting Superior But Actually Inferior? Correlates and Consequences of Workplace Arrogance. *Human Performance, 23*(5), 403–427. doi:10.1080/08959285.2010.515279

Judge, T. A., & Bono, J. E. (2001). Relationship of core self-evaluations traits—self-esteem, generalized self-efficacy, locus of control, and emotional stability—with job satisfaction and job performance: A metaanalysis. *The Journal of Applied Psychology*, *86*(1), 80–92. doi:10.1037/0021-9010.86.1.80 PMID:11302235

Kanfer, R. (1990), Motivation Theory and Industrial and Organizational Psychology. In M. D. Dunnette& L. M. Hough (Eds.), Handbook of Industrial and Organizational Psychology (2nd ed.; vol. 1). Palo Alto, CA: Consulting Psychologists Press.

Knight, D. K., Kim, H. J., & Crutsinger, C. (2007). Examining the effects of role stress on customer orientation and job performance of retail salespeople. *International Journal of Retail & Distribution Management*, *35*(5), 381–392. doi:10.1108/09590550710743735

Ma, H., & Jiang, A. L. (2007). Literature review of nursing leadership. *Chinese Nursing Management*, *7*(8), 36–38.

Moorman, R. H., & Blakely, G. L. (1995). Individualism-collectivism as an individual difference predictor of organizational citizenship behavior. *Journal of Organizational Behavior*, *16*(2), 127–142. doi:10.1002/job.4030160204

Motowidlo, S. J., & Van Scotter, J. R. (1994). Evidence that task performance should be distinguished from contextual performance. *The Journal of Applied Psychology*, *79*(4), 475–480. doi:10.1037/0021-9010.79.4.475

Mount, M. K., & Barrick, M. R. (1995). The Big Five personality dimensions: Implications for research and practice in human resources management. In K. M. Rowland & G. Ferris (Eds.), Research in personnel and human resources management (vol. 13, pp. 153-200). Greenwich, CT: JAI Press.

Murphy, K. R., & Cleveland, J. N. (1995). *Understanding performance appraisal: Social organizational, and goal-based perspectives*. Thousand Oaks, CA: Sage.

Nonaka, I. (1994). A Dynamic Theory of Organizational Knowledge Creation. *Organization Science*, *5*(1), 14–37. doi:10.1287/orsc.5.1.14

Organ, D. W. (1988). *Organizational citizenship behavior: The good soldier syndrome*. D.C. Heath and Company.

Poropat, A. (2002). The relationship between attributional style, gender and the FiveFactor Model of personality. *Personality and Individual Differences*, *33*(7), 1185–1201. doi:10.1016/S0191-8869(02)00008-9

Redfern, S. J., & Norman, I. J. (1990). Measuring the quality of nursing care: A consideration of different approaches. *Journal of Advanced Nursing*, *15*(11), 1260–1271. doi:10.1111/j.1365-2648.1990.tb01741.x PMID:2269748

Roe, R. A. (1999). Work performance: A mUltiple regulation perspective. In C. L. Cooper & I. T. Robertson (Eds.), International Review of Industrial and Organizational Psychology. Chichester, UK: Wiley.

Rosman, B. M. Y., Azlah, M. A., & Anwar, K. (2014). Assessing Reliability and Validity of Job Performance Scale among University Teachers. *Journal of Basic and Applied Scientific Research, 4*(1), 35–41.

Schmidt, F. L., Ones, D. S., & Hunter, J. E. (1992). Personnel selection. *Annual Review of Psychology, 42*(1), 627–670. doi:10.1146/annurev. ps.43.020192.003211

Schwirian, P. (1978). Evaluating the performance of nurses: A multidimensional approach. *Nursing Research, 27*(6), 347–351. doi:10.1097/00006199-197811000-00004 PMID:251246

Silverman, S. B., Johnson, R. E., McConnell, N., & Carr, A. (2012). Arrogance: A Formula for Leadership Failure. *The Industrial-Organizational Psychologist*, *50*(1), 21–28.

Sonnentag, S., Binnewies, C., & Mojza, E.J. (2010). Staying well and engaged when demands are high: the role of psychological detachment. *Journal of Applied Psychology, 95*(5), 965.

Sonnentag, S., & Frese, M. (2002). Performance Concepts and Performance Theory. In S. Sonnentag (Ed.), *Psychological Management of Individual Performance*. Chichester, UK: John Wiley & Sons, Ltd; doi:10.1002/0470013419

Spender, J. C. (1996). Organizational knowledge, learning and memory: Three concepts in search of a theory. *Journal of Organizational Change Management, 9*(1), 63–78. doi:10.1108/09534819610156813

Tett, R. P., Jackson, D. N., & Rothstein, M. (1991). Personality measures as predictors of job performance: A meta-analytic review. *Personnel Psychology*, *44*(4), 703–742. doi:10.1111/j.1744-6570.1991.tb00696.x

Tsoukas, H., & Vladimirou, E. (2001). What is organizational knowledge? *Journal of Management Studies*, *38*(7), 973–993. doi:10.1111/1467-6486.00268

Viswesvaran, C., & Ones, D. S. (2000). Perspectives on models of job performance. *International Journal of Selection and Assessment*, *8*(4), 216–226. doi:10.1111/1468-2389.00151

Wade, G. H. (1999). Professional Nurse Autonomy: Concept Analysis and Application to Nursing Education. *Journal of Advanced Nursing*, *30*(2), 310–318. doi:10.1046/j.1365-2648.1999.01083.x PMID:10457232

Waldenstro, U., Brown, S., McLachlan, H., Forster, D., & Brennecke, S. (2000). Does team midwife care increase satisfaction with antenatal, intrapartum, and postpartum care? A randomized controlled trial. *Birth (Berkeley, Calif.)*, *27*(3), 156–167. doi:10.1046/j.1523-536x.2000.00156.x PMID:11251496

Wandelt, M., & Phaneuf, M. (1974). Three instruments for measuring the quality of nursing care. *Hospital Topics*, *50*(8), 20–24. doi:10.1080/00185868.1972.9947925

Wiktorowicz, J. (2017). Competencies as a factor of economic deactivation: Application of exploratory factor analysis. *International Journal of Social Economics*, *44*(5), 605–619. doi:10.1108/IJSE-08-2015-0198

Williams, S., & Wong, T. (1999). Mood and organizational citizenship behavior: The effects of positive affect on employee organizational citizenship behavior intentions. *The Journal of Psychology*, *133*(6), 656–668. doi:10.1080/00223989909599771 PMID:10589519

Wright, T. A., & Cropanzano, R. (2000). Psychological well-being and job satisfaction as predictors of job performance. *Journal of Occupational Health Psychology*, *5*(1), 84–94. doi:10.1037/1076-8998.5.1.84 PMID:10658888

Zimet, G. D., Dahlem, N. W., Zimet, S. G., & Farley, G. K. (1988). The Multidimensional Scale of Perceived Social Support. *Journal of Personality Assessment*, *52*(1), 30–41. doi:10.1207/s15327752jpa5201_2 PMID:2280326

Chapter 5
How Do Competences Valorize Strategic Scope Dimensions?

ABSTRACT

This chapter deals with the concept of competence as a main dimension of organizational effectiveness with its mysterious relation with the concept of arrogance. In fact, competences are considered a main driver of any company, but its definition remains vague. In order to explore the relationship between competence and arrogance, the authors attempted to answer the following question: How do competences valorize strategic scope dimensions? In fact, they tried to view empirically show that competences can impact the strategic scope of any business through research and development and market and resources.

INTRODUCTION

Competences are an effective capacity for action. They are not a simple know-how, but also a Know-it-How, a special skill. They are in fact, strategic capacities, essential to resolve special problems in complex situations. From another side, having an inflated self-perception of power or a defense mechanism that closes people off can be seen as arrogance more than competence (Jones 2016). There is a precise evenness that should any individual in the competence look for. A blending between High Competence and High Arrogance provides quite successful people but destructive to the morale or relationship in some situations (Golson 2007 cited by Padua et

DOI: 10.4018/978-1-5225-5525-4.ch005

al. 2010). The splitter between arrogance and self-confidence is very thin but well defined. It is like between real ability and conceit[1]. However, the presence of competence remains a relevant factor for today and tomorrow, it should be vocational as a combination of abilities, skills, ways of thinking, and knowledge resources (Meyer et al. 2015). Thus, this chapter is composed by two parts: (1) the business strategic scope, and (2) the competence as an ambiguous concept.

The Business Strategic Scope

This first section, "The business strategic scope", is based on the development of a concept emanating from strategy and strategic actions that is called "the strategic scope". This term highlights the viability and the sustainability field of any business through valuable combination of resources, activities and assets at its disposal (Zenger & Huang 2015). Corporate managers are called to establish and develop solid foundations for future success that depend primarily on actions initiated now. Therefore, managers routinely face complex decision-making scenarios. In addition, they must respond to contradictory requests from different stakeholders. As understood through direct and careful observations by excellent managers in action as well as research output by highly skilled scholars, strategic thinking is characterized by its progressive nature. Hence, "the strategic scope" could be considered as a new strategic landscape of the organizational effectiveness. The authors provided in this research work an overview on the evolution of strategic thinking to explain the reasons behind the proposal of strategic scope (SS) concept. Then they presented a summary of the definitions of the concept. Finally, they turn into identifying the concept's main dimensions as well as its mechanisms of actions. An empirical study on Agrifood Tunisian companies will show how the concept and dimension are interrelating in an emerging economy.

Definition and Typology of Strategic Scope

Undeniably, any business strategy draws a set of objectives to achieve. These objectives may refer to the dimension, size and weight of the company's extend or scope. Allaire and Firsiritou (1993) and Fahey (1996) noted that the strategic scope remains a major factor in understanding any company's strategy. In fact, this concept involves the definition of the business/trade field and the place of deployment of the enterprise's resources. Indeed, the strategic scope traces the extent on which any company could establish its competitive advantage (Houthoofd & Heene 1997). Some studies have raised a variety of concepts related to the strategic scope, which we will try to develop in the following sections.

Typologies

Ge et al. (2007) have dealt in their research works with the scope of strategic change which refers to "the magnitude of changes in the mode of resource allocation of products, services and target markets. Therefore, the scope of strategic change explains how managers must adjust their strategy to change of environment. The change in strategy is related mainly to the resources allocation, market gaining share, the product development and so on (Li and Xu 2014). Determining the strategic scope leads systematically any company to assess its sector of activity, market opportunities and the means at its disposal in order to make best results. However, through literature review, the concept of scope was analyzed differently.

The Scope at the Group Level and Profit Center

Fahey (1996) focuses on the study of the scope at the level of group and profit center. He specifies that the determination of the scope revolves around three main issues, namely:

- Products offered in the market.
- Market needs to be satisfied.
- Resources, competences and technology to possess or develop in order to satisfy the product-market segments.

Thus, these three components compel the company to systematically evaluate its sector of activity, market opportunities and to seize the means at its disposal or it can acquires. Similarly, Fahey (1996) stipulates that the scope at the group level raises key questions and issues pertaining to the trade, partners, synergy and strategic challenges. In parallel, to expand the scope at the profit centers, each company should act on different axes, including product, customers, and geographic scope. Table 1 summarizes the essential questions related to each topic.

Table 1. The scope: Some key questions

At the Group Level	
Business/trade Scope	What are the company's current business/trades? What business (es)/trades does the company wants to integrate?
Scope of the partners	Which companies/entities would the company enter into some sort of partnership with to achieve its objectives?
Scope of the synergy	To what extent should the company's different activities in linked? Should it be done systematically?
Means to evolve the scope	Internal development, acquisitions, alliances, divestitures, aligning with partners or opposition..
Strategic Issues	Which sectors should the company invest more, maintain its current level of investment, reduce investment and/or disengage completely?
Strategic Challenges	How can the company enhance its group's presence in each of the sectors in which it operates? What could be the basis for a synergy between two or more profit centers?
At the Profit Centers	
Product scope	What range of products the company wants to commercialize?
Customer scope	Which market segments the company wants to reach? What customer needs does the company wants to answer?
Geographical scope	What geographic area(s) the company wants to offer its products to targeted customers it defined?
Vertical scope	What kind of business relationship the company wants to maintain (and/or develop) with its suppliers and its customers?
Partners scope	What entities the company can partner with to achieve its objectives?
Means to evolve the scope	Add or remove products and targets, enter or exit a geographical area, to align with partners or be an opponent.
Strategic Issues	Which products should the company invest more in, maintain its current level of investment, reduce investment and/or disengage completely?
Strategic Challenges	How can the opportunities be identified and seized? What is the best strategy to achieve this goal?

Fahey, 1996.

Product-Market Scope

For Allaire and Firsirotu (1993), the strategic scope called the frontiers of the strategic system, traces the variety of products offerings, geographical coverage and the coverage of buyers. A company's scope is largely related to the types of competences, management style and staff. A company will not be able to attend its full economic strength only if it uses optimally its tangible and intangible assets. However, every company must take into consideration several strategic dimensions that allow it to succeed (Wegberg 2004). Adcock (2000) noted that the determination of the product-market scope should answer three main basic questions (see Figure 1):

Figure 1. The marketing zone
Source: Adcok (2000).

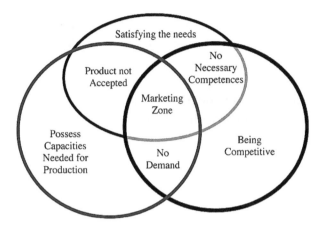

- What are the customers' needs that should be met?
- How should customers be satisfied?
- What are the main reasons that would lead the clients to buy the company's product/service?

Any company should keep balance between availability of competences, ability to be competitive in the market and meeting customers' expectations. Without this condition, determination or expansion of the strategic product-market scope cannot be made.

From another point of view, some researchers have argued that there are other strategic scope dimensions on which any company should act on in order to respond successfully to the environmental change, which are the business/trade scope, geographic scope and the organizational scope.

Business Scope

Companies need to assess the way in which the new economic reality affect business and create new opportunities. In this regard, business scope orients companies towards favorable and profitable segments. For example the case of economic liberalization that led some companies to concentrate on certain business segments which provide economic benefits (Anand et al. 2006).

Geographic Scope

Geographic scope traces the extent of a company in a local market and/or in foreign countries. In other words, the geographic scope traces the competitive standard. From a geographical perspective, companies may have two units of markets, domestic and foreign. Furthermore, some researchers distinguish between companies with a wide geographical spread, those with an average geographical extent and those with a small geographical area (Qian & Li 2002).

Organizational Scope

Organizational scope refers to alliances, mergers and acquisitions which provide companies extra resources and capabilities. It may also take the form of collaboration to achieve better results. We can take the case of vertical integration or horizontal alliances. Through strategic alliances, companies may benefit from sharing inputs and activities. Indeed, some authors have stressed the importance on the theory of resource dependence through alliances (Kauser & Shaw 2004). Moreover, alliances can allow companies to increase output and therefore the ideal and complementary exploitation of their resources (Oum et al. 2004). Other research workers have endorsed the idea that business success stems mainly from organizational alliances to enhance resources available, it is an organizational scope expansion (Brandenburger & Nalebuff 1995).

Technology Scope and Transfer Scope

Any new technology is, continuously, evaluated, developed and transferred. There is a strong link between research, development and transfer of technology in organizations. The ultimate goal of companies is to improve and expand their technological capacity (Valyasevi & Rolle 2002; Nobelius 2004). New technologies should be adapted to new productions. Every company is faced with the expansion of its transfer of technology scope that should answer a key question, namely "what is it to be transferred? (Nobelius 2004). This term refers to the scope of technology and fundamental knowledge to be transferred within the company such as general and specific information, computer knowledge, procedures and practices.

Syed-Ikhsan and Rowland (2004) define knowledge transfer as a process through which a unit (group, department or division) is affected by the experience of another. Syed-Ikhsan and Rowland (2004) speak about knowledge assets and consider any organization needs to identify where its knowledge resides. Moreover, Peffers and Tuunainen (2001) addressed the issue of information technology scope and analyzed the relationship between technology scope and product scope. Technological scope leads to technological development. All outputs are produced or delivered using means supported by new technologies (Chi et al. 2005). Firms need continually to ensure competitiveness on the market relying on updating knowledge from external knowledge which is a valuable source for R&D and innovation (Ritala et al. 2013).

Competitive Scope

Competitive scope can be defined as the extent of a company's actions on several competitive strategic "priorities" (Stock et al. 1998; Durand & Coeurderoy 2001). While some companies may focus only on one strategic priority, others may consider many strategic priorities such as cost, product quality, and the speed of product delivery. Thus, a high level of competitive scope indicates a variety of competitive priorities.

Delimitation of the Dimensions of the Strategic Scope Field

The goal of any business is to ensure the sustainability and continuity of its activity by acting on the different types of scopes mentioned above. Hwang and Park (2007) showed that the survival of any business imperatively passes through guaranteeing the continuity of the products/services commercialization on a market. This turns out to be the main pillar of a company's strategic scope. At the same time, several types of scopes are attached to the market, including product scope, customer scope, geographic scope, competitive scope, and business scope. Furthermore, Hwang and Park (2007) have also argued that a company's viability could be achieved by adopting new technologies, developing new work processes, etc. This leads to research and development as a dynamization factor. Technological and knowledge transfer scopes mentioned above form constitutive elements of the research & development dimension.

Finally, business survival depends also on the tangible, intangible and/or latent resources that support the business activities and constitute the third dimension of the strategic scope. In the next 3 sections three dimensions of the strategic scope will be developed further.

Research and Development

The research and development dimension is one dimension of the strategic scope, it traces principally technology and knowledge deployed and shared within the organization (Peffers et al. 2001; Valyasevi & Rolle 2002; Syed Ikhsan & Rowland 2004; Nobelius 2004; Dias 2008; Datta 2008). The new knowledge creation involves looking for new possibilities, new alternatives, creative and innovative new business practices. Knowledge management remains a concerted effort that improves the methods of creation, delivery, and use of knowledge (Davenport et al. 2008). Research and development remains the principal driver of change and continuous development, it is the dynamism motor for any company operating in a constantly changing and competitive environment (Studt 2008).

The Information as a Basic of the Research and Development

Information provides support to the management process; it is an instrument of communication in the company and a support and liaison instrument with an evolutive environment characterized by changes, uncertainty and complexity. Information is the basis of research and development and enables continuous adaptation to customer requirements (Bounfour 1998).

The Transfer of Technological Knowledge

At the research & development scope level, companies are always looking to enhance their technological knowledge. Indeed, transfer and sharing of different types of knowledge among members of the organization constitute a strategic factor for the creation of competitive advantages. Thus, to promote research & development, it becomes necessary for companies to observe the flow of knowledge that provides a quick and effective learning and therefore competitiveness (Nobelius 2004). At this level, adequate organizational context for knowledge sharing would facilitate the transfer, sharing and updating of technical and non- technical know-how. This will allow companies a different use of their knowledge and help them to carry out specific tasks. Technological progress has an immediate impact such as reducing costs, saving time, improving quality and increasing production diversification. For Castells (2001), nowadays companies are considered informational, they organize their production systems around productivity maximization principles based mainly on knowledge that ensures development and dissemination of new information technologies. In this regard, companies find in the knowledge and information technology a tool that would favor innovation that, in turn, would help to maintain and even extend their strategic fields scope.

Market

The second dimension of the strategic scope is the market. This is a place of direct confrontation between companies, in which they prove their image, positioning and competitiveness. Thus, the market dimension is related to products, customers, geography, competitiveness, business domain, etc. (Allaire & Firsiritou 1993; Fahey 1996; Stock et al. 1998; Quain & Li 2002; Wegberg 2004; Anand et al. 2006). Understanding the scope of marketing practices in the market and how they add value to the organization is very fundamental for the best functioning of the organization Marketing practices is fundamental to and the actual value it adds to the organization. Practicing good marketing activities and understanding the nature of activities that should be carried out is a fundamental task of determining the market scope (Dibb et al. 2014). Success or failure in the market determined the strategic scope of any firm (Hallwood 2014).

The Stages of a Market's Evolution

Market evolves and changes progressively, it shows a tendency to grow in phases from emergence to growth then to maturity and saturation and finally to decline. As part of the emergent phase, a product/service disposes of new features depending on customers' needs in a given geographical area/market. This new product is supposed to be supported by sufficient marketing resources in order to meet customers' expectations respond to their indifferences and get them to change their purchasing routines. In the maturity phase, total sales continuously and rapidly increase but in the saturation phase, the number of new consumers becomes lower and market segmentation takes a dominant character. Finally the decline phase is the outcome of the substitution, it is the result of technological innovations and changes in consumer tastes and values (Allaire & Firsiritou 1993).

Market Components

In general, the market may combine several components including products/ services offered, different types of customers and a competition which helps to improve the functioning of enterprises. However, every market has certain geography and a field of action in which any company carries out its trade through a business area. At this part, we will try to clarify the concept of the market by analyzing its main components.

The Product

Every business, develops, produces, distributes and supports products/ services in distinct markets. Companies should offer customers an essential advantage with respect in order to pursue an objective of competitiveness. They are therefore called upon to manage assortments and ensure a production capacity that promotes a broad and extensive range. In this context, every company opts for attacking a part of the market it did not cover, this is to practice expansion strategies that are possible downwards, upwards, and in both directions. So in terms of downwards extension many companies start by attacking the top or middle of the range. However, the upward extension is formed when a company well placed in a low range aims to enhance its product line in order to benefit from a growing market, weakening competitors and repositioning their images. Finally, for the extension in both directions the company is positioned in both directions and simultaneously tried to grow upwards and downwards (Kotler & Dubois 1992; Pitta & Pitta 2012).

Customers

Customer satisfaction has always been businesses' main concern. The question is to know and understand the customer needs to be able to provide compliant products and services. Now the client has a new power and can express it by putting suppliers in competition (Muller, 2001). Customers want to ensure that the satisfaction is maximal, fast and reasonably priced. This is what could directly or indirectly influence companies' market shares. In this perspective, customers become the focus of companies. Indeed, in an environment characterized by severe competition, products become with shorter life cycles commoditization (Pateyron & Solomon 1992). Gradually then we are witnessing a move from a mass consumption society to personalized consumption society.

Geographical Scope

Any company tries to occupy a market territory defined by its strategy and policy. Profit maximizing needs an expansion of geographical scope. Thus a dynamic company, especially which are still in maturity phase, seek to take place in new geographical markets (Allaire & Firsiritou 1993).

Competition

The changes experienced by the economic context during the last century have altered the relationship with time and space. We are witnessing a phenomenon of spatial expansion and temporal contraction. Indeed, the time lag between a new product design phase and its marketing has been significantly shortened (Blay 2002). Thus competition is being played increasingly on the basis of reactivity as the first to arrive to the market increases its chances to become a leader and gain advancement over others.

Resources

A company's activity and its performance are conditioned by several key factors such as the resources. The resources of a firm are defined as assets that are semi-permanently linked to the firm (Bounfour 1998). Barney (1991) states that resources can have an impact on the company's competitiveness if they are:

- Recoverable that means they have strategic value as they lead to exploit opportunities and/or neutralize threats from the environment.
- Rare, that means they are unique and cannot be found in competing or potentially competing firms.
- Imitable, which means cannot be imitated as they are specific to the firm and historically.
- Finally, non-substitutable, because competitors cannot substitute these resources to alternative resources to achieve the same results.

The use and combination of such resources would then provide companies with best results in terms of competitiveness. Indeed, they can create synergies and delay imitation by competitors. Meanwhile, corporate resources can be tangible or intangible, and it is the interaction and joint use of these two types of resources that strengthen a firm's competitive advantage.

Tangible Resources

Previously resources that were the most valuable were tangible resources, that is to say, financial and physical resources. Tangible resources refer to infrastructure components. They incorporate different elements to build a coherent and tailored infrastructure and also a reproducible process in terms of capacity (Zhu & Kraemer 2002; 2005).

Intangible Resources

Being competitive is considered as one of the intangible and immaterial resources of the company. The company's performance depends largely on the importance and the quality of its intangible and immaterial assets. The sustainability is related to the ability to maintain and increase success. The market value is also determined largely by intangible capital" (Pierrat & Martory 1995). The strategic management of organizations should move from a static vision of resources to one that is considered to dynamic vision and essentially of immaterial nature (Bounfour 2000).

The Latent Resources

Any business looks to enhance both its tangible and intangible resources. However, and with the current fierce competition, businesses have oriented their energies towards seeking partnerships and alliances to generate another type of resources: the latent resources (Arrègle et al. 1998). Successful alliances provide resource sharing from coordinated work and collaborative actions (Resource Dependency Theory) (Oum et al. 2004; Kauser & Shaw 2004; Anand et al. 2006). Alliances and partnerships are among the requirements of the enlargement of the strategic scope field which enhance resources through a combination of internal and external knowledge, developing new competences through inter-organizational cooperation and strengthening of the strategic positioning, in summary, accessing external resources help firms to obtain preferential resources (Arrègle et al. 1998; Hwang & Park 2007; Pulles et al. 2016).

Strategic Scope in Emerging Economy: Case of Tunisian Agrifood Industry

About 66 Tunisian Agrifood companies have been questioned on their strategic scope. As mentioned above and according to our literature review, three dimensions represented the strategic scope: (1) the market as a place of excellence and viability of the firm; (2) the second pillar is resources which is a support factor of the viability on the market; and (3) the third pillar is Research and Development which energizes and boosts the excellence and survival on the market.

The Exploratory Results

Analysis with SPSS and SmartPLS has demonstrated that items retained which represented the three dimensions in Tunisian companies are as follow:

- The dimension of Market is represented by the variation of product range offerings, the customers' needs satisfaction, the good marketing efforts provided and the new market gaining.
- Regarding the Research and Development, we found items related to the openness to innovations in the field, adaptation to new technologies, the continual updates to new software and applications which are under international norms, impregnation of technology new and diffusion within the company.
- Finally, as for the Resources, only latent resources are kept in this analysis. Latent resources come from the well-studied partnership between companies which rely on the rational sharing of the resources.

Validity and reliability conditions are verified in Table 2.

There are four criteria used in order to validate the validity and reliability of data collected.

Table 2. Reliability and validity measurements

Variables	Reliability		Validity	
	Internal Consistency Reliability		Convergent Validity	Discriminant Validity
	Cronbach's Alpha	Composite Reliability	Average Variance Extracted (AVE)	Fornell-Larcker Criterion
Market	0.809	0.862	0.513	0.716
R & D	0.783	0.851	0.534	0.731
Resources	1.000	1.000	1.000	1.000

The Variables Measures

Cronbach's alpha and Composite reliability are used to evaluate reliability and should be between 0.7 and 0.9 (Hair et al. 2012). Results shown in the table are considered satisfactory. Regarding the convergent validity which ensures if the measures of the same construct are correlated (Carricano & Poujol 2008), should has Values of Average Variance Extracted (AVE) greater than 0.5 (Hair et al. 2012). Finally, to evaluate discriminant validity which indicates how much items of each construct represent only their construct, we used Fornell-Larcher analysis (Hair et al. 2012).

Structural Links Validation and Confirmatory Results

The results (see Table 3) showed that R&D and Resources affected the market that means that all the theoretical links are validated. In the following table 3 the effect of R&D on the Market is considered large as the f^2 is above 0.35 while the effect of Resources on the market is moderate as the value is under 0.35 (Cohen 1988).

It turns out from the results above that the effect of R & D on market is more important than the effect of the resources. Given the evolving nature of the sector in which these companies operate, they need continually for

Table 3. Validation of structural links

Effects	Original Sample	T Statistics	p Values	f^2	Effect
R & D --> Market	0.502	5.112	0.000	0.506	Large
Resources --> Market	0.401	3.733	0.000	0.338	Moderate

new range of products that comes from R&D in order to ensure to ensure competitiveness. These Agrifood Tunisian companies give great importance to innovation and creativity. On the other side the impact of resources is still moderate. Tunisian companies in this sector do not exploit optimally their real resources. These companies have to trust their capacity, on others that can build with them beneficial partnership. This can be change by changing the culture and beliefs. Tunisian companies must build participative and open management system in order to be more competitive.

The concept of strategic scope helps strategists to define and structure better the strategic working. It helps them to define the extent on which they can be competitive and viable.

Today, companies are called upon, when determining or broadening their scope, to act primarily on the market, which is the main area of viability and sustainability. Thus, the market is the place of assurance of the achievement of viability, competitiveness and corporate influence objectives, and thus constitutes the first dimension of scale. The delimitation of the "market" scope implies multiple choices in terms of listening to the expectations of certain customer segments, product line developments and innovations, the choice of competitors to compete, the delimitation of the geographical scope in which the company works, etc.

At the same time, the desire to compete in the markets requires the obtaining of certain resources. These constitute the second dimension of the scope of the strategic field, support the basic scope that is the market and can come from the relationships of alliances and partnerships.

On the other hand, the company's resources should be exploited in an optimal way to better adapt to the ever-changing economic context. As a result, and for a good delineation of its scope, the company is called upon to look at a third major component of research and development. In this way, the company increases its chances by energizing the actions on the "market" scope. Research and development provides basic support that leads to the development of new ideas and designs to conquer new markets and retain current demand. In fact the extensive resources and research and development, support the action on the "market" scope.

Competence as an Ambiguous Concept

The multiplication of the theoretical studies dealing with competences has generated a certain ambiguity in the definitions. Lorino (2001) put emphasis on the importance of the notion of competence using the resources. It considers it as the ability to mobilize, combine and coordinate resources within a specific process of action in order to achieve a sufficient outcome in order to be recognized and evaluable. In addition, other authors such as Baker et al. (1997) have interpreted the concept of competences by referring to several meanings. Thus, they consider that the notion of competences can refer to strategic competences, that is to say the quality of the adjustment between a company's business strategy and its external competitive environment. Similarly, other authors talked about distinctive competences which are all the talents and technologies that offer the company competitive advantage in a given market. In addition, some researchers also spoke about individual competencies which are considered as a set of talents and knowledge that the individual needs so that he can perform his task appropriately.

The concept of competences could refer to the skills of ability. In this case, each individual or organization has a set of skills, thoughts and ideas that allow to acquire certain capacities. Similarly, it is necessary to speak of the congruence or harmony of the competences related to the concept of sufficiency indicating the concordance between the capacities of a company and its requirements. From another point of view, some authors spoke about the "insight / foresight" skills that enable the company to make discoveries generating what called "first-mover advantages". Finally, there are some authors referred to the "Frontline" execution competences that develop when the quality of a product or service varies greatly depending on the abilities of the staff.

Other authors have defined the concept of competences as collective learning allowing the organization to co-ordinate between the various talents ranging from production to the integration of multiple currents of technologies (Hamel and Prahalad 1990; Hamel and Prahalad 1994). Similarly, competences are seen as a unique combination of technologies, knowledge and talents that belong to a given firm in a well-defined market. These competences are the basis of the products and services offered and are therefore characterized by several attributes such as complexity, invisibility, sustainability, appropriation and non-substitutability.

It appears that in order to analyze competences, these authors have chosen several orientations and have focused on different notions, and this has generated the ambiguous character of competences. However, regardless of the field of study, competences are constructed of intangible assets, individual or group, that encompass the organization's abilities, talents, knowledge, experience, people, resources and intellectual properties. Consequently, competences allow firms access to a wide variety of markets, they contribute significantly to the perception of the benefits of products and services offered on the market. Similarly, competences refer to the entrepreneurial strengths of firms that offer them the ability to challenge, guide and compete in a given market (Gilgeous and Parveen 2001).

History of the Concept of Competence

The management model that predominated in the mid-19th century and into the early 20th century was that of the Scientific Organization of Labor dictated by Taylor. This model advocates "the one best way", that is, a single structure is appropriate. In addition, it emphasizes the importance of the provision of minimum work performance skills among workers. Thus work and responsibility for work were divided almost equally between the members of the management and the workers. We thus see the separation between conception and execution (Lalanke 1998; Dubey 2003). At that time, we did not spreak about competences, but rather about skills and abilities.

By the 1940s, some authors, including Shumpeter (1934 cited by Cadieux and Denis 2007), began using the concept of rare competences. Indeed, they assume that the possession of rare competences is an essential condition for maintaining the performance of any company. Around the 1960s, and more precisely in 1959, the theory of fundamental competences found its roots with Penrose (1959 quoted by Cadieux and Denis 2007) who considers that the growth of the company as well as its capacity to support a competitive advantage depend mainly on a combination of resources mobilized. In the eighties, a model dominated the managerial literature and revealed a method of confronting the firm with its competitive environment. This method is called the "Competitive Forces Approach". The firm uses several means to cope with its environment, namely, threats of substitution, bargaining power, profit, barriers to entry, etc. (Major et al. 2001).

Finally, and up to the present day, firms have come to understand that competitiveness can be summed up in resources. This is the reason for the appearance of the Resource Based Approach. As a result, the firm was considered to be a collection of resources (Wernerfelt 1984; Barney 1991). This approach states that managerial capacities including skills are the main sources of the competitive advantage of any firm (Major et al., 2001). Similarly, the evolution of the history of strategic management has focused on the concept of "critical capacities" (Aaker 1989) by introducing the roles of individuals, tacit knowledge and other aspects of internal structure of the firm. All this has led to a better explanation of the evolution of new conceptions in strategic management (Drejer 2002).

At the end of the 20th century, Hamel and Prahalad (1990) turned to the concept of an "integrated system of basic competences". The latter outlines the field of competition and forms part of an organization's collective learning, and more specifically how it can coordinate various production skills and integrate multiple streams of technology to remain competitive.

The historical overview shows that the appearance of the concept of competence was progressive. However, it has had a rich subsequent development and has constituted the privileged field of research of several authors, which has given a variety of definitions.

Naming of Competences

Although the concept of the competences is considered as ambiguous, some research works has shown certain unanimity by considering them as capabilities above all. The richness of the literature has prompted us to study the variety of appellations and typologies. Valuing competences leads to a variety of names, so there are several ways of naming them, each corresponding to a specific conception of competences.

The Congruence Competences

Baker et al. (1997) used the concept of "congruence competences" in this logic of adjustment between capacities and requirements. In this perspective, it is called an adjustment between the requirements of organizational success and the ability to provide and deliver the requirements (Vickery et al. 1993; Kim and Arnold 1992). These interpretations have led the authors to use the term strategic competences which refer to the adjustment between the business strategy adopted by the organization and the requirements imposed by the external environment.

In other research works, some thinkers have invented the concept of individual competences, often used in human resources management, which refers to a set of talents that each individual must possess in order to be able to assume responsibility (Boyatzis 1982). On the other hand, the counterpart of individual competences in terms of group interaction has been defined as the interpersonal competences which refer to the individual's ability to get along with others within an organization. Thus, it is not only individual competencies that generate the basis for interpersonal competences, but also meaningful interaction.

Community Competences

Jay (2000) spoke about the concept of community competences, which is based on four major indicators:

- Effective collaboration in problem identification and needs assessment,
- A working consensus on priorities and objectives,
- Accreditation on a change-oriented implementation process,
- and the ability to work coherently to formulate and implement objectives.

The effectiveness of community competences is based on group work, which must continually develop effective conflict resolution procedures. In this so-called community group, participation is seen as a process of development in which everyone engages in the community and contributes to the proper definition of objectives, methods and means. This community needs to have broad knowledge about the society in which it works and establish procedures that need to be well-placed to maintain community participation, interaction and performance.

The Managerial Competences

Stuart and Lindsay (1997) used the concept of managerial competencies starting from the concept of organizational skills as shown in Figure 2.

It appears from this figure that competences are influenced by the organizational culture which is a set of values that influence the methods of the manager and often valued by the organization. In fact, the state of value that is stipulated in the organization will provide areas of competence which are activities within the organization such as product sales, relationships with suppliers, etc. This state of value also provides "competencies", which form an integrated set of behaviors such as building external relationships, creating business opportunities, and so on. And competencies components that reflect talents, knowledge, personal characteristics such as communication skills, initiative, honesty, and so on.

Figure 2. Contextual framework of the managerial competences
Stuart & Lindsay 1997.

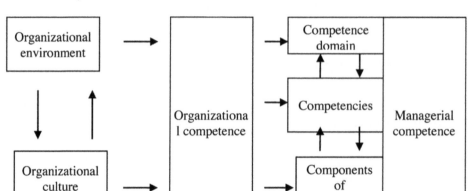

On the other hand, managerial competencies themselves can be divided into technical and behavioral competencies (May 1999). Indeed, for the technical competences, they are unique and can be common for the business or sector in which they work. For example, in any industry, financial officers need to have specific knowledge. Competences can be behavioral such as self-confidence or communication skills, negotiation skills, leadership and creative thinking.

The definition of managerial competences shows clearly the contribution of organizational dimensions such as culture. The skills of the company grow and also draw strength from the organization which remains an important factor in promoting the good working climate.

The Compliance Competences

The improvement of some services often requires compliance competences. The latter enable the achievement of some organizational objectives. We are talking about obedience or even adherence to the spirit of the law that allows certain services to be improved. According to the research of Edwards and Wolfe (2006), Compulsive Competence comes from coordination between three main elements: good obedience practice, good ethics practice and relationship with the regulator.

Intergroup Competences

Intergroup competences should be distinguished by a number of individuals with differences in their cultures, affiliation, hierarchy, geography, personal styles, socio-political affiliations, etc. These competences should have an effective interrelationship of talents.

Thus, four main points are at the basis of the intergroup competences. The first focus of competences is "self". It consists of becoming aware of cultural values and engaging in personal changes. The second focus of interest is relational; this concerns the commitment in the opening. The third is consciousness, which consists of connecting the personnel to the cultural and the societal. Finally, the fourth area of interest is summarized in the commitment to systemic change (Ramsey and Latting 2005).

Typologies of Competencies

Generally the competences of any company take three directions, namely the development of technologies to offer new products and/or services, knowledge of certain market variables (mainly customers and competitors) or the integration of Internal and external dimensions to generate synergies and boost available skills. It is in this spirit that Wang et al. (2003; 2004), distinguish between three typologies of skills, namely technological skills, market skills and integrative skills.

Technological Competences

Technological skills generally refer to the ability to develop new products and processes. It is therefore a set of theoretical and practical knowledge which is manifested in know-how, methods and procedures. Thus, technological competences require a deep understanding of scientific principles and the ability to generate new knowledge. Therefore, they represent an important potential source of development of competitive advantages, especially in technology markets (Kandampully 2002).

The Competences of the Market

Market competences are defined as the application processes, collective knowledge, talents and resources of the firm, linked to the market in order to realize better adaptation to business needs. At this level, two main elements of market competence are distinguished: knowledge of competitors and customers whose development depends on the size of the company's assets. By comparing them to technological competences, market competences appear to be much more client-oriented, since they refer to a set of cultural values and beliefs that put consumer requirements and tastes first "customer-oriented environment".

At the same time, Hamel and Prahalad (1994) distinguish between three types of competences:

- Competences linked to the access to the market: all the talents that place the firm close to customers, such as brand management, sales and marketing, logistics and distribution, Technical support, etc.
- Integrity competences: which are talents that enable the firm to operate faster and more efficiently than competitors. For example, improving quality, managing time cycles, just-in-time, etc.
- Functionality competences: which are the talents that allow the firm to characterize the products and services offered by the advantages and unique features and distinctive features of other competitors.

Integrative Competences

Integrative skills condition the climate for interaction, learning and internal coherence within firms. In this perspective, Torkkeli and Tuominen (2002) talk about organizational or integration competences, which facilitate the exchange of knowledge and expertise, and create a homogeneous working climate and interrelation between the different skills available in the organization.

Concretely, integrative skills allow us to align several elements, namely the various existing skills, organizational learning, strategic flexibility, turbulent environments and strategic positioning. Thus, any organization will need this kind of competences as it becomes essential to integrate the internal and external dimensions of the company in order to follow the technological trends and the requirements of the consumers. Integrative competences enable companies to combine the capabilities, information, perspectives and knowledge needed to develop products or services that most closely match customer requirements.

At this level, Hamel and Prahalad (1990; 1994) define competences as collective learning in the organization that coordinate talent and integrate multiple streams of technology. It thus becomes necessary for companies to develop their capacities to integrate technological change, to combine different functional specialties, to benefit from the effects of synergies through coordination between divisions and business units and to integrate and revitalize existing skills.

Core Competences

The Core competences were developed mainly at the end of the Nineties. Indeed, some authors stipulate that the concept of core competences can be represented by a system of roots that generate value and stability. In addition, research on this concept has given two central attributes. Indeed, these competences should be considered as a talent or a capacity of a firm rather than a resource property, then competences must help any company to achieve its objectives. In other words, these competences must be central to value generation activities (Mooney 2007; Ljungquist 2013).

At the same time, some authors such as Wang et al. (2003, 2004) presented several definitions of the core competences concept. Thus, they consider core competences as skills that enable the firm to deliver and deliver to its clients what is offered, to establish, embellish, and use its resources to maintain Competitive advantages. Moreover, these skills are productive resources made up of talents and technologies, collective learning, tacit and explicit knowledge that contribute through organizational processes to the coordination of functional activities (Drejer and Sorensen 2002). Other research has shown that core competences are said to be superior and give the firm the ability to generate and act on knowledge to help it to develop a basis for competitive advantage (Naver and Slater 1990; Woodruff 1997).

Similarly, Stalk et al. (1992) and Tampoe (1994) defined "core competencies" as an integrated set of core technology and core skills that provide the organization with a competitive advantage.

Distinctive Competences

Distinctive competences are skills that allow any company to detach itself in its competitive environment, which leads customers to notice the differentiation. Moreover, any distinctive competence should be sustained and preserved. This makes it difficult to be imitated by competitors. However, in confusion with the concept of distinctive competencies, the authors spoke about competitive advantages. The latter have been defined as properties that must generate a strong competitive position for the firm. The competitive advantage has been well developed in the "resource-based view" approach (Mooney 2007).

Dynamic Competences

The dynamic nature of competences enables companies to be even more competitive. Indeed, dynamic competences help firms to be proactive and reactive because the variety of the potential of the knowledge stock can be exploited to formulate and implement a diversification strategy (Teece 1987; Ljungquist 2013).

Dynamic skills can also be effective in implementing a defense strategy, as they generate means to respond to competitors' threats. Effectively, the selection of dynamic areas of competence such as organizational, marketing and technology skills are key issues for strategy formulation (SubbaNarasimha 2001).

Competences as Source of Competitiveness

Competences are essential to the survival of any business in the short and long term. Indeed, they are supposed invisible to competitors, difficult to be imitated and favor the development of the products and the implementation of the strategic vision in the market (Torkkeli and Tuominen 2002). The objective of this study is to view empirically how the competences (with its two dimensions developed below) can impact the strategic dimensions of any business. The authors made the focus on three dimensions of which represents the strategic pillars or the three dimensions of the strategic scope field (see section 1): Research and Development, Market and Resources.

Data Analysis

The data in our example are collected from some Tunisian companies (Economy in transition). We preceded, as usual in any data analysis, to verify firstly the validity and reliability conditions of the variables of our model which suppose the impact of two variables (the two dimensions of competences: conceptual and executive dimensions) on three dimensions of which represents the strategic pillars (Research and Development, Market and Resources).

RESULTS

The results are as shown in Table 4.

Cronbach's alpha and Composite reliability are used to evaluate reliability. Our results are considered satisfactory as their values should be between 0.7 and 0.9 (Hair et al. 2012). Concerning the convergent validity, Average Variance Extracted (AVE) and Fornell-Larcher values are considered satisfactory and they verify the discriminant validity (Hair et al. 2012).

The second step is validating the structural model path coefficients. The results show that conceptual competences have large effect on the resources while the executive competences have large effect on Research and development. The dimension of Market is explained moderately by the executive competences. All this can be noted from p and f^2 values[2]

We can conclude that there is dispersion in the effect of the competences dimensions on strategic pillars. Resources are valorized largely only by the conceptual dimension while the R&D are valorized largely by the executive. This means that Tunisian competences haven't yet the maturity of functioning in their competences as effects are dispersed. All the more so, the principal axis of the strategy which is the market isn't yet valorized largely. It is affected only and moderately by the executives' competences.

Tunisian companies and in general, any company has to work hard on the valorization of their competences. These latter have to impact primarily the market. There should be also equilibrium in the effect on R&D and Resources as these two dimensions supported the most important place of competitiveness which is the market.

Table 4. Reliability and validity measurements

Variables		Reliability		Validity	
		Internal Consistency Reliability		Convergent Validity	Discriminant Validity
		Cronbach's Alpha	Composite Reliability	Average Variance Extracted (AVE)	Fornell-Larcker Criterion
Competences	Conceptual	0.713	0.825	0.615	0.784
	Executive	0.713	0.824	0.542	0.736
Strategic dimensions	R&D	0.804	0.860	0.505	0.713
	Market	0.809	0.854	0.502	0.709
	Resources	0.611	0.825	0.706	0.840

Figure 3. The structural model path coefficients

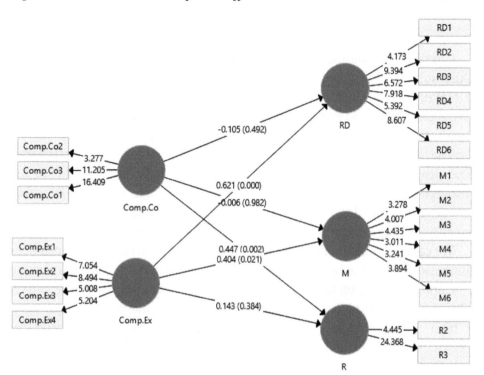

Table 5. The validation of structural links

Effects	Original Sample	T Statistics	*p* Values	*f²*	Effect
Comp.Co -> M	-0.006	0.023	0.982	0.000	Weak/no effect
Comp.Co -> R	**0.447**	**3.167**	**0.002**	**0.192**	**Large effect**
Comp.Co -> RD	-0.105	0.687	0.492	0.011	Weak/no effect
Comp.Ex -> M	**0.404**	**2.313**	**0.021**	**0.133**	**Moderate effect**
Comp.Ex -> R	0.143	0.871	0.384	0.020	Weak/no effect
Comp.Ex -> RD	**0.621**	**5.462**	**0.000**	**0.389**	**Large effect**

CONCLUSION

In conclusion, competences facilitate the acquisition and development of knowledge through organizational relationships, the dissemination of all that has been acquired and the exploitation and integration of all that has been learned. Competences allow for knowledge building and transfer throughout the organization, enhance creativity and develop new knowledge at different levels of the organization (Kak and Sushil 2002). Competences enable the firm to position itself strategically and to act rapidly on the market (Fleury and Fleury 2003). Competences assume responsibility for the recombination of resources and inputs in order to generate new ideas that meet the requirements of the environment (Banerjee 2003). Competences are considered as a main driver of any company that drives it towards competitiveness but its definition remains very large to the extent that we mixed it with the concept of the arrogance.

REFERENCES

Aaker, D. A., & Shansby, G. (1982). Positionning your product. *Business Horizons*, 25.

Adcock, D. (2000). *Marketing strategies for competitive advantage.* Chichester, UK: John Wiley & sons.

Allaire, Y., & Firsiritou, M. (1993). *L'entreprise stratégique: penser la stratégie.* édition Gaëtan Morin.

Anand, J., Brenes, E. R., Karnani, A., & Rodriquez, A. (2006). Strategic responses to economic liberalization in emerging economies: Lessons from experience. *Journal of Business Research*, *59*(3), 365–371. doi:10.1016/j.jbusres.2005.08.004

Arrègle, J. L., Amburgey, T., & Dacin, T. (1998). Le rôle des capacités organisationnelles dans le développement des réseaux d'entreprises: une application aux alliances. *Finance Contrôle Stratégie*, *1*(1), 7-25.

Baker, J. C., Mapes, J., New, C. C., & Szwejczewski, M. (1997). A hierarchical model of business competence. *Integrated Manufacturing Systems*, *8*(5), 265–272. doi:10.1108/09576069710179715

Banerjee, P. (2003). Resource dependence and core competence: Insights from Indian software firms. *Technovation*, *23*(3), 251–263. doi:10.1016/S0166-4972(01)00120-1

Barney, J. B. (1991). Firm resources and sustained competitive advantage. *Journal of Management*, *17*(1), 1. doi:10.1177/014920639101700108

Blay, O. T. (2002). Vers une nouvelle économie d'entreprise: Organisation et stratégie à l'aube de la nouvelle économie. *Economica.*

Bounfour, A. (1998). *Le management des ressources immatérielles.* Paris: DUNOD.

Boyatzis, R. E. (1994). Stimulating self-directed change: A required MBA course called Managerial Assessment and Development. *Journal of Management Education, 18*(3), 304–323. doi:10.1177/105256299401800303

Brandenburger, A., & Nalebuff, B. J. (1995). The Right Game: Use Game theory to Shape Strategy. *Harvard Business Review, 73*(4), 57–71.

Cadieux, L., & Denis, U. (2007). *Une lecture stratégique de la transmission d'entreprise: Le cas Guy Degrenne.* 5ème congré de l'académie de l'entreprenariat.

Castells, M. (2001). *La société en réseau, l'ère de l'information.* Paris: Fayard.

Chi, L., Jones, K. G., Lederer, A. L., Li, P., Newkirk, H. E., & Sethi, V. (2005). Environmental assessment in strategic information systems planning. *International Journal of Information Management, 25*(3), 253–269. doi:10.1016/j.ijinfomgt.2004.12.004

Cohen, J. (1988). *Statistical power analysis for the behavioral sciences.* Mahwah, NJ: Lawrence Erlbaum.

Datta, R. (2008). Ideation and the supply side of knowledge. *Knowledge Management Review, 11*(2), 14–17.

Davenport, T. H., Prusak, L., & Strong, B. (2008, March 10). Business Insight (A Special Report): Organization; Putting Ideas to Work: Knowledge management can make a difference - but it needs to be more pragmatic. *The Wall Street Journal.*

De Meyer, A., Dubuisson, S., & Le Bas, C. (1999). La Thématique des Compétences – Une Confrontation de Points de Vue Disciplinaires. In *Innovations et Performances – Approches Interdisciplinaires.* Éditions de l'Ecole des Hautes Etudes en Sciences Sociales.

Dias, B. (2008). Firm of the Future is an Intelligent Business. *Accounting Technology, 22.*

Dibb, S., Simões, C., & Wensley, R. (2014). Establishing the scope of marketing practice: Insights from practitioners. *European Journal of Marketing, 48*(1/2), 380–404. doi:10.1108/EJM-04-2011-0212

Drejer, A., & Sorenson, S. (2002). Succeeding with sourcing of competencies in technology-intensive industries. *Benchmarking, 9*(4), 388–401. doi:10.1108/14635770210442716

Dubey, C. (2003). *La gestion des compétences. Séminaire: changement et intervention dans les organisations.* Academic Press.

Durand, R., & Coeurderoy, R. (2001). Age, order of entry, strategic orientation, and organizational performance. *Journal of Business Venturing, 16*(5), 471–494. doi:10.1016/S0883-9026(99)00061-0

Edwards, J., & Wolfe, S. (2006). A compliance competence partnership approach model. *Journal of Financial Regulation and Compliance, 14*(2), 140–151. doi:10.1108/13581980610659459

Fleury, A., & Fleury, M. T. (2003). Competitive strategies and core competencies: Perspectives for the internationalisation of industry in Brazil. *Integrated Manufacturing Systems, 14*(1), 16–26. doi:10.1108/09576060310453317

Ge, Y. Q., Liu, Y., & Li, Y. (2007). Studies on the characteristics of strategic change. *Journal of Industrial Engineering and Engineering Management, 21*(2), 1–4.

Gilgeous, V., & Parveen, K. (2001). Core competency requirements for manufacturing effectiveness. Integrated Manufacturing Systems, 12(3), 217-228.

Golson, H. L. (2007). *Influence for Impact.* New York: McGrawhill.

Hair, J. F., Sarstedt, M., Ringle, C. M., & Mena, J. M. (2012). An Assessment of the Use of Partial Least Squares Structural Equation Modeling in Marketing Research. *Journal of Marine Science, 40*(3), 414–433.

Hallwood, C. P. (2014). Governing knowledge and the scope of the firm. *The International Journal of Organizational Analysis, 22*, 1, 2–13. doi:10.1108/IJOA-07-2010-0441

Hamel, G., & Prahalad, C. K. (1990). The core competence of the corporation. *Harvard Business Review*, 79–91.

Hamel, G., & Prahalad, C. K. (1994). *Competing for the future*. Cambridge, MA: Harvard Business School Press.

Hwang, Y., & Park, S. H. (2007). The Organizational Life Cycle as a Determinant of Strategic Alliance Tactics: Research Propositions. *International Journal of Management, 24*(3), 427.

Jay, J. (2000). Building capacity. Organizational competence and critical theory. *Journal of Organizational Change Management, 13*(3), 264–274. doi:10.1108/09534810010330913

Jones, J. (2016). *How Do Confidence and Arrogance Work in the Workplace? Organizational and Employee Development*. Society for Human Resource Management. Retrieved from https://www.shrm.org/resourcesandtools/hr-topics/organizational-and-employee-development/pages/how-do-confidence-and-arrogance-work-in-the-workplace.aspx

Kandampully, J. (2002). Innovation as the core competency of a service organisation: The role of technology, knowledge and networks. *European Journal of Innovation Management, 5*(1), 18–26. doi:10.1108/14601060210415144

Kauser, S., & Shaw, V. (2004). The influence Of Behavioural and Organizational Characteristics on the Success of International strategic Alliances. *International Marketing Review, 21*(1), 17–52. doi:10.1108/02651330410522934

Kim, J. S., & Arnold, P. (1992). Manufacturing competence and business performance: A framework and empirical analysis. *International Journal of Operations & Production Management, 13*(10), 4–25. doi:10.1108/01443579310045518

Kotler, P., & Dubois, B. (1992). *Marketing management*. Paris: Publi-Union.

Lalanke, B. (1998). 100 ans de management. *L'essentiel du management*, 103-115.

Li, Y., & Xu, J. (2014). Board independence, CEO succession and the scope of strategic change: Empirical research on the effectiveness of independent directors. *Nankai Business Review International, 5*(3), 309–325. doi:10.1108/NBRI-05-2014-0023

Ljungquis, U. (2007). Core competency beyond identification: presentation of a model. *Management Decision, 45*(3), 393.

Ljungquist, U. (2013). Adding dynamics to core competence concept applications. *European Business Review, 25*(5), 453–465. doi:10.1108/EBR-09-2012-0052

Lorino, P., & Tarondeau, J-C. (2006). De la stratégie aux processus stratégiques. *Revue Française de gestion, 160*(1), 307-328.

Major, E., Asch, D., & Hayes, M. C. (2001). Foresight as a core competence. *Futures, 33*(2), 91–107. doi:10.1016/S0016-3287(00)00057-4

May, A. (1999). Developing management competencies for fast changing organisations. *Career Development International, 4*(6), 336–339. doi:10.1108/13620439910288022

Meyer, G., Brünig, B., & Nyhuis, P. (2015). Employee competences in manufacturing companies – an expert survey. *Journal of Management Development, 34*(8), 1004–1018. doi:10.1108/JMD-06-2014-0056

Meyer, A., Dubuisson, S., & Le Bas, C. (1999). La Thématique des Compétences– Une Confrontation de Points de Vue Disciplinaires. In *Innovations et Performances – Approches Interdisciplinaires.* Éditions de l'Ecole des Hautes Etudes en Sciences Sociales.

Mooney, A. (2007). Core Competence, Distinctive Competence, and Competitive Advantage: What Is the Difference? *Journal of Education for Business, 83*(2), 110–116. doi:10.3200/JOEB.83.2.110-115

Nobelius, D. (2004). Linking product development to applied research: Transfer experiences from an automotive company. *Technovation, 24*(4), 321–334. doi:10.1016/S0166-4972(02)00073-1

Oum, T. H., Park, J. H., Kim, K., & Yu, C. (2004). The effect of horizontal alliances on firm productivity and profitability: Evidence from the global airline industry. *Journal of Business Research, 57*(8), 844–853. doi:10.1016/S0148-2963(02)00484-8

Padua, R. N., Lerin, M. M., Tumapon, T. T., & Pañares, Z. A. (2010). Patterns and Dynamics of an Arrogance-Competence Theory in Organizations. *Liceo Journal of Higher Education Research Cutting Edge Research, 6*(2), 2094–1064.

Pateyron, E. A., & Salomon, R. (1992). *Les nouvelles technologies de l'information et l'entreprise*. Paris: Economica.

Peffers, K., & Tuunainen, V. K. (2001). Leveraging geographic and information technology scope for superior performance: An exploratory study in international banking. *The Journal of Strategic Information Systems*, *10*(3), 175–200. doi:10.1016/S0963-8687(01)00051-8

Penrose, E. T. (1959). *The theory of the growth of the firm*. Basise Blackwell & Moth Ltd.

Pitta, D., & Pitta, E. (2012). Transforming the nature and scope of new product development. *Journal of Product and Brand Management*, *21*(1), 35–46. doi:10.1108/10610421211203097

Pulles, N. J., Veldman, J., & Schiele, H. (2016). Winning the competition for supplier resources: The role of preferential resource allocation from suppliers. *International Journal of Operations & Production Management*, *36*(11), 1458–1481. doi:10.1108/IJOPM-03-2014-0125

Quain, G., & Li, J. (2002). Multinationality, global market diversification and profitability among the largest US firms. *Journal of Business Research*, *55*(4), 325–335. doi:10.1016/S0148-2963(00)00153-3

Ramsey, V. J., & Latting, J. K. (2005). A Typology of Intergroup Competencies. *The Journal of Applied Behavioral Science*, *41*(3), 3, 265, 285. doi:10.1177/0021886305277974

Kak & Sushil. (2002). Sustainable Competitive Advantage with Core Competence: A Review. *Global Journal of Flexible Systems Management*, *3*(4), 23-39.

Ritala, P., Henttonen, K., Salojärvi, H., Sainio, L.-M., & Saarenketo, S. (2013). Gone fishing for knowledge?: The effect of strategic orientations on the scope of open knowledge search. *Baltic Journal of Management*, *8*(3), 328–348. doi:10.1108/BJOM-Apr-2012-0019

Stalk, G. J., Evans, P., & Shulman, L. E. (1992). Competing on capabilities: The new rules of corporate strategy. *Harvard Business Review*. PMID:10117369

Stock, G. N., Greis, N. P., & Kasarda, J. D. (1998). Logistics, strategy and structure: A conceptual Framework. *International Journal of Operations & Production Management*, *18*(1), 37–52. doi:10.1108/01443579810192772

Strategy statement: Articulating your competitive advantage, objectives and scope. (2013). Retrieved from http://www.marsdd.com/mars-library/strategy-statement-articulating-your-competitive-advantage-objectives-and-scope/

Stuart, R., & Lindsay, P. (1997). Beyond the frame of management competencies: Towards a contextually embedded framework of managerial competence in organizations. *Journal of European Industrial Training, 21*(1), 26–33. doi:10.1108/03090599710156410

Studt, T. (2008). Technology Will Continue to be the Driver of Change. *R & D Highlands Ranch, 50*(3), 12.

Subbanarasimha, P. N. (2001). Strategy in turbulent environments: The role of dynamic competence. *Managerial and Decision Economics, 22*(4-5), 201–212. doi:10.1002/mde.1017

Syed-Ikhsan, S. O. S., & Rowland, F. (2004). Knowledge Management in a Public Organization: A Study On the Relationship Between Organizational Elements and The performance of Knowledge Transfer. *Journal of Knowledge Management, 8*(2), 95–111. doi:10.1108/13673270410529145

Tampoe, M. (1994). Exploiting the core competences of your organization. *Long Range Planning, 27*(4), 66–77. doi:10.1016/0024-6301(94)90057-4

Teece, D. J. (1987). The competitive challenge: Strategies for industrial innovation and renewal. Cambridge, MA: Ballinger Publishing.

Torkkeli, M., & Tuominen, M. (2002). The contribution of technology selection to core competencies. *International Journal of Production Economics, 77*(3), 271–284. doi:10.1016/S0925-5273(01)00227-4

Valyasevi, R., & Rolle, R. S. (2002). An overview of small-scale food fermentation technologies in developing countries with special reference to Thailand: Scope for their improvement. *International Journal of Food Microbiology, 75*(3), 231–239. doi:10.1016/S0168-1605(01)00711-5 PMID:12036145

Vickery, S. K., Drodge, C., & Markland, R. E. (1993). Production competence and business strategy: Do they affect business performance? *Decision Sciences, 24*(2), 435–455. doi:10.1111/j.1540-5915.1993.tb00482.x

Wang, Y., & Lo, H.-P. (2003). Customer-focused performance and the dynamic model for competence building and leveraging. A resource-based view. *Journal of Management Development, 22*(6), 483–526. doi:10.1108/02621710310478486

Wang, Y., Lo, H.-P., & Yang, Y. (2004). The constituents of core competencies and firm performance: Evidence from high-technology firms in China. *Journal of Engineering and Technology Management, 21*(4), 249–280. doi:10.1016/j.jengtecman.2004.09.001

Wegberg, M. V. (2004). Compatibility Choice by Multi-market Firms. *Information Economics and Policy, 16*(2), 235–254. doi:10.1016/j.infoecopol.2003.09.011

Wernerfelt, B. (1984). A resource-based view of the firm. *Strategic Management Journal, 5*(2), 171–180. doi:10.1002/smj.4250050207

Woodruff, R. B. (1997). Customer value: The next source for competitive advantage. *Journal of the Academy of Marketing Science, 25*(2), 2. doi:10.1007/BF02894350

Zenger, T. R., & Huang, J. X. (2015, March 9). Limits to the scale and scope of the firm. *Economic Institutions of Strategy,* 267-286.

Zhu, K., & Kraemer, K. L. (2002). E-commerce metrics for net-enhanced organizations: Assessing the value of e-commerce to firm performance in the manufacturing sector. *Information Systems Research, 13*(3), 275–295. doi:10.1287/isre.13.3.275.82

Zhu, K., & Kraemer, K. L. (2005). Post-adoption variations in usage and value of e-business by organizations: Cross-country evidence from the retail industry. *Information Systems Research, 16*(1), 61–84. doi:10.1287/isre.1050.0045

ENDNOTES

[1]   https://www.interviewedge.com/articles/Competencies-Selfconfidence-or-Arrogance.html

[2]   A value of f square (f^2) between 0.02 and 0.15 indicates a weak effect whereas a value between 0.15 and 0.35 indicates a moderate effect while f square above 0.35 indicates a large effect (Cohen, 1988).

Chapter 6
Case Study:
A Young Entrepreneur Agronomist Between Arrogance and Competence

ABSTRACT

In order to explore the relationship between competence and arrogance, the authors developed a case study based on real facts that a young ergonomist entrepreneur was confronted with. The entrepreneur need only "over trust" and a strong personality, an arrogance that permits him to live more experience and then acquire expertise. This chapter is in continuity with the previous. It offers to the reader a different perspective in order to investigate this ambiguous relationship between arrogance and competence in the field of entrepreneurship.

SHOULD ENTREPRENEUR CONSIDER COMPETENCE AS RESOURCES?

Several authors define competences as a set of skills, know-how, activities and routines, and distinguish them from resources that are assets to be valued (Gordon and Tarafdar 2007). Moreover, by referring to the work of Reynaud (2001), we noted the existence of a certain nuance between the concept of resources and competences. Indeed, resources at disposal of entrepreneur can be defined as the tangible and intangible assets that he holds, that is to say the elements necessary for the functioning.

DOI: 10.4018/978-1-5225-5525-4.ch006

Hafeez et al. (2002) confirmed that resources are different from competences and constitute everything that can be a strength or weakness of the company, they include raw materials, equipment, finance, the image of the firm, etc. This means tangible and intangible resources. On the other hand, competences are valued capacities which allow any entrepreneur to deliver added value to clients and thus constitute a network of capacities. Similarly, competences are not mere capacities but rather enhanced capacities. They are usual and simple applications of activities and processes, and primary source of development of competitive advantages.

Competences are an inherent quality of an individual or group of individuals who can refine a resource. They are seen as capacities to support a coordinated deployment of assets in order to achieve a given objective (Ljungquist 2007).

According to Escrig Tena and Bou-Llusar (2005), competences are considered as specific capabilities and talents used to properly deploy resources and support the coordinated deployment of assets. They refer to cognitive characteristics that contribute to the achievement of activities and the attainment of specific objectives.

From another point of view, some authors such as Major et al. (2001), consider that competences allow to evaluate the different possibilities of action and investment in the future with maximum realism. The aim is to facilitate the opening up and development of future paths, taking into account the scarce of resources.

The Competence of Entrepreneur Between Design and Delivery

Competences appear as a complex combinatorial of different types of knowledge and abilities to produce a result (De Meyer et al. 1999). Gilbert and Parlier (1992) consider that competences encompass *"the body of knowledge, capacity for action, and behavior, structured according to purpose and in a given type of situation"*. Thus, the authors are unanimous in saying that competences call for knowledge as well as action and practice. Indeed, knowledge refers to the concept of design whereas action, behavior and the ability to produce a result refer to the notion of execution, perform and delivery. These two notions were developed by two approaches, namely the French approach and the Anglo-Saxon approach (Saint-Onge 1999).

The French Approach

The French school distinguishes three levels of competence:

Knowledge: Which gathers the specific book and theoretical knowledge that characterizes the governance, study, realization, sales and support capacities of the products and services of any company. (Grundstein 2002).

In the same way, Banerjee (2003) asserts that competences are composed, among other things, of what is called "The domain Thrust Competence", that is to say, the totality of theoretical knowledge and specific to the domain or profession. It is in fact the stable and conceptual response of the firm to its environment. It is therefore important to train employees in their fields. At the same time, Prahalad and Hamel (1990; 1994) distinguish the conceptual competencies that are realized by the knowledge acquired in order to open up new perspectives in managerial perspectives and to create competitive advantages.

- Know-how: this type of knowledge represents the competences that can be acquired through practice and which can be at the same time individual or collective. They are characterized by the capacity of a company to act. This type of competence (know-how) consists of a set of tangible elements such as "databases, procedures, plans, models, algorithms, analysis and synthesis documents". Know-how can also be made up of a set of intangible elements such as *"skills, trades secrets, routines, knowledge of history and decision-making contexts, knowledge of the environment (customers, Competitors, technologies, socio-economic influences)"* (Grundstein 2002).

In this perspective, Banerjee (2003) spoke about "The domain knowledge competence" and "The first order competences", to designate the acquisition of expertise through the experience of the staff. Similarly, Prahalad and Hamel (1990; 1994) talked about operational skills that are translated into more professional experiences and managerial practices.

The know-how that is embodied in relational abilities or attitudes. It represents any company's ability to connect with its environment. The concept of "relational skills" refers to *"the transaction cost approach, which, in conjunction with complementary resources and skills, not only reduces transaction costs, but also protects against Risk of opportunistic behavior of the partners"*(Persais 2001).

The Anglo-Saxon Approach

The Anglo-Saxon approach differs from the French approach in that it adopts a classification of competences by referring only to the following two levels:

- **The Essential Competences:** Refers to all the essential knowledge required to perform tasks related to a specific position. The latter are of two types, explicit and tacit. For the explicit knowledge, it forms the set of knowledge "formalized, specialized, redundant and presented in the form of data, plans, synthesis documents, etc". In the case of tacit knowledge, competences include all the know-how of a company, *"they are acquired through practice, passed on through collective learning and linked to talents, skills, trade secrets, etc.* "(Grundstein 2002).
- **The Soft Competences:** They give an advantage in terms of performance to the person who holds them. Certain competences that are unique, non-substitutable and non-transferable provide companies with competitive advantages. The development of know-how, considered as a support for the competitiveness of the company, thus constitutes the main basis of competences (Tremblay and Sire 1999).

It appears that, for the French or Anglo-Saxon approach, competencies revolve around two main concepts, the first of which traces the conceptual character that we will call conceptual capacities. The latter form all the capacities of individuals to form methods and ideas of work. The second concept refers to the capacities related to the practice that we called the skills of execution and delivery. The latter form the ability to put into practice the concepts already developed.

Entrepreneur, Competent, or Arrogant?

Entrepreneurship is considered usually as one of the most important solution that can face unemployment. Many young people from all over the world express their wants to embark and open their own business. On the other side many countries are required to provide millions of job opportunities by "the year 2020 with keeping the same living standards" (Ayed 2017). In parallel, entrepreneur needs to be competent and disposes of one profile that leads him to success. The big question is that when we study these characteristics, we can feel arrogance in that. For example, for some researchers, entrepreneur must embrace purpose and mission, he should take the leap and believe in what he is doing and find his own way of how doing things, he should be convinced and trustful that things believed never to be done can be done (Molinsky 2016). Entrepreneur is an opportunity spotter, someone who takes risk and seeks to capitalize what he is doing in order to create value (Habiby and Coyle 2010; Hagel 2016). Entrepreneur is someone offensive, needs traits of Focus, Advantage, Creativity, Ego, Team and Social (FACETS) (Thompson 2004). Entrepreneur must be armed with achievement, "internal locus of control, a moderate risk-taking propensity, a tolerance for ambiguity, self-confidence, innovativeness (Cromie 2000), autonomy, independence (Cromie et al. 1992), dominance and self-esteem (Chakravarthy and Lorange 2008) and the spirit of initiative.

Synopsis

The story began in 1994 when the young future entrepreneur Mr "M" was graduated in animal and fodder production (with congratulations of the jury). He was so ambitious and enthusiast that he believed he could easily implant and succeed his own project. He liked very well his field and thought he had all the gift and skills to be a good breeder. He dreamed to become one of the leaders of the animal and fodder producers.

In addition, and just after the graduation, his father (a great trader in the region) advised him to apply at the Ministry of Agriculture as there were some vacant positions offered. This in order to gain experience and relationship before going to launch his own project. The young entrepreneur refused categorically the proposal of his father by claiming that he liked to have just a small experience in the private sector before launching his own project. So he started working as an agricultural manager, he fulfilled his mission successfully and fully satisfied his boss. A few months later he decided to look for another job offers with better and more attractive salary.

After a while, the young entrepreneur changed his job. He proved his skills and assumed appropriately the responsibilities and tasks assigned to him especially at the technical level. Unfortunately, a few months later he applied again for a new position of technical director in a large company specialized in the breeding of rabbit. The young entrepreneur was very successful and his boss was proud of him. He even offered him some benefits (home and car) and wanted him to stay with him as long as possible. However, and precisely after 16 months of working, the young agronomist asked again for his resignation because he wanted to go back to his hometown since his father died. His boss asked him to stay and even offered him other benefits but the young man refused. He wanted to come back to comfort and stay with his family members as he was the eldest son.

After a while, the young agronomist had a proposal from a businessman to be hired as an agricultural manager in a farm specialized in cattle breeding. He began to work in this function but unfortunately, this situation lasted only thirteen months and the young agronomist was again impressed by a new offer from one of his relatives. The latter wanted from him to go in entrepreneurship and start to launch together a company specialized in the Sales and marketing of chicken meat and dairy products. Thus, the young "M" claimed that this project is the dream of his life, he resigned and launched a new company called NEAPOLIS. His family members helped him financially to invest in this new area.

Over time, several problems arose between the two partners and just after two years, the young entrepreneur agronomist decided to end the association with his partner and open another own point of sales. So he bought the share of his partner and the NEAPOLIS Company became at his total property with a capital of about $ 25,000. He started working and the profit attained monthly an average of about $ 1,000. After a period of time, one of his relatives, proposed to him to buy his farm with an ease of payment. The total of price was about 90 000 $ (sale over ten years with a one year of grace).

With this new offer, the young entrepreneur agronomist believed that his dream would become a reality as he realized that his favorite domain would always remain animal production. So, he accepted this offer, sold the NEAPOLIS Company and go to invest all the money got in the buying of this farm. He was fully committed to his new project and fully convinced that he would succeed in his project.

Unfortunately, 16 months later, the young entrepreneur agronomist declared his bankruptcy. He opened again a small point of sale of meat of chickens and dairy products. Again once more, his mother had financed this project just to guarantee for him a source of income.

The Objective of the Case

This case is addressed to students who would be entrepreneurs and studying in business administration and wishing to create their own projects. The main objective is to make students understand that starting a professional life is not an easy task and needs to pay a lot of attention to things that are initially simple but in reality, count hidden mistakes to be avoided.

This case also illustrates theoretical concepts useful for understanding the reality of business. Thus, it refers to the concept of individual competences, their dimensions and their implementation. It aims to analyze entrepreneur's capacities and their positioning in relation to open business opportunities. This case will cite a real example of the experience of a young entrepreneur agronomist living in a given period as well as the errors committed during the period in question. The objective is to provide students a general idea about the reality of entrepreneurship as well as the highlights to take into account in order to avoid any failure. Understanding the concept of the limited rationality seems very important to avoid any bad consequences.

In addition, we will aim, through this case, to introduce students considered as future entrepreneurs to draw up a competency grid, to identify the shortcomings to be faced resulting from a lack of competence and consequently requiring a profound diagnostic of training needs. In fact, the themes and tools mainly mobilized are competences, career and risk management, and strategic management.

In addition to the introduction of these basic concepts, this exercise should allow students to acquire communication skills following the class discussion guided by the teacher and based on some questions that we will be shown in the following. This exercise should also allow students to acquire capacities of logical structuring of ideas. By this case, students should also be able to differentiate between a problem and a symptom of a problem.

Finally, this case can be taught and integrated in a course of entrepreneurship or project management. Prerequisite courses such as corporate strategy or management of organizations are preferred to be taken before.

The Origin of the Case

This is a real case experienced by a young entrepreneur agronomist, the author's brother of this case, who has long dreamed of becoming an expert in the domain. The errors committed during fifteen years have led him to question everything especially after his declaration of bankruptcy. The lesson he learned is that going through a tricky business path and without realizing the reality has led him to disclose his experience to all beginners in order to tell them: "Be careful, time is expensive, you must always have wisdom to learn from errors and not to commit them again". It should be noted that the official authorizations to disseminate this case according to the code of ethics are taken into consideration. On the contrary, the subject would have declared his honor to initiate his experiment to the young entrepreneur's beginners as well as to make them to be aware of any fatal error that can upset success in the business paths.

The pedagogical guidelines to be addressed to the students before starting the exercise: The pedagogical value of the case

According to the research work of Tamilia (2000), the pedagogical case is the object of a philosophy of learning different from the traditional method. The analysis of the case puts into practice the talents acquired by the students. The more, students are close to the practice, the more effective they are. Students must also practice more decision-making and not only discuss issues.

Students should know that the analysis of this case is considered as a democratic process requiring participation in a discussion session with their colleagues and their teacher. The latter should be the guide of the students who organizes the exchange of ideas. Students should not be afraid of others' criticisms by spreading their points of view. The benefits gained from the treatment of this case are fixed to the efforts devoted by the students to work this case as well as the time spent. Students should be good listeners and speakers. Saying a point of view is just for participation but also primarily to contribute to the valorization of the discussion. Students should organize their ideas and thoughts before pronouncing them. Communication skills will surely be improved as a result of this exercise as a result of their participation and exploitation of the points of views of others.

Finally, it should be noted that students may not have easy access to the necessary information. They should consider this to be normal and should provide more efforts and strive by the tools available to solve their problems.

The analysis of this case should allow students to:

- To organize the collected information in a logical structure: that is to say that each student must present his points of view by illustrating them with rational and convincing arguments (the why).
- To know how to diagnose a problem, that means, to distinguish between a problem and a symptom of a problem.
- To know how to identify and evaluate alternative actions and,
- To generate solutions to solve the identified problems (Tamilia 2000).

In the Classroom

Working Method

This case may be discussed during a three-hour session during which three parts will be included. The first part will concern the launching of the discussion with the students. A second part will be constructed of four exercises. Each exercise has purpose to teach students theoretical concepts and show them how to put into practice these theories. The third part is consecrated to test of the capacities of structuring ideas by the students.

Part 1: Questions for Students to Prepare Them for Class Discussion

The teacher can ask a question by which students will begin to overcome the barriers of discussion and participation in class. A very classical question in its form, easy to answer, its envisaged responses are varied and the risk for students to "commit nonsense" is low. This will lead to a discussion without obstacles. Moreover, the objective is purely of a communicational and pedagogical nature.

Students will have the opportunity to understand the difference between a problem and a symptom of a problem. For example, if one of the students answers that the major problem of the young entrepreneur agronomist is bankruptcy, the professor will accept his answer and open other paths for reflection by asking other questions like this: do you think this is the main problem of this young entrepreneur agronomist? If he is given $ 200,000, do you think that his problem will be solved? Do you think that he will make good decisions and exploit successfully this amount of money? As a result, its bankruptcy is only the results of real problems in the person in question. At this level, the teacher can disclose some techniques and tools that can help any manager to discover the real problems and not the symptoms. For example, he can show to students a technique by which everyone concerned can ask the question "why" five times, some steps to follow to find the real problem and not to limit to symptoms.

As a result, he would be able to find a real reason for any problem or situation or conflict. In addition, the "4WH" technique can be the object of such a resolution by allowing to define the different components of a well-defined subject. It is a question of systematically answering the following questions: "What is it? ", "Who is concerned ", " Where is it happening? ", " When does this happen? ", and "How does it happen?" All of this is in one goal, to face the real problem and to try to find the appropriate remedies to deal with the situation.

In addition, the teacher can also introduce students to creative tools in order to identify all possible obstacles to achieving such goals. For example, there is the disaster scenario method by which any entrepreneur before launching his own project, can consider possible obstacles to the implementation of such actions. It is to define the most negative scenario by answering the following question: "What and how to do to fail?" This is called the disaster scenario method. It is a reflective pedagogy that every entrepreneur must adopt especially in the phase of launching of a new project. Answer such questions "What if it does not work? "," What do we do if ...? "What have we prepared if ...? ", etc.

Part 2: Some Questions to Introduce Key Concepts and Their Applications

Working Method

In this stage, the teacher teaches the students theoretical definitions of the key concepts used and evaluates their abilities to put these concepts into practice. For each question, the teacher must open a brainstorming session during which the student will have to say everything he thinks but has to provide efforts to argument and justify his answer with rationality. The student should always bear in mind that any answer must be justified by the "why". In the following, some questions that the teacher can ask them with the detail of their key answers proposals.

Question 1: *What are the Main Criteria for Assessing the Individual Competences of this Young Entrepreneur Agronomist?*

The teacher should listen carefully to the students' answers and guide them gradually to a theoretical answer that we propose in the following:

Answer 1: Before going on to assess the competences of this young entrepreneur agronomist, it would be essential to define their evaluation criteria. Indeed, it should be noted that managerial literature has always, in its definitions of competences, distinguished between notions of design and execution. Thus, with the appearance of the Taylorian model based on the Scientific Organization of Labor, the boundary between design and execution was clear. At the present time, authors advocate that competencies can be understood on both the conceptual and the executive sides, the latter can be distinct or complementary. Competence thus appears as a complex combinatorial of different types of knowledge and ability to produce a result. These two notions (conceptual and executive) were developed by the French approach which distinguishes three levels of competence.

Question 2: *Draw a Grid of Competences of this Young Entrepreneur Agronomist*

After a first discussion, the professor can give students a competency chart to be filled in according to the case text. This filling must be accompanied by a discussion with the students in order to validate the results found.

Answer 2: See Table 1.

After analyzing this grid, we can say that this young entrepreneur agronomist has strengths especially in technical knowledge in animal production. Also,

Table 1. Grid of competences of the Young Entrepreneur Agronomist

Assessment Criteria of Competences	Satisfactory	To Improve	Unavailable
The Know			
Technically	*		
commercially			*
The Know-How			
Technically	*	*	
commercially			*
The Know-Being			
Motivation	*		
Will	*		
dynamism	*		
continuity			*
patience			*
Risk-Taking			*

his know-how is rich and can be valued and developed since he has a will and motivation to work, he likes well his domain and his job and wants really to move forward. On the other hand, we have noticed that he did not succeed when he launched commercial business. He missed competences, rationality and professionalism. So he still lacked conceptual capacities and execution skills at the commercial level and also lacked certain know-how because he was not patient every time he started his project. He never assures continuity because he quickly changes his job and he does not realize what it means the risk. This reminds us of "*arrogance-competence theory in human organizations is developed by the axiomatic approach to theory development*" (Padua et al. 2010). Each person has arrogance-competence pair characteristics for himself. Competences trace the good trait characteristics of a person. In the other side arrogance presents the species of pride, dignity, estimation, power that exalts the importance of estimation. People disposing of high arrogance and high competence are quite successful but can also be destructive to morale and relationships (Padua et al. 2010).

Question 3: *What are the Errors Made by this Young Entrepreneur Agronomist in the Management of his Project?*

Answer 3: When launching any new project, entrepreneurs are asked to think about how to create value. Today, we talk about the creation of social value (the constitution of the relational network), the institutional value (consecration of the entity) and also mainly, the economic value (creation of material wealth). It seems that in the case of this young entrepreneur, the creation of economic value was a priority, since it is in its early stages, he wanted essentially to value his resources to go in the following to invest in on other projects.

For many researchers, the creation of economic value is mainly due to good strategic management and the dynamization of the three motors of wealth valorization, which are strategic motors, financial motors and "corporate" motors.

In our case, the young entrepreneur, did not boost continuously these three motors. Thus, concerning the strategic motors, he did not have a clear configuration of costs (cost of buying the firm compared to its current income, continuous investments with the help of his family members, that is to say without taking into account that all these are really costs). In addition, we did not feel that this young entrepreneur had a clear vision on his competitive positioning. He did not try to fully develop and valorize his intangible assets

Table 2. The characteristics of people belonging to each quadrant

	Description Characteristics
High Arrogance-High Competence	1. These people are often quite successful but they can also be destructive to morale and relationships, and ultimately to the organization. 2. As leaders, they tend to oppress subordinates. Bosses with this combination create subordinates who become adept at passive aggression. Of course they say all the right words and show appropriate compliance, but they secretly take pleasure in the inevitable obstacles and setbacks the high competence/arrogance style creates. And they will watch passively as the leader fails when in fact they could help.
Low Arrogance - High Competence	1. These are the people who provide solid problem solutions and do so in a way that's not offensive or abrasive. You want all of these folks you can get in your organization. But if the low arrogance is due to insecurity, you may need to do a lot of work to encourage them to take the initiative and go to bat for their solutions. 2. They're likely to expect their work to speak for them and may have trouble selling themselves when necessary and appropriate. 3. They're more likely to be facilitative and supportive in a leadership role than aggressive, charismatic or forceful.
Low Arrogance-Low Competence	1. These people aren't likely to rise to the executive ranks unless they're related to someone in power. 2. They may be delightful people to spend time with, but they don't have the cleverness to solve complex business problems or the arrogance to bluff their way through. 3. They're too dumb to know when somebody's peeing on their leg and too nice to tell them to quit if they realize it.
High Arrogance Low Competence	1. They're dangerous. They don't realize the limits of their ability and don't have the good sense to ask for a second opinion. 2. They can make a big splash early in their careers but they'll usually flame out. 3. Their unfounded self confidence can propel them far beyond their true abilities. Then, they can take the organization down unless they're very lucky.

Golson 2007 cited by Padua et al. 2010.

(Example taking training session in commerce). Finally, we have not noticed a willingness of this young entrepreneur to reduce the uncertainty (continuous changes in the business), this leads to increase risks and decrease confidence on self.

For the second type of motor, which is finance, the young entrepreneur relies heavily on the subsidies of his family members in his investments. This leads him to have a "fuzzy" capital structure and therefore can have a negative effect on the optimal allocation of financial resources. Similarly, we did not feel a rigorous attempt to reduce costs because re-investments and re-launches of projects were frequent and continuous without any objectivity.

Finally, we come to the third type of motors which is the "corporate". In summary, the young entrepreneur agronomist did not properly manage his reputation. One time seems as a commercial and one another as agronomist and animal producer of different types (cattle, chicken, and rabbit). He should have put in place a system of steering that encourages him to achieve high performance in one area.

It was necessary to say that the young entrepreneur had a limited rationality because he committed many mistakes without reaching any objective. The gap exists between action and achievement of objectives (Simon 1991). This entrepreneur seems to be limited in his habits and reflexes, his values and his conception of the objectives. Behavior remains a set of means, objectives and information that require to be managed effectively[1].

Question 4: *Given his Current Profile, What Types of Risks that this Young Entrepreneur Agronomist can Face in his day-to-day Management?*

Answer 4:

- **The Strategic Risks:** Risks of bad strategic choices that means the risk of obtaining the desired results with the chosen strategies. This young entrepreneur has to establish a plan to implement his strategy. He has to compare his progress to the business plan for each period.
- **The Risks of Non-Compliance:** Risk of loss due to non-compliance with recommended business practices. This young entrepreneur lacks the managerial and commercial knowledge. He must attend training seminars in the field especially at entrepreneurship.
- **Operational Risks:** Risks resulting from human error, system failures, inadequate processes or external factors. The management of these operational risks must include the ongoing assessment of control measures. There must be business continuity programs that provide measures for emergency response.

The risks of reputational damage: such as risks of loss of reputation, credibility or brand image resulting from past misconduct. The young entrepreneur must ensure his continuity and position himself in the field in which he has launched.

Question 5: *Opening up of Horizons: What Steps Should be Taken to Develop a Diagnosis of Training Needs? Make a Proposal!*

Answer 5: In order to draw up an effective training plan for the staff concerned, it would be important to carry out first diagnosis in order to make the right decisions and to target the actions necessary for proper functioning. This diagnosis can be done at three levels.

At the individual level, it's about assessing the strengths and weaknesses of existing staff.

At the enterprise level by studying the type of job in detail (job description, skills and knowledge, required skills, etc.). This can make it possible to know the trainings that can be proposed. In addition, determining the needs of training can start from the problems reported in the company, and then detect whether one of the improvement responses can be training or not.

At the strategic level, by examining the profile of the future employee and the training to be put in place to ensure his improvement. It is about anticipating new competences to acquire.

The Training Needs Assessment Is of a Three-Step Process

Step 1: *Define the Company's Objectives*

What goals should the company set? What is his overall project? What are the axes of development to be implemented? What are the human and material resources to be mobilized? What is of priority and urgency? What is immediate to do?

Step 2: *Determine Available Competences*

What is the profile of each staff? His training, his career, his abilities, aspirations, sense of belonging in terms of evolution, flexibility, stability, change of activity. At this level, some tools should be used such as the competency assessment grid, the professional interview, the skills assessment.

Step 3: *Identify Training Needs*

This involves identifying the gap between existing skills and the skills required for the business development of the company. Based on the needs identified for each of the above categories and for each employee interviewed, it would be appropriate to define training priorities in terms of audiences and practical objectives.

This involves conducting semi-structured interviews with staff to assess their potential, their motivations, their visions, their working and customer relations philosophies. At the end of these interviews, we need to be able to develop a Competency Analysis Grid (CAG). This tool will allow to have a global vision of the skills, and to identify the axes of training for the collaborators. This grid would be fed by the answers given during the individual interviews.

Part 3: Final Exercise Which Aims Structuring Logically Ideas Among Students

At the end of the discussion, the teacher can ask students to map out a logical structure of the links between the different concepts that are: limited rationality, career, strategy, risk and success. The teacher can help students by asking them to distinguish between the explanatory variables and the variables to be explained. Any answer which is the object of the result of an effort of reflection will be welcome provided that the student rationally argues his logical reasoning.

REFERENCES

Banerjee, P. (2003). Resource dependence and core competence: Insights from Indian software firms. *Technovation, 23*(3), 251–263. doi:10.1016/S0166-4972(01)00120-1

De Meyer, A., Dubuisson, S., & Le Bas, C. (1999). La Thématique des Compétences – Une Confrontation de Points de Vue Disciplinaires. In *Innovations et Performances – Approches Interdisciplinaires*. Éditions de l'Ecole des Hautes Etudes en Sciences Sociales.

Escrig-Tena, A. B., & Bou-Llusar, J. C. (2005). A Model for Evaluating Organizational Competencies: An Application in the Context of a Quality Management Initiative. *Decision Sciences, 36*(2), 221–258. doi:10.1111/j.1540-5414.2005.00072.x

Frioui, M. (2006). *Le cadre institutionnel et la problématique managériale: Cas vivants de management*. les presses de l'imprimerie Top Printing.

Gilbert, P., & Parlier, M. (1992). La compétence: Du mot-valise au concept opératoire. *Actualité de la Formation Permanente, 116*, 14–18.

Golson, H. L. (2007). *Influence for Impact*. New York: McGrawhill.

Grundstein, M. (2002). *De la capitalisation des connaissances au renforcement des compétences dans l'entreprise étendue.* 1er Colloque du groupe de travail Gestion des Compétences et des Connaissances en Génie Industriel Vers l'articulation entre Compétences et Connaissances. GCC-GI02 12-13 décembre 2002 – Nantes (France).

Hafeez, K., Zhang, Y., & Malak, N. (2002). Determining key capabilities of a firm using analytic hierarchy process. *International Journal of Production Economics, 76*(1), 39–51. doi:10.1016/S0925-5273(01)00141-4

Hamel, G., & Prahalad, C. K. (1990). The core competence of the corporation. *Harvard Business Review*, 79–91.

Hamel, G., & Prahalad, C. K. (1994). *Competing for the future.* Cambridge, MA: Harvard Business School Press.

Haywood-Farmer, J. (2008). *An Introductory Note On The Case Method.* Richard Ivey School of Business.

Kamprath, M., & Mietzner, D. (2015). The impact of sectoral changes on individual competences: A reflective scenario-based approach in the creative industries. *Technological Forecasting and Social Change, 95*, 252–275. doi:10.1016/j.techfore.2015.01.011

Ljungquis, U. (2007). Core competency beyond identification: presentation of a model. *Management Decision, 45*(3), 393.

Ljungquist, U. (2013). Adding dynamics to core competence concept applications. *European Business Review, 25*(5), 453–465. doi:10.1108/EBR-09-2012-0052

Major, E., Asch, D., & Hayes, M. C. (2001). Foresight as a core competence. *Futures, 33*(2), 91–107. doi:10.1016/S0016-3287(00)00057-4

Meyer, A., Dubuisson, S., & Le Bas, C. (1999). La Thématique des Compétences– Une Confrontation de Points de Vue Disciplinaires. In *Innovations et Performances – Approches Interdisciplinaires.* Éditions de l'Ecole des Hautes Etudes en Sciences Sociales.

Padua, R. N., Lerin, M. M., Tumapon, T. T., & Pañares, Z. A. (2010). Patterns and Dynamics of an Arrogance-Competence Theory in Organizations. *Liceo Journal of Higher Education Research Cutting Edge Research, 6*(2).

Persais, E. (2001). Le caractère stratégique des compétences relationnelles. Xième Conférence de l'Association Internationale de Management Stratégique. Faculté des Sciences de l'administration, Université Laval, Québec.

Saint-Onge, S. (1999). Rémunérer les Compétences: Où en Sommes-Nous? *Gestion*, *23*(4), 24–33.

Sasser, W. E., & Beckham, H. (2008). *Thomas Green: Power, Office Politics, and a Career in Crisis.* Academic Press.

Tamilia, R. (2000). *Pedagogical value of case analysis. Recueil de lectures et notes de cours MBA 8132 et DCM 7131. École des sciences de gestion. Département stratégie des affaires. Université du Québec à Montréal.* Edition Guérin.

Tremblay, M., & Sire, B. (1999). Rémunérer les compétences plutôt que l'activité? *Revue Française de Gestion*, *126*, 129–139.

ENDNOTE

[1]   http://www.businesspme.com/articles/economie/123/rationalite-limitee.html

Related Readings

To continue IGI Global's long-standing tradition of advancing innovation through emerging research, please find below a compiled list of recommended IGI Global book chapters and journal articles in the areas of workplace arrogance, job satisfaction, and job performance. These related readings will provide additional information and guidance to further enrich your knowledge and assist you with your own research.

Adada, N., Shatila, A., & Mneymneh, N. M. (2017). Technology Leadership: Bridging the Gap between Problems and Solutions in Lebanese Schools. In R. Styron Jr & J. Styron (Eds.), *Comprehensive Problem-Solving and Skill Development for Next-Generation Leaders* (pp. 293–312). Hershey, PA: IGI Global. doi:10.4018/978-1-5225-1968-3.ch014

Ali, N. (2015). Afghanistan: Leadership Development: A Comparison between Men and Women Managers. In S. Jones & S. Graham (Eds.), *Cases on Sustainable Human Resources Management in the Middle East and Asia* (pp. 212–228). Hershey, PA: IGI Global. doi:10.4018/978-1-4666-8167-5.ch008

Anantharaman, R. N., Rajeswari, K. S., Angusamy, A., & Kuppusamy, J. (2017). Role of Self-Efficacy and Collective Efficacy as Moderators of Occupational Stress Among Software Development Professionals. *International Journal of Human Capital and Information Technology Professionals*, 8(2), 45–58. doi:10.4018/IJHCITP.2017040103

Athota, V. S. (2017). Foundations and Future of Well-Being: How Personality Influences Happiness and Well-Being. In S. Háša & R. Brunet-Thornton (Eds.), *Impact of Organizational Trauma on Workplace Behavior and Performance* (pp. 279–294). Hershey, PA: IGI Global. doi:10.4018/978-1-5225-2021-4.ch012

Badawoud, T. (2015). Egypt: Sustainable HR within the CSR Policies in a Multinational Hospitality Group. In S. Jones & S. Graham (Eds.), *Cases on Sustainable Human Resources Management in the Middle East and Asia* (pp. 229–245). Hershey, PA: IGI Global. doi:10.4018/978-1-4666-8167-5.ch009

Baniata, B. A., & Alryalat, H. (2017). The Effect of Strategic Orientations Factors to Achieving Sustainable Competitive Advantage. *International Journal of E-Entrepreneurship and Innovation*, 7(1), 1–15. doi:10.4018/IJEEI.2017010101

Barron, I., & Novak, D. A. (2017). i-Leadership: Leadership Learning in the Millennial Generation. In P. Ordoñez de Pablos, & R. Tennyson (Eds.), Handbook of Research on Human Resources Strategies for the New Millennial Workforce (pp. 231-257). Hershey, PA: IGI Global. doi:10.4018/978-1-5225-0948-6.ch011

Basu, K. (2017). Change Management and Leadership: An Overview of the Healthcare Industry. In P. Ordoñez de Pablos & R. Tennyson (Eds.), *Handbook of Research on Human Resources Strategies for the New Millennial Workforce* (pp. 47–64). Hershey, PA: IGI Global. doi:10.4018/978-1-5225-0948-6.ch003

Bergethon, K. P., & Davis, D. C. (2016). Emotional Leadership: Leadership Styles and Emotional Intelligence. In A. Normore, L. Long, & M. Javidi (Eds.), *Handbook of Research on Effective Communication, Leadership, and Conflict Resolution* (pp. 63–77). Hershey, PA: IGI Global. doi:10.4018/978-1-4666-9970-0.ch004

Beycioglu, K., & Wildy, H. (2015). Principal Preparation: The Case of Novice Principals in Turkey. In K. Beycioglu & P. Pashiardis (Eds.), *Multidimensional Perspectives on Principal Leadership Effectiveness* (pp. 1–17). Hershey, PA: IGI Global. doi:10.4018/978-1-4666-6591-0.ch001

Bhat, V., & Person, A. (2016). Differences in the Factors Influencing Job Satisfaction among Scientists and Engineers. *International Journal of Applied Management Sciences and Engineering*, 3(1), 1–10. doi:10.4018/IJAMSE.2016010101

Blomme, R. J., & Lub, X. D. (2017). Routines as a Perspective for HR-Professionals: Diversity as a Driver for Routines. In P. Ordoñez de Pablos & R. Tennyson (Eds.), *Handbook of Research on Human Resources Strategies for the New Millennial Workforce* (pp. 337–350). Hershey, PA: IGI Global. doi:10.4018/978-1-5225-0948-6.ch017

Blomme, R. J., & Morsch, J. (2016). Organizations as Social Networks: The Role of the Compliance Officer as Agent of Change in Implementing Rules and Codes of Conduct. In A. Goksoy (Ed.), *Organizational Change Management Strategies in Modern Business* (pp. 110–121). Hershey, PA: IGI Global. doi:10.4018/978-1-4666-9533-7.ch006

Bridgeforth, J. S. (2017). Multicultural Leadership in Higher Education. In R. Styron Jr & J. Styron (Eds.), *Comprehensive Problem-Solving and Skill Development for Next-Generation Leaders* (pp. 139–164). Hershey, PA: IGI Global. doi:10.4018/978-1-5225-1968-3.ch007

Bronzetti, G., Baldini, M. A., & Sicoli, G. (2017). Intellectual Capital Report in the Healthcare Sector: An Analysis of a Case Study. In P. Ordoñez de Pablos & R. Tennyson (Eds.), *Handbook of Research on Human Resources Strategies for the New Millennial Workforce* (pp. 272–285). Hershey, PA: IGI Global. doi:10.4018/978-1-5225-0948-6.ch013

Bronzetti, G., Baldini, M. A., & Sicoli, G. (2017). The Measurement of Human Capital in Family Firms. In P. Ordoñez de Pablos & R. Tennyson (Eds.), *Handbook of Research on Human Resources Strategies for the New Millennial Workforce* (pp. 371–392). Hershey, PA: IGI Global. doi:10.4018/978-1-5225-0948-6.ch019

Brown, M. A. Sr. (2018). *Motivationally Intelligent Leadership: Emerging Research and Opportunities* (pp. 1–139). Hershey, PA: IGI Global. doi:10.4018/978-1-5225-3746-5

Busari, A. H., & Mughal, Y. H. (2017). Two Ways Interaction between Lower Order Terms of Left Brain and Right Brain Cognitive Style and Relationship between Satisfaction and Turnover Intention. *International Journal of Information Systems and Social Change*, 8(1), 71–83. doi:10.4018/IJISSC.2017010105

Byrd-Poller, L., Farmer, J. L., & Ford, V. (2017). The Role of Leaders in Facilitating Healing After Organizational Trauma. In S. Háša & R. Brunet-Thornton (Eds.), *Impact of Organizational Trauma on Workplace Behavior and Performance* (pp. 318–340). Hershey, PA: IGI Global. doi:10.4018/978-1-5225-2021-4.ch014

Camillo, A. A., & Camillo, I. C. (2016). The Ethics of Strategic Managerial Communication in the Global Context. In A. Normore, L. Long, & M. Javidi (Eds.), *Handbook of Research on Effective Communication, Leadership, and Conflict Resolution* (pp. 566–590). Hershey, PA: IGI Global. doi:10.4018/978-1-4666-9970-0.ch030

Carlos, V. S., & Rodrigues, R. G. (2016). The Use of Online Social Networks in Higher Education and Its Influence on Job Performance. In A. Normore, L. Long, & M. Javidi (Eds.), *Handbook of Research on Effective Communication, Leadership, and Conflict Resolution* (pp. 330–353). Hershey, PA: IGI Global. doi:10.4018/978-1-4666-9970-0.ch018

Cejka, P., & Mohelska, H. (2017). National Culture Influence on Organisational Trauma: A Conceptual Framework Review. In S. Háša & R. Brunet-Thornton (Eds.), *Impact of Organizational Trauma on Workplace Behavior and Performance* (pp. 162–186). Hershey, PA: IGI Global. doi:10.4018/978-1-5225-2021-4.ch007

Charoensukmongkol, P. (2015). Social Media Use and Job Performance: Moderating Roles of Workplace Factors. *International Journal of Cyber Behavior, Psychology and Learning*, 5(2), 59–74. doi:10.4018/IJCBPL.2015040105

Chen, E. T. (2016). Virtual Team Management for Higher Performance. In A. Normore, L. Long, & M. Javidi (Eds.), *Handbook of Research on Effective Communication, Leadership, and Conflict Resolution* (pp. 298–310). Hershey, PA: IGI Global. doi:10.4018/978-1-4666-9970-0.ch016

Chiadamrong, N., & Tham, T. T. (2016). Investigating Relationships Between Supply Chain Capabilities, Competitive Advantage, and Business Performance: A Comparative Study between Thai and Vietnamese Food Industries. *International Journal of Information Systems and Supply Chain Management*, 9(4), 58–81. doi:10.4018/IJISSCM.2016100104

Choi, Y. (2017). Human Resource Management and Security Policy Compliance. *International Journal of Human Capital and Information Technology Professionals*, 8(3), 68–81. doi:10.4018/IJHCITP.2017070105

Clark, C., & Stowers, G. (2016). Speaking with Trunks, Dancing with the "Pink Elephants": Troubling E-Racism, E-Classism, and E-Sexism in Teaching Multicultural Teacher Education. In A. Normore, L. Long, & M. Javidi (Eds.), *Handbook of Research on Effective Communication, Leadership, and Conflict Resolution* (pp. 78–97). Hershey, PA: IGI Global. doi:10.4018/978-1-4666-9970-0.ch005

Cleve, R. A., Işık, İ., & Pecanha, V. D. (2017). Sexual Identities in the Workplace: Avoiding Organizational Trauma When Disclosure Occurs – Current Perspectives. In S. Háša & R. Brunet-Thornton (Eds.), *Impact of Organizational Trauma on Workplace Behavior and Performance* (pp. 188–220). Hershey, PA: IGI Global. doi:10.4018/978-1-5225-2021-4.ch008

Cockburn, T., & Smith, P. A. (2016). Leadership in the Digital Age: Rhythms and the Beat of Change. In A. Normore, L. Long, & M. Javidi (Eds.), *Handbook of Research on Effective Communication, Leadership, and Conflict Resolution* (pp. 1–20). Hershey, PA: IGI Global. doi:10.4018/978-1-4666-9970-0.ch001

Cockburn, T., Smith, P. A., Martins, B. M., & Valles, R. S. (2016). Conflict of Interest or Community of Collaboration?: Leadership, SME Network Dialectics, and Dialogs. In A. Normore, L. Long, & M. Javidi (Eds.), *Handbook of Research on Effective Communication, Leadership, and Conflict Resolution* (pp. 210–232). Hershey, PA: IGI Global. doi:10.4018/978-1-4666-9970-0.ch012

Çolakoğlu, S., Chung, Y., & Tarhan, A. B. (2016). Strategic Human Resource Management in Facilitating Organizational Change. In A. Goksoy (Ed.), *Organizational Change Management Strategies in Modern Business* (pp. 172–192). Hershey, PA: IGI Global. doi:10.4018/978-1-4666-9533-7.ch009

Connolly, R., & Kenny, G. (2016). Dataveillance and Information Privacy Concerns: Ethical and Organizational Considerations. In A. Normore, L. Long, & M. Javidi (Eds.), *Handbook of Research on Effective Communication, Leadership, and Conflict Resolution* (pp. 606–626). Hershey, PA: IGI Global. doi:10.4018/978-1-4666-9970-0.ch032

Cross, D. E. (2016). Globalization and Media's Impact on Cross Cultural Communication: Managing Organizational Change. In A. Normore, L. Long, & M. Javidi (Eds.), *Handbook of Research on Effective Communication, Leadership, and Conflict Resolution* (pp. 21–41). Hershey, PA: IGI Global. doi:10.4018/978-1-4666-9970-0.ch002

Daves, D. P. (2017). Principles of Effective Leadership. In R. Styron Jr & J. Styron (Eds.), *Comprehensive Problem-Solving and Skill Development for Next-Generation Leaders* (pp. 40–56). Hershey, PA: IGI Global. doi:10.4018/978-1-5225-1968-3.ch002

Davis, D. C., & Scaffidi-Clarke, N. M. (2016). Leading Virtual Teams: Conflict and Communication Challenges for Leaders. In A. Normore, L. Long, & M. Javidi (Eds.), *Handbook of Research on Effective Communication, Leadership, and Conflict Resolution* (pp. 196–209). Hershey, PA: IGI Global. doi:10.4018/978-1-4666-9970-0.ch011

De Ruiter, M., Blomme, R. J., & Schalk, R. (2016). Reducing the Negative Effects of Psychological Contract Breach during Management-Imposed Change: A Trickle-Down Model of Management Practices. In A. Goksoy (Ed.), *Organizational Change Management Strategies in Modern Business* (pp. 122–142). Hershey, PA: IGI Global. doi:10.4018/978-1-4666-9533-7.ch007

de Soir, E., & Kleber, R. (2017). Understanding the Core of Psychological Trauma: Trauma in Contemporary French Theory. In S. Háša & R. Brunet-Thornton (Eds.), *Impact of Organizational Trauma on Workplace Behavior and Performance* (pp. 57–75). Hershey, PA: IGI Global. doi:10.4018/978-1-5225-2021-4.ch003

Delmas, P. M. (2017). Research-Based Leadership for Next-Generation Leaders. In R. Styron Jr & J. Styron (Eds.), *Comprehensive Problem-Solving and Skill Development for Next-Generation Leaders* (pp. 1–39). Hershey, PA: IGI Global. doi:10.4018/978-1-5225-1968-3.ch001

Durst, S., & Aggestam, L. (2017). Using IT-Supported Knowledge Repositories for Succession Planning in SMEs: How to Deal with Knowledge Loss? In P. Ordoñez de Pablos & R. Tennyson (Eds.), *Handbook of Research on Human Resources Strategies for the New Millennial Workforce* (pp. 393–406). Hershey, PA: IGI Global. doi:10.4018/978-1-5225-0948-6.ch020

Efeoğlu, E. I., & Ozcan, S. (2017). The Relationship Between Social Problem Solving Ability and Burnout Level: A Field Study Among Health Professionals. In B. Christiansen & H. Chandan (Eds.), *Handbook of Research on Human Factors in Contemporary Workforce Development* (pp. 268–282). Hershey, PA: IGI Global. doi:10.4018/978-1-5225-2568-4.ch012

Ellis, B., & Normore, A. H. (2016). Effective Engagement and Communication between First-Line Police Supervisors and Police Officers. In A. Normore, L. Long, & M. Javidi (Eds.), *Handbook of Research on Effective Communication, Leadership, and Conflict Resolution* (pp. 479–493). Hershey, PA: IGI Global. doi:10.4018/978-1-4666-9970-0.ch025

Elouadi, S., & Ben Noamene, T. (2017). Does Employee Ownership Reduce the Intention to Leave? In P. Ordoñez de Pablos & R. Tennyson (Eds.), *Handbook of Research on Human Resources Strategies for the New Millennial Workforce* (pp. 111–127). Hershey, PA: IGI Global. doi:10.4018/978-1-5225-0948-6.ch006

Elufiede, O. J., & Flynn, B. B. (2017). Mentor the Leader: A Transformational Approach. In R. Styron Jr & J. Styron (Eds.), *Comprehensive Problem-Solving and Skill Development for Next-Generation Leaders* (pp. 188–209). Hershey, PA: IGI Global. doi:10.4018/978-1-5225-1968-3.ch009

Estis, J. M. (2017). Changing Culture through Active Learning. In R. Styron Jr & J. Styron (Eds.), *Comprehensive Problem-Solving and Skill Development for Next-Generation Leaders* (pp. 96–115). Hershey, PA: IGI Global. doi:10.4018/978-1-5225-1968-3.ch005

Fernandes, V. (2016). Reframing Continuous School Improvement in Australian Schools. In A. Normore, L. Long, & M. Javidi (Eds.), *Handbook of Research on Effective Communication, Leadership, and Conflict Resolution* (pp. 98–124). Hershey, PA: IGI Global. doi:10.4018/978-1-4666-9970-0.ch006

Gairín, J., Fernández-de-Álava, M., & Barrera-Corominas, A. (2015). Considering Latin American School Management from a Skills-Based Perspective. In K. Beycioglu & P. Pashiardis (Eds.), *Multidimensional Perspectives on Principal Leadership Effectiveness* (pp. 59–87). Hershey, PA: IGI Global. doi:10.4018/978-1-4666-6591-0.ch004

Gallego, J. (2017). Organizational Trauma and Change Management. In S. Háša & R. Brunet-Thornton (Eds.), *Impact of Organizational Trauma on Workplace Behavior and Performance* (pp. 140–161). Hershey, PA: IGI Global. doi:10.4018/978-1-5225-2021-4.ch006

Ghaem, A. R. (2015). Iran: Sustainable HRM Practices in SMEs. In S. Jones & S. Graham (Eds.), *Cases on Sustainable Human Resources Management in the Middle East and Asia* (pp. 277–293). Hershey, PA: IGI Global. doi:10.4018/978-1-4666-8167-5.ch012

Giannouli, V. (2017). Emotional Aspects of Leadership in the Modern Workplace. In B. Christiansen & H. Chandan (Eds.), *Handbook of Research on Human Factors in Contemporary Workforce Development* (pp. 24–59). Hershey, PA: IGI Global. doi:10.4018/978-1-5225-2568-4.ch002

Giousmpasoglou, C., & Marinakou, E. (2017). Culture and Managers in a Globalised World. In P. Ordoñez de Pablos & R. Tennyson (Eds.), *Handbook of Research on Human Resources Strategies for the New Millennial Workforce* (pp. 1–27). Hershey, PA: IGI Global. doi:10.4018/978-1-5225-0948-6.ch001

Goldstein, A. (2015). China: Managing a Diverse and Multicultural Workforce in Multinationals in a Growth Economy: Understanding the Chinese Workforce. In S. Jones & S. Graham (Eds.), *Cases on Sustainable Human Resources Management in the Middle East and Asia* (pp. 1–42). Hershey, PA: IGI Global. doi:10.4018/978-1-4666-8167-5.ch001

Goldstein, A. (2015). China: Managing a Diverse and Multicultural Workforce in Multinationals in a Growth Economy: Understanding the Expatriate Workforce. In S. Jones & S. Graham (Eds.), *Cases on Sustainable Human Resources Management in the Middle East and Asia* (pp. 43–75). Hershey, PA: IGI Global. doi:10.4018/978-1-4666-8167-5.ch002

Graham, S. (2015). Indochina: Starting up an HR Function from Scratch. In S. Jones & S. Graham (Eds.), *Cases on Sustainable Human Resources Management in the Middle East and Asia* (pp. 150–158). Hershey, PA: IGI Global. doi:10.4018/978-1-4666-8167-5.ch005

Green, W. S. (2017). Increasing Leadership Capacity through Emotional Intelligence. In R. Styron Jr & J. Styron (Eds.), *Comprehensive Problem-Solving and Skill Development for Next-Generation Leaders* (pp. 57–75). Hershey, PA: IGI Global. doi:10.4018/978-1-5225-1968-3.ch003

Grobler, B. (2015). The Relationship between Emotional Competence and Instructional Leadership and Their Association with Learner Achievement. In K. Beycioglu & P. Pashiardis (Eds.), *Multidimensional Perspectives on Principal Leadership Effectiveness* (pp. 373–407). Hershey, PA: IGI Global. doi:10.4018/978-1-4666-6591-0.ch017

Guilott, M. C., Parker, G. A., & Wheat, C. A. (2017). Tools to Change School Culture: Learning About Learning Together. In R. Styron Jr & J. Styron (Eds.), *Comprehensive Problem-Solving and Skill Development for Next-Generation Leaders* (pp. 165–186). Hershey, PA: IGI Global. doi:10.4018/978-1-5225-1968-3.ch008

Gul, S. (2016). Alternative Dispute Resolution: A Legal Perspective. In A. Normore, L. Long, & M. Javidi (Eds.), *Handbook of Research on Effective Communication, Leadership, and Conflict Resolution* (pp. 126–143). Hershey, PA: IGI Global. doi:10.4018/978-1-4666-9970-0.ch007

Gupton, S. L. (2017). Technology's Impact on Higher Education: Implications for next Generation Leaders. In R. Styron Jr & J. Styron (Eds.), *Comprehensive Problem-Solving and Skill Development for Next-Generation Leaders* (pp. 278–292). Hershey, PA: IGI Global. doi:10.4018/978-1-5225-1968-3.ch013

Hameed, Z., Khan, I. U., Chudhery, M. A., & Ding, D. (2017). Incivility and Counterproductive Work Behavior: A Moderated Mediation Model of Emotional Regulation and Psychological Distress. *International Journal of Applied Behavioral Economics*, 6(3), 1–22. doi:10.4018/IJABE.2017070101

Hassan, A., & Rahimi, R. (2017). Insights and Rumination of Human Resource Management Practices in SMEs: Case of a Family Run Tour Operator in London. In P. Ordoñez de Pablos & R. Tennyson (Eds.), *Handbook of Research on Human Resources Strategies for the New Millennial Workforce* (pp. 258–271). Hershey, PA: IGI Global. doi:10.4018/978-1-5225-0948-6.ch012

Hendel, R. J. (2017). Leadership for Improving Student Success through Higher Cognitive Instruction. In R. Styron Jr & J. Styron (Eds.), *Comprehensive Problem-Solving and Skill Development for Next-Generation Leaders* (pp. 230–254). Hershey, PA: IGI Global. doi:10.4018/978-1-5225-1968-3.ch011

Hieker, C., & Rushby, M. (2017). Diversity in the Workplace: How to Achieve Gender Diversity in the Workplace. In B. Christiansen & H. Chandan (Eds.), *Handbook of Research on Human Factors in Contemporary Workforce Development* (pp. 308–332). Hershey, PA: IGI Global. doi:10.4018/978-1-5225-2568-4.ch014

Hörnqvist, M. (2015). Principals' Understandings of Education Based on Research: A Swedish Perspective. In K. Beycioglu & P. Pashiardis (Eds.), *Multidimensional Perspectives on Principal Leadership Effectiveness* (pp. 149–170). Hershey, PA: IGI Global. doi:10.4018/978-1-4666-6591-0.ch008

Inglezakis, I. (2016). Surveillance of Electronic Communications in the Workplace and the Protection of Employees' Privacy. In A. Normore, L. Long, & M. Javidi (Eds.), *Handbook of Research on Effective Communication, Leadership, and Conflict Resolution* (pp. 591–605). Hershey, PA: IGI Global. doi:10.4018/978-1-4666-9970-0.ch031

Ion, G., Tomàs, M., Castro, D., & Salat, E. (2015). Analysis of the Tasks of School Principals in Secondary Education in Catalonia: Case Study. In K. Beycioglu & P. Pashiardis (Eds.), *Multidimensional Perspectives on Principal Leadership Effectiveness* (pp. 39–58). Hershey, PA: IGI Global. doi:10.4018/978-1-4666-6591-0.ch003

Isik, I. (2017). Organizations and Exposure to Trauma at a Collective Level: The Taxonomy of Potentially Traumatic Events. In S. Háša & R. Brunet-Thornton (Eds.), *Impact of Organizational Trauma on Workplace Behavior and Performance* (pp. 18–56). Hershey, PA: IGI Global. doi:10.4018/978-1-5225-2021-4.ch002

Jackson, K., & Rasheed, R. (2016). Communication, Culture, and Discord: A Lesson in Leadership Failure. In A. Normore, L. Long, & M. Javidi (Eds.), *Handbook of Research on Effective Communication, Leadership, and Conflict Resolution* (pp. 182–195). Hershey, PA: IGI Global. doi:10.4018/978-1-4666-9970-0.ch010

Jackson, T. C. (2015). Internal HR Security Compliance and Risk Management Systems in a Major International Bank in a North African Country. In S. Jones & S. Graham (Eds.), *Cases on Sustainable Human Resources Management in the Middle East and Asia* (pp. 260–276). Hershey, PA: IGI Global. doi:10.4018/978-1-4666-8167-5.ch011

Jeong, S., Lim, D. H., & Park, S. (2017). Leadership Convergence and Divergence in the Era of Globalization. In P. Ordoñez de Pablos & R. Tennyson (Eds.), *Handbook of Research on Human Resources Strategies for the New Millennial Workforce* (pp. 286–309). Hershey, PA: IGI Global. doi:10.4018/978-1-5225-0948-6.ch014

Jerabek, I., & Muoio, D. (2017). The Stress Profile: The Influence of Personal Characteristics on Response to Occupational Trauma. In S. Háša & R. Brunet-Thornton (Eds.), *Impact of Organizational Trauma on Workplace Behavior and Performance* (pp. 77–119). Hershey, PA: IGI Global. doi:10.4018/978-1-5225-2021-4.ch004

Jha, J. K., & Singh, M. (2017). Human Resource Planning as a Strategic Function: Biases in Forecasting Judgement. *International Journal of Strategic Decision Sciences*, 8(3), 120–131. doi:10.4018/IJSDS.2017070106

Johnson, R. D., & Yanson, R. (2015). Job Satisfaction and Turnover Intentions during Technology Transition: The Role of User Involvement, Core Self-Evaluations, and Computer Self-Efficacy. *Information Resources Management Journal*, 28(4), 38–51. doi:10.4018/IRMJ.2015100103

Jones, S. (2015). China: Managing a Diverse and Multicultural Workforce in Multinationals in a Growth Economy: Issues in Practice. In S. Jones & S. Graham (Eds.), *Cases on Sustainable Human Resources Management in the Middle East and Asia* (pp. 76–122). Hershey, PA: IGI Global. doi:10.4018/978-1-4666-8167-5.ch003

Kanape-Willingshofer, A., & Bergner, S. (2015). Individual Differences and Educational Leadership. In K. Beycioglu & P. Pashiardis (Eds.), *Multidimensional Perspectives on Principal Leadership Effectiveness* (pp. 171–206). Hershey, PA: IGI Global. doi:10.4018/978-1-4666-6591-0.ch009

Keil, L. J., & Jerome, A. M. (2016). Leadership in a Time of Crisis: Jim Tressel's Ousting from The Ohio State University. In A. Normore, L. Long, & M. Javidi (Eds.), *Handbook of Research on Effective Communication, Leadership, and Conflict Resolution* (pp. 162–181). Hershey, PA: IGI Global. doi:10.4018/978-1-4666-9970-0.ch009

Khoury, G. C., & McNally, B. (2016). The Role of the Leadership Style in Creating Conflict and Tension in a Higher Education Institution. In A. Normore, L. Long, & M. Javidi (Eds.), *Handbook of Research on Effective Communication, Leadership, and Conflict Resolution* (pp. 233–247). Hershey, PA: IGI Global. doi:10.4018/978-1-4666-9970-0.ch013

Kılıç, B. (2017). An Organizational Trauma Intervention: A Case From Turkey. In S. Háša & R. Brunet-Thornton (Eds.), *Impact of Organizational Trauma on Workplace Behavior and Performance* (pp. 264–277). Hershey, PA: IGI Global. doi:10.4018/978-1-5225-2021-4.ch011

Kirstein, K. D. (2016). Developing Trust within International Teams: The Impacts of Culture on Team Formation and Process. In A. Normore, L. Long, & M. Javidi (Eds.), *Handbook of Research on Effective Communication, Leadership, and Conflict Resolution* (pp. 385–404). Hershey, PA: IGI Global. doi:10.4018/978-1-4666-9970-0.ch021

Kock, N. (2017). Which is the Best Way to Measure Job Performance: Self-Perceptions or Official Supervisor Evaluations? *International Journal of e-Collaboration, 13*(2), 1–9. doi:10.4018/IJeC.2017040101

Kock, N., Moqbel, M., Barton, K., & Bartelt, V. (2016). Intended Continued Use Social Networking Sites: Effects on Job Satisfaction and Performance. *International Journal of Virtual Communities and Social Networking, 8*(2), 28–46. doi:10.4018/IJVCSN.2016040103

Kondakci, Y., Zayim, M., & Beycioglu, K. (2015). Continuous Change in Educational Organizations. In K. Beycioglu & P. Pashiardis (Eds.), *Multidimensional Perspectives on Principal Leadership Effectiveness* (pp. 305–322). Hershey, PA: IGI Global. doi:10.4018/978-1-4666-6591-0.ch014

Kučera, D. (2017). The Potential of Spirituality for the Treatment of Organizational Trauma. In S. Háša & R. Brunet-Thornton (Eds.), *Impact of Organizational Trauma on Workplace Behavior and Performance* (pp. 295–317). Hershey, PA: IGI Global. doi:10.4018/978-1-5225-2021-4.ch013

Kythreotis, A., & Antoniou, P. (2015). Exploring the Impact of School Leadership on Student Learning Outcomes: Constraints and Perspectives. In K. Beycioglu & P. Pashiardis (Eds.), *Multidimensional Perspectives on Principal Leadership Effectiveness* (pp. 349–372). Hershey, PA: IGI Global. doi:10.4018/978-1-4666-6591-0.ch016

Labat, M. B., Eadens, D. W., Labat, C. A., & Eadens, D. M. (2017). Motivational Factors for Pursuing Degrees in Educational Administration. In R. Styron Jr & J. Styron (Eds.), *Comprehensive Problem-Solving and Skill Development for Next-Generation Leaders* (pp. 210–228). Hershey, PA: IGI Global. doi:10.4018/978-1-5225-1968-3.ch010

Lazaridou, A. (2015). Reinventing Principal Preparation in Illinois: A Case Study of Policy Change in a Complex Organization. In K. Beycioglu & P. Pashiardis (Eds.), *Multidimensional Perspectives on Principal Leadership Effectiveness* (pp. 18–38). Hershey, PA: IGI Global. doi:10.4018/978-1-4666-6591-0.ch002

Leonard, E. E. (2017). 21st Century Educational Leadership. In R. Styron Jr & J. Styron (Eds.), *Comprehensive Problem-Solving and Skill Development for Next-Generation Leaders* (pp. 313–332). Hershey, PA: IGI Global. doi:10.4018/978-1-5225-1968-3.ch015

Long, L. W., Javidi, M., Hill, L. B., & Normore, A. H. (2016). Credible Negotiation Leadership: Using Principled Negotiation to Improve International Negotiation. In A. Normore, L. Long, & M. Javidi (Eds.), *Handbook of Research on Effective Communication, Leadership, and Conflict Resolution* (pp. 430–455). Hershey, PA: IGI Global. doi:10.4018/978-1-4666-9970-0.ch023

Malik, A. (2016). The Role of HR Strategies in Change. In A. Goksoy (Ed.), *Organizational Change Management Strategies in Modern Business* (pp. 193–215). Hershey, PA: IGI Global. doi:10.4018/978-1-4666-9533-7.ch010

Margalina, V. M., De-Pablos-Heredero, C., & Botella, J. L. (2015). Achieving Job Satisfaction for Instructors in E-Learning: The Relational Coordination Role. *International Journal of Human Capital and Information Technology Professionals*, *6*(4), 64–79. doi:10.4018/IJHCITP.2015100104

Marinakou, E., & Giousmpasoglou, C. (2017). Gendered Leadership as a Key to Business Success: Evidence from the Middle East. In P. Ordoñez de Pablos & R. Tennyson (Eds.), *Handbook of Research on Human Resources Strategies for the New Millennial Workforce* (pp. 200–230). Hershey, PA: IGI Global. doi:10.4018/978-1-5225-0948-6.ch010

Martins, A., Martins, I., & Pereira, O. (2017). Challenges Enhancing Social and Organizational Performance. In P. Ordoñez de Pablos & R. Tennyson (Eds.), *Handbook of Research on Human Resources Strategies for the New Millennial Workforce* (pp. 28–46). Hershey, PA: IGI Global. doi:10.4018/978-1-5225-0948-6.ch002

Martins, A., Martins, I., & Pereira, O. (2017). Embracing Innovation and Creativity through the Capacity of Unlearning. In P. Ordoñez de Pablos & R. Tennyson (Eds.), *Handbook of Research on Human Resources Strategies for the New Millennial Workforce* (pp. 128–147). Hershey, PA: IGI Global. doi:10.4018/978-1-5225-0948-6.ch007

Matuska, E. M., & Grubicka, J. (2017). Employer Branding and Internet Security. In B. Christiansen & H. Chandan (Eds.), *Handbook of Research on Human Factors in Contemporary Workforce Development* (pp. 357–378). Hershey, PA: IGI Global. doi:10.4018/978-1-5225-2568-4.ch016

Mestry, R., & Naicker, S. R. (2015). Exploring Distributive Leadership in South African Public Primary Schools in the Soweto Region. In K. Beycioglu & P. Pashiardis (Eds.), *Multidimensional Perspectives on Principal Leadership Effectiveness* (pp. 283–304). Hershey, PA: IGI Global. doi:10.4018/978-1-4666-6591-0.ch013

Miller, P. (2015). Becoming a Principal: Exploring Perceived Discriminatory Practices in the Selection of Principals in Jamaica and England. In K. Beycioglu & P. Pashiardis (Eds.), *Multidimensional Perspectives on Principal Leadership Effectiveness* (pp. 132–147). Hershey, PA: IGI Global. doi:10.4018/978-1-4666-6591-0.ch007

Mishra, K. E., Mishra, A. K., & Walker, K. (2016). Leadership Communication, Internal Marketing, and Employee Engagement: A Recipe to Create Brand Ambassadors. In A. Normore, L. Long, & M. Javidi (Eds.), *Handbook of Research on Effective Communication, Leadership, and Conflict Resolution* (pp. 311–329). Hershey, PA: IGI Global. doi:10.4018/978-1-4666-9970-0.ch017

Mitchell, R. J., & Von Zoller, K. (2016). The Link between Communicative Intelligence and Procedural Justice: The Path to Police Legitimacy. In A. Normore, L. Long, & M. Javidi (Eds.), *Handbook of Research on Effective Communication, Leadership, and Conflict Resolution* (pp. 456–478). Hershey, PA: IGI Global. doi:10.4018/978-1-4666-9970-0.ch024

Moore, B. (2017). Authentic Leadership: Applications in Academic Decision-Making. In R. Styron Jr & J. Styron (Eds.), *Comprehensive Problem-Solving and Skill Development for Next-Generation Leaders* (pp. 76–94). Hershey, PA: IGI Global. doi:10.4018/978-1-5225-1968-3.ch004

Mukhopadhyay, P. (2017). Investigation of Ergonomic Risk Factors in Snacks Manufacturing in Central India: Ergonomics in Unorganized Sector. In B. Christiansen & H. Chandan (Eds.), *Handbook of Research on Human Factors in Contemporary Workforce Development* (pp. 425–449). Hershey, PA: IGI Global. doi:10.4018/978-1-5225-2568-4.ch019

Muralidharan, E., & Pathak, S. (2017). National Ethical Institutions and Social Entrepreneurship. In B. Christiansen & H. Chandan (Eds.), *Handbook of Research on Human Factors in Contemporary Workforce Development* (pp. 379–402). Hershey, PA: IGI Global. doi:10.4018/978-1-5225-2568-4.ch017

Naik, K. R., & Srinivasan, S. R. (2017). Distinctive Leadership: Moral Identity as Self Identity. In P. Ordoñez de Pablos & R. Tennyson (Eds.), *Handbook of Research on Human Resources Strategies for the New Millennial Workforce* (pp. 90–110). Hershey, PA: IGI Global. doi:10.4018/978-1-5225-0948-6.ch005

Naito, Y. (2017). Factors Related to Readjustment to Daily Life: A Study of Repatriates in Japanese Multinational Enterprises. In B. Christiansen & H. Chandan (Eds.), *Handbook of Research on Human Factors in Contemporary Workforce Development* (pp. 403–424). Hershey, PA: IGI Global. doi:10.4018/978-1-5225-2568-4.ch018

Nawaz, T. (2017). Expatriation in the Age of Austerity: An Analysis of Capital Mobilization Strategies of Self-Initiated Expatriates. In P. Ordoñez de Pablos & R. Tennyson (Eds.), *Handbook of Research on Human Resources Strategies for the New Millennial Workforce* (pp. 177–199). Hershey, PA: IGI Global. doi:10.4018/978-1-5225-0948-6.ch009

O'Neill, S. (2015). School Leadership and Pedagogical Reform: Building Student Capacity. In K. Beycioglu & P. Pashiardis (Eds.), *Multidimensional Perspectives on Principal Leadership Effectiveness* (pp. 103–131). Hershey, PA: IGI Global. doi:10.4018/978-1-4666-6591-0.ch006

Özdemir, S., & Kılınç, A. Ç. (2015). Teacher Leadership: A Conceptual Analysis. In K. Beycioglu & P. Pashiardis (Eds.), *Multidimensional Perspectives on Principal Leadership Effectiveness* (pp. 257–282). Hershey, PA: IGI Global. doi:10.4018/978-1-4666-6591-0.ch012

Özgeldi, M. (2016). Role of Human Resources in Change. In A. Goksoy (Ed.), *Organizational Change Management Strategies in Modern Business* (pp. 216–229). Hershey, PA: IGI Global. doi:10.4018/978-1-4666-9533-7.ch011

Palm, K. (2017). A Case of Phased Retirement in Sweden. In P. Ordoñez de Pablos & R. Tennyson (Eds.), *Handbook of Research on Human Resources Strategies for the New Millennial Workforce* (pp. 351–370). Hershey, PA: IGI Global. doi:10.4018/978-1-5225-0948-6.ch018

Patro, C. S. (2017). Performance Appraisal System Effectiveness: A Conceptual Review. In B. Christiansen & H. Chandan (Eds.), *Handbook of Research on Human Factors in Contemporary Workforce Development* (pp. 156–180). Hershey, PA: IGI Global. doi:10.4018/978-1-5225-2568-4.ch007

Patro, C. S. (2017). Welfare Regime: A Critical Discourse. In B. Christiansen & H. Chandan (Eds.), *Handbook of Research on Human Factors in Contemporary Workforce Development* (pp. 110–131). Hershey, PA: IGI Global. doi:10.4018/978-1-5225-2568-4.ch005

Pena, P. A., Van den Broucke, S., Sylin, M., Leysen, J., & de Soir, E. (2017). Definitions, Typologies, and Processes Involved in Organizational Trauma: A Literature Review. In S. Háša & R. Brunet-Thornton (Eds.), *Impact of Organizational Trauma on Workplace Behavior and Performance* (pp. 1–17). Hershey, PA: IGI Global. doi:10.4018/978-1-5225-2021-4.ch001

Perez-Montoro, M., & Sanz, S. (2016). Communities of Practice in Organizational Learning Strategies. In A. Normore, L. Long, & M. Javidi (Eds.), *Handbook of Research on Effective Communication, Leadership, and Conflict Resolution* (pp. 249–266). Hershey, PA: IGI Global. doi:10.4018/978-1-4666-9970-0.ch014

Pietiläinen, V., Salmi, I., Rusko, R., & Jänkälä, R. (2017). Experienced Stress and the Value of Rest Stops in the Transportation Field: Stress and Transportation. In B. Christiansen & H. Chandan (Eds.), *Handbook of Research on Human Factors in Contemporary Workforce Development* (pp. 249–267). Hershey, PA: IGI Global. doi:10.4018/978-1-5225-2568-4.ch011

Pyle, A. S. (2016). Surviving the Conflict of Self-Inflicted Organizational Crises. In A. Normore, L. Long, & M. Javidi (Eds.), *Handbook of Research on Effective Communication, Leadership, and Conflict Resolution* (pp. 144–161). Hershey, PA: IGI Global. doi:10.4018/978-1-4666-9970-0.ch008

Radzuan, N. R., & Kaur, S. (2016). Engineering Students' Communication Apprehension and Competence in Technical Oral Presentations. In A. Normore, L. Long, & M. Javidi (Eds.), *Handbook of Research on Effective Communication, Leadership, and Conflict Resolution* (pp. 371–383). Hershey, PA: IGI Global. doi:10.4018/978-1-4666-9970-0.ch020

Rintoul, H. M. (2016). The Role of Leadership and Communication: Re-Conceptualizing Graduate Instruction Online. In A. Normore, L. Long, & M. Javidi (Eds.), *Handbook of Research on Effective Communication, Leadership, and Conflict Resolution* (pp. 515–530). Hershey, PA: IGI Global. doi:10.4018/978-1-4666-9970-0.ch027

Roach, C. M., & Davis-Cooper, G. (2016). An Evaluation of the Adoption of the Integrated Human Resource Information System in Trinidad and Tobago. *International Journal of Public Administration in the Digital Age, 3*(3), 1–17. doi:10.4018/IJPADA.2016070101

Romanowski, M. H. (2015). Qatar's Educational Reform: Critical Issues Facing Principals. In K. Beycioglu & P. Pashiardis (Eds.), *Multidimensional Perspectives on Principal Leadership Effectiveness* (pp. 88–102). Hershey, PA: IGI Global. doi:10.4018/978-1-4666-6591-0.ch005

Roy, S. R. (2015). *Promoting Trait Emotional Intelligence in Leadership and Education* (pp. 1–341). Hershey, PA: IGI Global. doi:10.4018/978-1-4666-8327-3

Ruffin, T. R., Hawkins, J. M., & Lee, D. I. (2016). Organizational Leadership and Health Care Reform. In A. Normore, L. Long, & M. Javidi (Eds.), *Handbook of Research on Effective Communication, Leadership, and Conflict Resolution* (pp. 42–62). Hershey, PA: IGI Global. doi:10.4018/978-1-4666-9970-0.ch003

Saad, M. M., & Moawad, R. (2015). Egypt: Identifying Sustainable Leadership Competencies for Local and Multinational Businesses at a Time of Chaos. In S. Jones & S. Graham (Eds.), *Cases on Sustainable Human Resources Management in the Middle East and Asia* (pp. 246–259). Hershey, PA: IGI Global. doi:10.4018/978-1-4666-8167-5.ch010

Safi, H. (2015). Afghanistan: Managing Conflict and Employee Relations between Americans and Afghans. In S. Jones & S. Graham (Eds.), *Cases on Sustainable Human Resources Management in the Middle East and Asia* (pp. 190–211). Hershey, PA: IGI Global. doi:10.4018/978-1-4666-8167-5.ch007

Sarafidou, J., & Xafakos, E. (2015). Transformational Leadership and Principals' Innovativeness: Are They the "Keys" for the Research and Innovation Oriented School? In K. Beycioglu & P. Pashiardis (Eds.), *Multidimensional Perspectives on Principal Leadership Effectiveness* (pp. 324–348). Hershey, PA: IGI Global. doi:10.4018/978-1-4666-6591-0.ch015

Seino, K., Nomoto, A., Takezawa, T., & Boeltzig-Brown, H. (2017). The Diversity Management for Employment of the Persons With Disabilities: Evidence of Vocational Rehabilitation in the United States and Japan. In B. Christiansen & H. Chandan (Eds.), *Handbook of Research on Human Factors in Contemporary Workforce Development* (pp. 333–356). Hershey, PA: IGI Global. doi:10.4018/978-1-5225-2568-4.ch015

Shen, L., & Austin, L. (2017). Communication and Job Satisfaction. In B. Christiansen & H. Chandan (Eds.), *Handbook of Research on Human Factors in Contemporary Workforce Development* (pp. 201–225). Hershey, PA: IGI Global. doi:10.4018/978-1-5225-2568-4.ch009

Simuth, J. (2017). Psychological Impacts of Downsizing Trauma. In S. Háša & R. Brunet-Thornton (Eds.), *Impact of Organizational Trauma on Workplace Behavior and Performance* (pp. 120–139). Hershey, PA: IGI Global. doi:10.4018/978-1-5225-2021-4.ch005

Smith, P., & Cames, O. (2016). CAMES: An Approach to Project Management Based on Action Research and the Ideal Speech Situation. In A. Normore, L. Long, & M. Javidi (Eds.), *Handbook of Research on Effective Communication, Leadership, and Conflict Resolution* (pp. 531–544). Hershey, PA: IGI Global. doi:10.4018/978-1-4666-9970-0.ch028

Solvoll, T. (2016). Mobile Communication in Hospitals: Is It Still a Problem? In A. Normore, L. Long, & M. Javidi (Eds.), *Handbook of Research on Effective Communication, Leadership, and Conflict Resolution* (pp. 545–564). Hershey, PA: IGI Global. doi:10.4018/978-1-4666-9970-0.ch029

Starr-Glass, D. (2017). The Misappropriation of Organizational Power and Control: Managerial Bullying in the Workplace. In B. Christiansen & H. Chandan (Eds.), *Handbook of Research on Human Factors in Contemporary Workforce Development* (pp. 87–109). Hershey, PA: IGI Global. doi:10.4018/978-1-5225-2568-4.ch004

Stein, K. C., & Kim, T. (2017). Teacher Collaborative Inquiry and Democracy in Schools: Possibilities and Challenges. In R. Styron Jr & J. Styron (Eds.), *Comprehensive Problem-Solving and Skill Development for Next-Generation Leaders* (pp. 255–276). Hershey, PA: IGI Global. doi:10.4018/978-1-5225-1968-3.ch012

Stevenson, C. N. (2016). Communicating across the Generations: Implications for Higher Education Leadership. In A. Normore, L. Long, & M. Javidi (Eds.), *Handbook of Research on Effective Communication, Leadership, and Conflict Resolution* (pp. 494–514). Hershey, PA: IGI Global. doi:10.4018/978-1-4666-9970-0.ch026

Szymanski, M., & Schindler, E. (2017). Embracing Organizational Trauma: Positive Effects of Death Experiences on Organizational Culture – Three Short Case Studies. In S. Háša & R. Brunet-Thornton (Eds.), *Impact of Organizational Trauma on Workplace Behavior and Performance* (pp. 247–263). Hershey, PA: IGI Global. doi:10.4018/978-1-5225-2021-4.ch010

Taliadorou, N., & Pashiardis, P. (2015). Emotional Intelligence and Political Skill Really Matter in Educational Leadership. In K. Beycioglu & P. Pashiardis (Eds.), *Multidimensional Perspectives on Principal Leadership Effectiveness* (pp. 228–256). Hershey, PA: IGI Global. doi:10.4018/978-1-4666-6591-0.ch011

Teimouri, H., Jenab, K., Moazeni, H. R., & Bakhtiari, B. (2017). Studying Effectiveness of Human Resource Management Actions and Organizational Agility: Resource Management Actions and Organizational Agility. *Information Resources Management Journal*, 30(2), 61–77. doi:10.4018/IRMJ.2017040104

Tomasiak, M. A., & Chamakiotis, P. (2017). Understanding Diversity in Virtual Work Environments: A Comparative Case Study. In B. Christiansen & H. Chandan (Eds.), *Handbook of Research on Human Factors in Contemporary Workforce Development* (pp. 283–307). Hershey, PA: IGI Global. doi:10.4018/978-1-5225-2568-4.ch013

Tran, B. (2016). Communication: The Role of the Johari Window on Effective Leadership Communication in Multinational Corporations. In A. Normore, L. Long, & M. Javidi (Eds.), *Handbook of Research on Effective Communication, Leadership, and Conflict Resolution* (pp. 405–429). Hershey, PA: IGI Global. doi:10.4018/978-1-4666-9970-0.ch022

Tran, B. (2017). Impact of Organizational Trauma on Workplace Behavior and Performance: Workplace Bullying Due to (In)Competency. In S. Háša, & R. Brunet-Thornton (Eds.), Impact of Organizational Trauma on Workplace Behavior and Performance (pp. 221-245). Hershey, PA: IGI Global. doi:10.4018/978-1-5225-2021-4.ch009

Tran, B. (2017). The Art and Science in Communication: Workplace (Cross-Cultural) Communication Skills and Competencies in the Modern Workforce. In B. Christiansen & H. Chandan (Eds.), *Handbook of Research on Human Factors in Contemporary Workforce Development* (pp. 60–86). Hershey, PA: IGI Global. doi:10.4018/978-1-5225-2568-4.ch003

Traymbak, S., Kumar, P., & Jha, A. (2017). Moderating Role of Gender between Job Characteristics and Job Satisfaction: An Empirical Study of Software Industry Using Structural Equation Modeling. *International Journal of Human Capital and Information Technology Professionals*, 8(2), 59–71. doi:10.4018/IJHCITP.2017040104

Trichas, S. (2015). New Methods Exploring Facial Expressions in the Context of Leadership Perception: Implications for Educational Leaders. In K. Beycioglu & P. Pashiardis (Eds.), *Multidimensional Perspectives on Principal Leadership Effectiveness* (pp. 207–227). Hershey, PA: IGI Global. doi:10.4018/978-1-4666-6591-0.ch010

Umamaheswari, S., & Krishnan, J. (2017). Retention Factor: Work Life Balance and Policies – Effects over Different Category of Employees in Ceramic Manufacturing Industries. In P. Ordoñez de Pablos & R. Tennyson (Eds.), *Handbook of Research on Human Resources Strategies for the New Millennial Workforce* (pp. 329–336). Hershey, PA: IGI Global. doi:10.4018/978-1-5225-0948-6.ch016

Uyen, N. V. (2015). Vietnam: Understanding Vietnamese Business Culture. In S. Jones & S. Graham (Eds.), *Cases on Sustainable Human Resources Management in the Middle East and Asia* (pp. 123–149). Hershey, PA: IGI Global. doi:10.4018/978-1-4666-8167-5.ch004

Wahyuningtyas, R., & Anggadwita, G. (2017). Perspective of Managing Talent in Indonesia: Reality and Strategy. In P. Ordoñez de Pablos & R. Tennyson (Eds.), *Handbook of Research on Human Resources Strategies for the New Millennial Workforce* (pp. 407–420). Hershey, PA: IGI Global. doi:10.4018/978-1-5225-0948-6.ch021

Washington, G. D., & Shen, L. (2017). Emotional Intelligence and Job Stress. In B. Christiansen & H. Chandan (Eds.), *Handbook of Research on Human Factors in Contemporary Workforce Development* (pp. 226–248). Hershey, PA: IGI Global. doi:10.4018/978-1-5225-2568-4.ch010

Wingreen, S. C., LeRouge, C. M., & Nelson, A. C. (2017). Managing IT Employee Attitudes that Lead to Turnover: Integrating a Person-Job Fit Perspective. *International Journal of Human Capital and Information Technology Professionals*, 8(1), 25–41. doi:10.4018/IJHCITP.2017010102

Yildirim, F., Abukan, B., & Oztas, D. (2017). Determining the Needs for Employee Assistance Programs (EAPs): A Comparative Study on Public and Private Sector Employees. In P. Ordoñez de Pablos & R. Tennyson (Eds.), *Handbook of Research on Human Resources Strategies for the New Millennial Workforce* (pp. 65–89). Hershey, PA: IGI Global. doi:10.4018/978-1-5225-0948-6.ch004

You, J., Kim, J., & Lim, D. H. (2017). Organizational Learning and Change: Strategic Interventions to Deal with Resistance. In P. Ordoñez de Pablos & R. Tennyson (Eds.), *Handbook of Research on Human Resources Strategies for the New Millennial Workforce* (pp. 310–328). Hershey, PA: IGI Global. doi:10.4018/978-1-5225-0948-6.ch015

You, J., Kim, J., & Miller, S. M. (2017). Organizational Learning as a Social Process: A Social Capital and Network Approach. In B. Christiansen & H. Chandan (Eds.), *Handbook of Research on Human Factors in Contemporary Workforce Development* (pp. 132–155). Hershey, PA: IGI Global. doi:10.4018/978-1-5225-2568-4.ch006

Zheng, W., Wu, Y. J., & Xu, M. (2017). From Democratic Participation to Shared Values: Improving Employee-Employer Interactions to Achieve Win-Win Situations. In P. Ordoñez de Pablos & R. Tennyson (Eds.), *Handbook of Research on Human Resources Strategies for the New Millennial Workforce* (pp. 421–432). Hershey, PA: IGI Global. doi:10.4018/978-1-5225-0948-6.ch022

Zinger, D. (2016). Developing Instructional Leadership and Communication Skills through Online Professional Development: Focusing on Rural and Urban Principals. In A. Normore, L. Long, & M. Javidi (Eds.), *Handbook of Research on Effective Communication, Leadership, and Conflict Resolution* (pp. 354–370). Hershey, PA: IGI Global. doi:10.4018/978-1-4666-9970-0.ch019

About the Authors

Khaled Tamzini received his Master's degree in Management sciences and his Post-graduate diploma in Human Resource Management from the High Institute of Management of Tunis (1997-1999). He received his PhD degree with honors from the Faculty of Economic Sciences and management Sciences of Tunis in 2014. He founded and directed during 5 years (2006-2011) a recruitment agency. He justifies an experience of over 10 years (since 2001) as a senior trainer for the account of several national companies in the field of Human Resources Management. Dr. Tamzini is actually an Assistant professor of Strategic Human Resource Management at the IHCS of Sousse (Tunisia) where he teaches Human Resource management and Strategic management. He is a member of the Research laboratory "LARIME" and panel member of the International Association of Strategic Management (France). He is a reviewer for several international scientific meeting as the Academy of Management Meeting, the Academy of International Business, the European Academy of Management Conference... His research interests include the Resource-Based View, Knowledge Management, Talent management, Employer branding, Human resource marketing, Human Capital, Sustained Competitive Advantage and Strategic Human Resource Management.

Tahar Lazhar Ayed received his B.Sc. in economics and Social Sciences from Tunis El Manar University 1997 and his MBA in Marketing and Data Analysis from the University of Quebec At Montreal, Canada in 2002. He earned his Ph.D. in Business strategies from Tunis Al Manar university in 2009. He is now serving as an Assistant Professor (Visitor) of Strategies and Data analysis in College of Business at Umm Al-Qura University, KSA where he joined in 2012 and a senior consultant at the Institute of Consulting, Umm Al Qura University, KSA. He worked as a Marketing Manager at CFH Security in Canada from 2000 to 2004, a Lecturer at the School of Economics and Commerce (Tunis, Tunisia) from 2004 to 2006, a lecturer and assistant Professor at the School Of Commerce (Sfax, Tunisia) from 2006 to 2012.He teaches Principles of Management, Data Analysis, Research methodology, cost accounting, Business and Marketing strategies, etc. Dr Ayed has published books and scientific papers in international indexed journals.

Index

A

Agro-food industry 1, 13
arrogance 1-12, 22-27, 33-34, 38-39, 41,
44, 46-52, 54-55, 74-76, 83-84, 91,
109-111, 117-118, 143, 151, 154, 162

C

Case Study 151
competence 3-4, 51, 111, 117-118, 131-136,
138-140, 151-153, 157, 162
culture 1, 13-15, 18-22, 94, 131, 135-136
customer satisfaction 24, 33-34, 44, 46-47,
50-51, 64, 74, 91, 126

D

deployment 118, 152

E

employee satisfaction 34, 44, 57-62, 64, 73
entrepreneurship 151, 154, 156-157

F

financial performance 14, 33-34, 44, 48, 51

G

gulf region 84, 95, 108

H

hospitality sector 54, 63-64, 71-74, 83, 93
hubris 1, 4-5, 7-8

I

innovation 14, 18-19, 34, 44, 123, 125, 131
intangible 120, 123, 128, 132, 151-153, 162

J

job performance 5, 11, 24, 64, 74, 83-89,
91-93, 95, 97, 99, 104-111
job satisfaction 54-55, 57-66, 71-76, 83,
90-91, 111

N

narcissism 1, 4-7, 10-11, 26
nurses 83-84, 93-97, 100-108

O

organizational performance 1-2, 5, 10-15,
17, 19, 22-24, 26-27, 33-34, 38, 44,

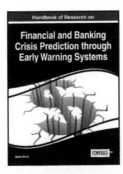

Stay Current on the Latest Emerging Research Developments

Become an IGI Global Reviewer for Authored Book Projects

Premier Reference Source

Emerging GIS Applications for Emergency and Disaster Management

Premier Reference Source

Managerial Strategies and Green Solutions for Project Sustainability

Premier Reference Source

Comparative Approaches to Using R and Python for Statistical Data Analysis

Premier Reference Source

Solutions for High-Touch Communications in a High-Tech World

The overall success of an authored book project is dependent on quality and timely reviews.

In this competitive age of scholarly publishing, constructive and timely feedback significantly decreases the turnaround time of manuscripts from submission to acceptance, allowing the publication and discovery of progressive research at a much more expeditious rate. Several IGI Global authored book projects are currently seeking highly qualified experts in the field to fill vacancies on their respective editorial review boards:

Applications may be sent to:
development@igi-global.com

Applicants must have a doctorate (or an equivalent degree) as well as publishing and reviewing experience. Reviewers are asked to write reviews in a timely, collegial, and constructive manner. All reviewers will begin their role on an ad-hoc basis for a period of one year, and upon successful completion of this term can be considered for full editorial review board status, with the potential for a subsequent promotion to Associate Editor.

If you have a colleague that may be interested in this opportunity, we encourage you to share this information with them.

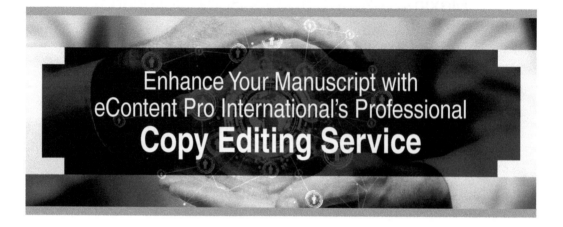

Information Resources Management Association

Advancing the Concepts & Practices of Information Resources Management in Modern Organizations

Become an IRMA Member

Members of the **Information Resources Management Association (IRMA)** understand the importance of community within their field of study. The Information Resources Management Association is an ideal venue through which professionals, students, and academicians can convene and share the latest industry innovations and scholarly research that is changing the field of information science and technology. Become a member today and enjoy the benefits of membership as well as the opportunity to collaborate and network with fellow experts in the field.

IRMA Membership Benefits:

- **One FREE Journal Subscription**
- **30% Off Additional Journal Subscriptions**
- **20% Off Book Purchases**
- Updates on the latest events and research on Information Resources Management through the IRMA-L listserv.
- Updates on new open access and downloadable content added to Research IRM.
- A copy of the Information Technology Management Newsletter twice a year.
- A certificate of membership.

IRMA Membership $195

Scan code or visit **irma-international.org** and begin by selecting your free journal subscription.

Membership is good for one full year.

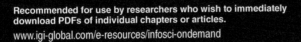

9 781522 555254